MARK TWAIN's AMERICA

MARK TWAIN'S

A Celebration in

AMERICA
Words and Images

HARRY L. KATZ
AND THE
LIBRARY OF CONGRESS

L B

LITTLE, BROWN AND COMPANY

NEW YORK   BOSTON   LONDON

Little, Brown and Company
Hachette Book Group
1290 Avenue of the Americas, New York, NY 10019
littlebrown.com

First Edition: October 2014

Little, Brown and Company is a division of Hachette
Book Group, Inc. The Little, Brown name and logo are
trademarks of Hachette Book Group, Inc.

The publisher is not responsible for websites (or their
content) that are not owned by the publisher.

Case binding: *The Mammoth Trees* (Sequoia gigantea),
California (Calaveras County). Lithograph printed in
color, Middleton, Strobridge & Co., Cincinnati, Ohio,
published by A. J. Campbell, ca. 1860 (p. 76).

Endpapers: *The Adventures of Tom Sawyer, from the book by
Mark Twain.* Portrait map by Everett Henry, 1953 (front);
*The Adventures of Huckleberry Finn, from the book by Mark
Twain.* Portrait map by Everett Henry, 1959 (back).

page i Detail from seventieth-birthday program and menu
(p. 177)

page ii–iii Detail from *Bird's Eye View of New York &
Brooklyn* (p. 30)

page iii (inset) Detail from Mark Twain in London (p. 112)

page vi–vii *Virginia City, Nevada Territory, 1861* (p. 62)

page viii *Samuel Clemens.* Photograph mounted on gray
board, unattributed, 1865.

page 1 Detail from seventieth-birthday program and menu
(p. 177)

page 2 Mark Twain. Photograph by A. F. Bradley, 1907.

page 5 Mark Twain. Photograph by Charles E. Bolles,
ca. 1902.

page 6 Mark Twain at Stormfield. Photograph by Frederic
Bulkeley Hyde, 1908.

page 15 *The Author's Memories.* Illustration from *A Tramp
Abroad* (p. 122).

Designed by Laura Lindgren

ISBN 978-0-316-20939-7
LCCN 2014937934

10 9 8 7 6 5 4 3 2 1

SC

Printed in China

To Mara Gai; and to Phyllis Rhodes and Chris Wasko, Twainiacs.

In memory of Charlotte Devereux Aladjem, who had a little fun every day.

CONTENTS

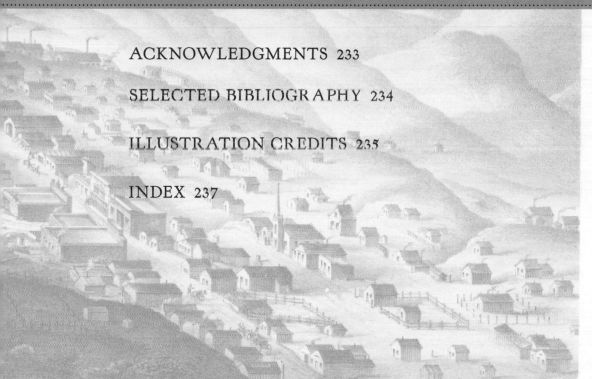

PREFACE

Mark Twain, described in his lifetime as America's favorite humorist—a title that fits even today—has been the subject of hundreds of books. Many of them can be found in the collections of the Library of Congress, so it might seem reasonable to ask: Does the world need yet another volume?

It is precisely because of the Library's collections that this book exists, and why it is unique among Twain literature. The story of Mark Twain is well known: Sam Clemens, the poor boy who grew up on the banks of the Mississippi River, became the world-renowned literary man of his age, a writer whose aphorisms are, more than one hundred years after his death, quoted daily in print, online, and in conversation. This volume is a biography of that man, but it is, moreover, a portrait of the times that nurtured his creative spirit, and its narrative is enhanced with more than two hundred images, many drawn from the collections of the Library of Congress.

From our rich Prints and Photographs collections, you will find photographs, portraits, and caricatures of Twain and his family and friends but also images of the river that supplied the foundation for his life and art; of the frontier West, where he first applied his talent for humorous writing—and where Samuel Clemens became Mark Twain; and of the tumultuous times that followed the Civil War, with fortunes made and lost, railroads crisscrossing the country, race and labor relations in flux, women demanding their rightful place in society, and America exerting its influence abroad for the first time in its history.

Mark Twain addressed all of these topics in his tales, sketches, essays, novels, and public speeches. His unique voice was the voice of an American at once celebrating his country's glorious achievements and exasperated with its shortcomings. Many of Twain's writings can be found in our general collections, as well as in our Rare Book and Special Collections, which contain precious and artfully illustrated first editions of his beloved works. From our Manuscripts, our Newspapers and Periodicals, and our Geography and Map divisions come items that round out a complex portrait of a man and his times.

Other books on Mark Twain have used materials from the Library of Congress, but none has reached so deeply into our collections to provide a portrait of the artist and the country that inspired him. In adding fresh insights into a man we thought we knew so well, *Mark Twain's America* is a salute from one American institution to another.

–James H. Billington, Librarian of Congress

Samuel Clemens, unattributed, 1865.
Photograph mounted on gray board.

FOREWORD by LEWIS H. LAPHAM

Mark Twain undertook the project of an autobiography in 1870 at the age of thirty-five, still a young man but already established as the famous author of *Innocents Abroad* and confident that he could navigate the current of his life by drawing upon the lessons learned thirteen years earlier as a steamboat pilot on the Mississippi River. As he noted in *Life on the Mississippi,*

> *There is one faculty which a pilot must incessantly cultivate until he has brought it to absolute perfection.... That faculty is memory. He cannot stop with merely thinking a thing is so-and-so, he must know it.... One cannot easily realize what a tremendous thing it is to know every trivial detail of twelve hundred miles of river and know it with absolute exactness.*

Twain expected the going to be as easy as a straight stretch of deep water under the light of a noonday sun. It wasn't. His memory was too close to absolute perfection, and he soon ran across snags and shoals unlike the ones to which he was accustomed south of Memphis and north of Vicksburg, an embarrassment he admitted in 1899 to a reporter from the *London Times:* "You cannot lay bare your private soul and look at it. You are too much ashamed of yourself. It is too disgusting" (p. 16).*

But Twain doesn't abandon his attempt at autobiography, because the longer he stays the course– for thirty-four years and through as many drafts of misbegotten manuscript while also writing nine other books, among them *Huckleberry Finn*–the more clearly he comes to see that what he intends is not the examination of an inner child or the confessions of a cloistered id. His topic is of a match with that of

the volume here in hand–America and the Americans making their nineteenth-century passage from an agrarian democracy to an industrial oligarchy, to Twain's mind a great and tragic tale, and one that no other writer of his generation was better positioned to tell because none had seen the country at so many of its compass points or become as acquainted with so many of its oddly assorted inhabitants.

Born in Missouri in 1835 on the frontier of what was still Indian territory, Twain as a boy of ten had seen the flogging and lynching of Negro slaves, had been present in his twenties not only at the wheel of the steamboats *Pennsylvania* and *Alonzo Child* but also at the pithead of the Comstock Lode when in 1861 he joined the going westward to the Nevada silver mines and the California goldfields, there to keep company with underage murderers and overage whores. In San Francisco he writes newspaper sketches and satires, becomes known as "The Wild Humorist of the Pacific Slope" who tells funny stories to the dancing girls and gamblers in the city's waterfront saloons.

Back east in the 1870s, Twain settles in Hartford, Connecticut, an eminent man of letters and property, and for the next thirty years, oracle for all occasions and star attraction on the national and international lecture stage, his wit and wisdom everywhere a wonder to behold–at banquet tables with presidents Ulysses S. Grant and Theodore Roosevelt, in New York City's Tammany Hall with swindling politicians and thieving financiers, on the program at the Boston Lyceum with Oliver Wendell Holmes, Horace Greeley, Petroleum V. Nasby, and Ralph Waldo Emerson. He also traveled forty-nine times across the Atlantic, and once across the Indian Ocean, as a dutiful tourist surveying the sights in Rome, Paris, and the Holy Land; as an itinerant sage entertaining crowds in Australia and Ceylon.

Laughter was Twain's stock-in-trade, and he

---

* All parenthetical page numbers in this essay refer to *Autobiography of Mark Twain, Volume 1: The Complete and Authoritative Edition* (Berkeley: University of California Press, 2010).

produced it in sufficient quantity to make bearable the acquaintance with grief he knew to be generously distributed among all present in a Newport drawing room or a Nevada brothel. Whether the audience was drunk or sober, swaddled in fur or armed with pistols, Twain recognized it as likely in need of comic relief. "The hard and sordid things in life," he once said, "are too hard and too sordid and too cruel for us to know and touch them year after year without some mitigating influence." He bottled the influence under whatever label drummed up a crowd–burlesque, satire, parody, sarcasm, ridicule–any or all of it guaranteed to fortify the blood and restore the spirit.

Twain coined the phrase the "Gilded Age" as a pejorative, to mark the calamity that was the collision of the democratic ideal with the democratic reality, the promise of a free, forbearing, and tolerant society run aground on the reef of destruction formed by the accruals of vanity and greed that Twain understood to be not a society at all but a state of war. The ostrich feathers and the mirrored glass, he associated with the epithet *citified,* "suggesting the absence of all spirituality, and the presence of all kinds of paltry materialisms and mean ideals and mean vanities and silly cynicisms." His struggling with his own paltry materialisms further delayed the composition of the autobiography. For thirty-four years he couldn't get out of his own way, kept trying to find a language worthy of a monument, to dress up the many manuscripts in literary velvets and brocades.

Eventually faced with the approaching sandbar of his death, he puts aside his pen and ink and elects to dictate, not write, what he construes as his "bequest to posterity." He begins the experiment in 1904 in Florence, where he has rented a handsome villa in which to care for his cherished, dying wife. To William Dean Howells, close friend and trusted editor, he writes to say, "I've struck it!" a method that removes all traces of a style that is "too prim, too nice," too slow and artificial in its movement for the telling of a story (pp. 20–22).

"Narrative," he had said at the outset of his labors,

should flow as flows the brook down through the hills and the leafy woodlands . . . a brook that never goes straight for a minute, but goes, and goes briskly, and sometimes ungrammatically, and sometimes fetching a horseshoe three-quarters of a mile around and at the end of the circuit flowing within the yard of the path it traversed an hour before; but always going, and always following at least one law, always loyal to that law, the law of narrative, which has no law. Nothing to do but make the trip; the how of it is not important so that the trip is made. (p. 224)

Twain's wife does not survive her season in the Italian sun, and at the age of seventy-one soon after his return to America, he casts himself adrift on the flood tide of his memory, dictating at discursive length to a series of stenographers while "propped up against great snowy white pillows" in a Fifth Avenue town house three blocks north of Washington Square. He delivers the deposition over a period of nearly four years, from the winter of 1906 until a few months before his death in the spring of 1910, here and there introducing into the record miscellaneous exhibits–previously published speeches, anecdotes and sketches, newspaper clippings, brief biographies, letters, philosophical digressions, and theatrical asides.

The autobiography he offers as an omnium-gatherum, its author reserving the right to digress at will, talk only about whatever interests him at the moment, "drop it at the moment its interest threatens to pale." He leaves the reader free to adopt the same approach, to come across Twain at a meeting of the Hartford Monday Evening Club in 1884 (at which the subject of discussion is the price of cigars and the befriending of cats) and to skip over as many pages as necessary to find Twain in Honolulu in 1866 with the survivors of forty-three days at sea in an open boat, or discover him in Calcutta in 1896 in the company of Mary Wilson, "old and gray-haired, but…very handsome," a woman whom he had much admired in her prior incarnation as a young woman in 1849 in Hannibal, Missouri:

We sat down and talked. We steeped our thirsty souls in the reviving wine of the past, the pathetic past, the beautiful past, the dear and lamented past; we uttered the names that had been silent upon our lips for fifty years, and it was as if they were made of music; with reverent hands we unburied our dead, the mates of our youth, and caressed them with our speech; we searched the dusty chambers of our memories and dragged forth incident after incident, episode after episode, folly after folly, and laughed such good laughs over them, with the tears running down. (p. 157)

The turn of Twain's mind is democratic. He holds his fellow citizens in generous and affectionate regard not because they are rich or beautiful or famous but because they are his fellow citizens. His dictations he employs as "a form and method whereby the past and the present are constantly brought face-to-face resulting in contrasts which newly fire up the interest all along like contact of flint with steel" (p. 441). Something seen in Paris in 1894 reminds him of something else seen in Virginia City in 1864; an impression of the first time he saw Florence in 1892 sends him back to St. Louis in 1845.

The intelligence that is wide-wandering, intuitive, and sympathetic is also, in the parsing of it by Bernard De Voto, the historian and editor of Twain's papers, "undeluded, merciless and final." His comedy drifts toward the darker shore of tragedy as he grows older and loses much of his liking for what he comes to regard as "the damned human race," his judgment rendered "in the absence of respect-worthy evidence that the human being has morals."

Twain doesn't absent himself from the company of the damned. He knows himself made, like all other men, as "a poor, cheap, wormy thing…a sarcasm, the Creator's prime miscarriage in invention, the moral inferior of all the animals…the superior to them all in one gift only, and that one not up to *his* estimation of it–intellect" (p. 184). The steamboat pilot's delight in that one gift holds fast only to the end of his trick at the wheel of his life. Mankind as a species he writes off as a miscarriage in invention, but he makes exceptions–a very great many exceptions–for the men, women, and children (usually together with any and all of their uncles, nieces, grandmothers, and cousins) whom he has come to know and hold dear over the course of his travels. The autobiography is crowded with their portraits sketched in an always loving few sentences or a handsome turn of phrase. Humor is still "the great thing, the saving thing after all," but as the gilded spirit of the age becomes everywhere more oppressive under the late-nineteenth-century chandeliers, Twain pits the force of his merciless and undeluded wit against "the peacock shams" of the world's "colossal humbug." He doesn't traffic in the mockery of a cynic or the bitterness of the misanthrope. Nor does he expect his ridicule to correct the conduct of Boss Tweed, improve the morals of Commodore Vanderbilt, or stop the same-day deliveries of the politicians to the banks.

His purpose is therapeutic. A man at play with the freedoms of his mind, believing that it is allegiance to the truth and not the flag that rescues the citizens of a democracy from the prisons of their selfishness and greed, Twain aims to blow away with a blast of laughter the pestilent hospitality tents of a society making itself sick with its consumption of "sweet-smelling, sugar-coated lies." He offers in their stead the reviving wine of the dear lamented past, and his autobiography stands, as does his presence in this book, as the story of an observant pilgrim heaving the weighted lead of his comprehensive and comprehending memory into the flow and stream of time.

MARK TWAIN's AMERICA

INTRODUCTION

Before there were bloggers and YouTube sensations, talk-radio hosts, rock stars, and reality-television celebrities, stand-up comedians and Steampunk, political pundits and cable television commentators, there was Mark Twain. In today's media-rich environment, he would likely rule the airwaves and dominate the Internet, expressing his opinions on education, immigration, religion, race, current events, and historical trends in a provocative blend of online anecdotes and observations, rambling rants and trenchant sound bites.

More than one hundred years after his death, Mark Twain remains a phenomenon, an Everyman appealing to everyone. The first volume of his unexpurgated autobiography, released in 2010, was a bestseller; volume two followed in 2013. His books and essays have been digitized for access on the World Wide Web, while his popular quotations adorn diverse websites, Listservs, and the latest social networks. Still trendy and trending, relevant and respected, in our divided times Mark Twain may be the one thing we can all agree on.

In his own time, presidents and paupers loved his books; young children saved pennies to buy his stories, while grown-ups debated his political observations and celebrated his genius. In today's parlance, he spoke to the 99 percenters as well as the 1 percenters, attracting Main Street Americans along with Wall Street titans. He was passionate, persuasive, and often politically incorrect. A mugwump and muckraker, he started out as a moderate Whig, supported the Republicans in the immediate aftermath of the Civil War, joined the Democrats after Reconstruction to vote for Grover Cleveland, and finally disavowed both party platforms as an independent voice.

The foundation for Mark Twain's wide appeal lies rooted in the character of his creator, Samuel L. Clemens. Born in a two-room cabin on the edge of civilization in 1835 Missouri, Clemens died seventy-five years later in a palatial estate outside New York City. In creating Mark Twain, Clemens self-consciously blended memory and imagination, fact and fiction, blurring the line between his personal life and professional persona. At times, we know only what he tells us; Clemens was a consummate storyteller, rarely letting facts spoil a good tale and using aphorisms to explain himself and his worldview. In Twain's world, there were often several sides to the story, and then there was the truth. He found truth, and wisdom, on the Mississippi River, in the South that framed his childhood and shaped his career. He unearthed nuggets of humanity in the West, under primitive conditions and layers of outrageous misdirection, like buried ore in a mine. Back East, he became a giant on the lecture circuit and a sight on the sidewalks, publicly human and humane, America's most popular and prolific author.

He looked strange and talked, walked, and dressed differently from everyone around him. He wore a sealskin coat in proper Boston and a white suit before a congressional committee in Washington. He lived and worked simply in the midst of slaves, miners, teamsters, laborers, boatmen, artists, editors, and engravers, yet he could mingle with high society, dine with royalty, and befriend some of America's richest and most powerful men and women.

His perspective was unique; between his boyhood in Hannibal, Missouri, and his death in Redding, Connecticut, he traveled the world, living abroad for a decade with his family. In some sense he remained an outsider—a Gladwellian outlier. Clemens overcame every obstacle and took seemingly every opportunity to develop his persona, promote the Mark Twain brand, and stir interest in his opinions.

He became an oracle and, for many, the nation's conscience. A transcendent celebrity, he made his health, welfare, and shifting fortunes available to his readers, who lived vicariously through his books, letters, and sketches. His life seemed an open book, as if he wished to share equally his luck and his haunting losses; his public loved him for his honesty, responding emotionally to his well-publicized triumphs, failures, and personal tragedies.

From politics to pets, his observations and opinions expressed in books, articles, interviews, and letters on virtually every aspect of modern life have made him one of the world's most oft-quoted figures. He is also one of our most recognizable; like George Washington, Benjamin Franklin, Daniel Webster, and Abraham Lincoln before him, Twain made sure he was seen, and saw himself, in portraits and caricatures published in magazines and newspapers everywhere.

We remember Twain primarily for his words, but pictures—drawings and comic sketches—were critical to his work and identity. They enhanced his publications, promoted his work and image, and documented his legend. Newspapers and books in Mark Twain's America were filled with illustrations, as publishers sought to attract a popular, newly literate audience. Sam Clemens understood the persuasive power of images at an early age; he was just sixteen and assisting in his brother Orion's print shop when he attacked a rival editor with a series of satirical woodcuts. Throughout his career, Clemens collaborated with illustrators, occasionally embellishing articles and letters with his own cartoons, sketches, and doodles.

The Library of Congress collections include rare and unpublished works by the artists, cartoonists, and photographers who sought out Mark Twain, attracted by his strong personality and striking looks. Portraits of Twain and pictures of his life and times illustrate beyond words the trajectory of his career and his relationships with family, friends, colleagues, and contemporaries. Bright caricatures, dark portraits, and candid photographs suggest his complex character, the manic energy that drove him, and the deep melancholy he knew from his earliest years. Scenes depicting the places in which he lived and the circles in which he traveled add to our sense of the man and help fill out the complex picture of his life. Seen within a larger context of period views and contemporary illustrations, Twain's extraordinary character stands out.

Although he drew from the past, Twain represented the future; he read voraciously, following with great interest the technological and scientific breakthroughs of the day. He flouted literary and social conventions, extending their boundaries to encompass the real world and characters he knew from his travels and encounters. He built an empire of words—becoming, like no other before him, an international celebrity, popular icon, moral authority, and literary legend. In a speech toward the end of his life, he said that the best fame "permeates the great crowd of people you never see and never mingle with; people with whom you have no speech, but who read your books and become admirers of your work and have an affection for you. You may never find it out in the world, but there it is.... They have nothing but compliments, they never see the criticisms, they never hear any disparagement of you, and you will remain in the home of their hearts' affection forever and ever."

And so, for Mark Twain, it is.

✤ 1835 ✤

Born Samuel Langhorne Clemens on November 30 in Florida, Missouri, to John M. and Jane L. Clemens. Is the sixth of seven children but only three siblings will survive childhood: his brother Orion (1825–1897), Henry (1838–1858), and Pamela (1827–1904).

✤ 1836 ✤

Begins life frequently ill. Lives in the town of Florida, where father purchases house on Main Street.

✤ 1837 ✤

Continues to live in Florida. John M. Clemens is appointed to a commission to develop Salt River and becomes a county judge.

✤ 1838 ✤

Henry Clemens, Sam's younger brother, is born June 13. Of all his siblings, Sam will become closest to Henry.

✤ 1839 ✤

John M. Clemens sells his Florida, Missouri, property and moves family to Hannibal in November.

Sam's sister, Margaret Clemens, dies August 17 of bilious fever at age nine.

✤ 1840 ✤

Begins attending school in Hannibal.

✤ 1841 ✤

Jane L. Clemens joins Presbyterian Church.

John M. Clemens sits in circuit court jury that sends abolitionists to prison.

✤ 1842 ✤

Orion Clemens begins working in St. Louis.

John M. Clemens trades a slave for ten barrels of tar.

Older brother Benjamin Clemens dies at age ten.

✤ 1843 ✤

Spends the first of several summers on the Quarles family farm near Florida.

John M. Clemens is elected Justice of the Peace in Hannibal.

✤ 1844 ✤

Contracts measles by climbing into a friend's sickbed during epidemic.

✤ 1845 ✤

Takes first steamboat ride to St. Louis.

Missouri charters Hannibal as a city.

Olivia Langdon (Clemens) is born, in Elmira, New York, on November 27.

✤ 1846 ✤

Family sells furniture to raise money.

John M. Clemens tries unsuccessfully to sell land he had purchased in Tennessee in the 1820s as investment. He chairs the committee promoting a road to St. Joseph in November. He becomes candidate for circuit court clerk.

✤ 1847 ✤

John M. Clemens dies March 24.

Court names Orion Clemens administrator of his father's estate.

Sam works at odd jobs, then begins attending John D. Dawson's one-room schoolhouse on April 14. Goes to work for the *Hannibal Gazette*.

✛ 1848 ✛

Sam goes to work as an apprentice for Joseph Ament's *Missouri Courier.*

✛ 1849 ✛

Sam stops attending school regularly.

Cholera epidemic hits the Hannibal region.

✛ 1850 ✛

Joins the Cadets of Temperance, a group that prohibits drinking, smoking, and the use of profanity. Later, the group would appear in the character of Tom Sawyer, who "joined the new order of Cadets of Temperance being attracted by the showy character of their 'regalia.' He promised to abstain from smoking, chewing, and profanity as long as he remained a member. Now he found out a new thing–namely, that to promise not to do a thing is the surest way in the world to make a body want to go and do that very thing." (*The Adventures of Tom Sawyer,* chapter 22)

Orion starts the *Western Union* in the summer. Sam begins to work for Orion in September.

Orion sells part of the family's Tennessee land.

✛ 1851 ✛

Begins working for Orion as a printer.

Orion buys *Hannibal Journal* and consolidates it with the *Western Union.*

Sam begins to run Orion's newspaper while Orion is away.

✛ 1852 ✛

Sam continues periodically to run the *Western Union* while also writing for the paper, using his first pen name, W. Epaminondas Adrastus Perkins, for these works. Publishes "The Dandy Frightening the Squatter" in Boston's *Carpet-Bag* in May with his initials, "S. L. C.," as his byline, his first national publication.

✛ 1853 ✛

Fire guts Orion Clemens's newspaper offices.

Sam leaves Hannibal for St. Louis. Will work as an itinerant printer in New York City and Philadelphia between August 1853 and February 1854.

Orion sells the paper, moves to Muscatine, Iowa. Sam corresponds for *Muscatine Journal* from Philadelphia.

✛ 1854 ✛

Visits Washington, DC, then returns to New York City.

From summer through the following June, lives in St. Louis and travels, working as jour printer, or journeyman printer, to be able to find employment wherever he desired.

Writes travel letters for Orion's *Muscatine Journal.*

✛ 1855 ✛

Makes his first attempt to become a steamboat pilot July 15.

Writes occasional travel letters for Orion's newspaper.

✛ 1856 ✛

Lives in Keokuk, Iowa, then moves to Cincinnati, Ohio.

Writes Thomas Jefferson Snodgrass letters for the *Keokuk Daily Post.*

✛ 1857 ✛

Lives in a Cincinnati boardinghouse. On February 28, leaves Cincinnati for New Orleans aboard the steamboat *Paul Jones.*

In March, is a cub pilot on the *Paul Jones.* The rest of the year, lives on the Mississippi River, where he cubs on the *Crescent City, Rufus J. Lackland, John J. Roe, William M. Morrison, Pennsylvania,* and *D. A. January.*

✛ 1858 ✛

Continues to live on the Mississippi River: on the *New Falls City, Pennsylvania, Alfred T. Lacey, John H. Dickey, White Cloud, New Falls City,* and *Aleck Scott.*

On June 5, after fighting with pilot William Brown, Clemens leaves the *Pennsylvania* in New Orleans–eight days before its boilers explode; the explosion severely injures his brother Henry, who is a clerk on the *Pennsylvania.* Henry dies eight days later.

⁘ 1859 ⁘

Clemens pilots the *Alfred T. Lacey, J. C. Swon, Edward J. Gay,* and *A. B. Chambers.* Receives steamboat piloting license.

Publishes "River Intelligence" on May 17 under the pseudonym Sergeant Fathom in *New Orleans Crescent.*

⁘ 1860 ⁘

Pilots the *City of Memphis* after renewing his piloting license. Joins his last steamboat, the *Alonzo Child.*

Publishes "Pilot's Memoranda" in the *St. Louis Missouri Republican.*

⁘ 1861 ⁘

Stays on the *Alonzo Child* until January 29.

Renews piloting license on March 20. President Lincoln signs Orion Clemens's commission as secretary of the Nevada Territory on March 27. On April 25, his piloting career ends when the Civil War stops river traffic.

Campaigns with Confederate irregulars around Marion County. His experiences will be the basis of "The Private History of the Campaign That Failed," an 1885 sketch of a group of "ragtag boys" excited but utterly naïve about joining up to fight in the war.

Begins journey to Nevada with his brother Orion: to St. Joseph as a passenger on the *Nebraska,* then by stagecoach July 26–August 14.

Clemens and "Johnny K–" stake timber claims at Lake Tahoe and start a forest fire, September 20.

Clerks for Nevada Territorial Legislature October–November.

Prospects at Unionville in December.

⁘ 1862 ⁘

Mines in Aurora, Nevada. Visits Mono Lake with Calvin Higbie, a mining partner who will appear in *Roughing It.*

Settles in Virginia City, Nevada, in August. Works for the *Virginia City Territorial Enterprise* September through May 1864, covering the Nevada legislature November to December 1862.

⁘ 1863 ⁘

Adopts the pen name Mark Twain on February 2.

Visits San Francisco May through July, then Lake Tahoe, before a return to San Francisco in September.

Writes occasionally for *San Francisco Daily Morning Call.*

Reports on Nevada Constitutional Convention October 26 through mid-December.

⁘ 1864 ⁘

Elected Governor of the Third House by Nevada journalists in January. (Third House was a mock legislative body; Twain was addressed as "Governor Twain.")

Publishes sketches in the *New York Mercury.*

Lives in San Francisco May through December; meets Bret Harte and works for *San Francisco Daily Morning Call.*

Prospects in Tuolumne and Calaveras counties December to February 1865.

⁘ 1865 ⁘

Stays at Angels Camp, where he first hears the jumping-frog story January 22. In late February, returns to San Francisco until March 1866.

Experiences November 8 earthquake in San Francisco.

In San Francisco, writes for several publications, publishing "Jim Smiley and His Jumping Frog" in November.

⁘ 1866 ⁘

Sails to Hawaii as *Sacramento Union* correspondent; stays there March to July.

Orion Clemens leaves Nevada in May.

Gives his first lecture on the Sandwich Islands in San Francisco on October 2.

Travels October–November on a sixteen-engagement lecture tour in northern California and western Nevada.

Sails for New York December 15. Aboard the ship *America* in the Pacific, writes the first of twenty-six letters to *Alta California;* meets Edgar Wakeman, a famous sea captain, the model for "captain characters" in many of Twain's novels.

✢ 1867 ✢

Arrives in New York on January 12 and lives there until June.

On March 1, signs up for the *Quaker City* cruise; will continue to write travel letters for the *Alta California* from the *Quaker City* excursion.

Delivers first New York City lecture at Cooper Union on May 6.

Publishes *The Celebrated Jumping Frog of Calaveras County, and Other Sketches* in May.

Sails on the *Quaker City* to Europe and the Holy Land June 10, returning to New York City November 19.

Lives in Washington, DC, until February 1868 as the private secretary of Senator William M. Stewart, author of the Fifteenth Amendment, granting suffrage to all men regardless of race, color, or previous condition of servitude.

Invited on December 1 by Elisha Bliss Jr., president of the American Publishing Company, of Hartford, Connecticut, to write a book about the *Quaker City* voyage.

Revisits New York City; meets Olivia (Livy) Langdon on December 27.

✢ 1868 ✢

Sails to California in March to gives lectures throughout northern California and western Nevada April–July. Completes *Innocents Abroad*.

Returns to New York City; will move between New York City, Elmira, and Hartford until November, when he embarks on another lecture tour in the East until March 1869. Courts Livy while in Elmira and becomes secretly engaged to her November 26.

✢ 1869 ✢

On February 4, engagement to Livy is formally announced.

Buys interest in the *Buffalo Express*.

Publishes *Innocents Abroad* in July.

November–January 1870, completes a forty-five-engagement lecture tour in New England, Pennsylvania, New Jersey, New York, and Washington, DC.

✢ 1870 ✢

Lives in Buffalo, New York, until March 1871.

On February 2, Mark Twain marries Olivia Langdon, in Elmira, New York.

Jervis Langdon, Olivia's father, dies of cancer August 6.

Signs contract to write *Roughing It.*

Twain and Olivia's first child, Langdon Clemens, is born prematurely November 7 in Buffalo.

✢ 1871 ✢

Lives in Buffalo and then Elmira while looking for a new home in Hartford and visiting New York and Washington, DC, on business.

Puts Buffalo home and newspaper interests up for sale March 2. Rents a house in Hartford's Nook Farm.

October–March 1872, goes on a lecture tour through the East.

Patents elastic garment strap invention later known as suspenders.

✢ 1872 ✢

Lives in Hartford and lectures in the Midwest and East. Journeys alone to England from August to November.

Publishes *Roughing It* in February.

Susy Clemens, first daughter, is born in Elmira March 19.

Langdon Clemens dies in Hartford June 2, age eighteen months.

✢ 1873 ✢

Signs deed to Nook Farm property in Hartford.

Writes *The Gilded Age* with Charles Dudley Warner; it is published in December.

With Livy and Susy, visits England, Scotland, and Ireland.

Returns to England with Charles Warren Stoddard, a journalist for the *San Francisco Chronicle* and a friend from the West, for a lecture tour.

Patents a self-pasting scrapbook.

✢ 1874 ✢

Clara Clemens, second daughter, is born in Elmira June 8.

Twain, Olivia, and the children move into their unfinished Hartford home on September 19. In November, begins hiking with Joseph Twichell from Hartford to Boston on a regular basis.

Publishes an authorized edition of *The Choice Humorous Works of Mark Twain.*

Pays Gilbert B. Densmore $400 for the script of a play about Colonel Sellers, main character of *The Gilded Age.* Begins rehearsing *The Gilded Age* in New York City; it runs September–January 1875.

✢ 1875 ✢

Publishes "Old Times on the Mississippi" as a serial in the *Atlantic Monthly.*

Attends Henry Ward Beecher's adultery trial in Brooklyn.

✢ 1876 ✢

Begins research for *The Prince and the Pauper;* begins to write *Huckleberry Finn.* Publishes *The Adventures of Tom Sawyer* in London in June.

Speaks on behalf of presidential candidate Rutherford B. Hayes in Hartford September 30.

✢ 1877 ✢

June to August, stays at Elmira with family while making frequent trips to New York City and Hartford.

Ah Sin, play concocted by Twain and Bret Harte from Harte's poem "The Heathen Chinee," opens in Washington, DC, May 7. *Ah Sin* runs in New York July–September.

Publishes *A True Story, and the Recent Carnival of Crime* in September.

On December 17, speaks at a Boston banquet honoring John Greenleaf Whittier's seventieth birthday. Attempts a burlesque in a spirit of humor, but it goes over terribly, leaving the room silent. With the help of William Dean Howells, Ralph Waldo Emerson, and Oliver Wendell Holmes, he comes to find that he is forgiven.

Has a telephone installed in his Hartford home.

✢ 1878 ✢

Works on *A Tramp Abroad* before contracting for a book on Europe.

Sails to Europe with Olivia, Clara, and Susy April 11. Journey to Germany, the Swiss and French Alps, and Italy.

✢ 1879 ✢

Twain and family continue their trip through Europe: Paris, Belgium, the Netherlands, England. Leave from Liverpool September 3 for New York City. They are in Hartford with visits to Elmira for the remainder of the year.

In September, Ulysses S. Grant returns to America after two years abroad, and on November 13, Twain speaks at a Chicago banquet honoring General Grant.

✢ 1880 ✢

Publishes *A Tramp Abroad* in March.

Writes *The Prince and the Pauper* in the course of this year.

Begins investing in the Paige Compositor.

Third daughter, Jean Clemens, is born in Elmira July 26.

Gives a welcome speech when Ulysses S. Grant visits Hartford October 16 and another speech on October 26 on behalf of James Garfield's presidential candidacy.

✢ 1881 ✢

Redecorates the Hartford home.

In April, makes Charles L. Webster his business manager; in July, gives Webster power of attorney in his publishing interests.

✢ 1882 ✢

Travels with publisher James Osgood and stenographer Roswell Phelps to St. Louis. Contracts to publish a memoir centered on his life on the Mississippi River. Goes to New Orleans and Minnesota by steamboat. Also visits Hannibal. During his travels, also works on *Huckleberry Finn.*

✢ 1883 ✢

Finishes *Life on the Mississippi* in January and visits Canada to establish the book's copyright in May; publishes it that same month.

Spends the rest of this year in either Hartford or Elmira.

Finishes *Adventures of Huckleberry Finn* in July.

✛ 1884 ✛

Spends most of year in Hartford or Elmira. In November, begins lectures in the eastern states and in the Midwest with George Washington Cable.

Founds Charles L. Webster & Co. publishing firm.

Offers to publish Grant's memoirs.

In December, publishes extract of *Huckleberry Finn* in *Century* magazine and the complete work in London.

✛ 1885 ✛

Contracts to publish Grant's *Memoirs* and publishes *Adventures of Huckleberry Finn* in New York.

Finishes lecture tour with George W. Cable in the Midwest, where he stops to visit Hannibal.

In March, Livy's adaptation of *The Prince and the Pauper* is staged and Twain makes Charles L. Webster a partner in his publishing company.

General Ulysses S. Grant dies July 23; in December, Webster & Co. issues the first volume of Grant's *Memoirs* and Twain publishes "The Private History of a Campaign That Failed."

Patents Mark Twain's Memory Builder.

✛ 1886 ✛

Revises partnership contract with Webster, giving Webster a more prominent place in the company.

Addresses Senate committee on copyright protection.

Col. Sellers is produced in Hartford.

Forms a partnership with Paige to develop the Paige Compositor.

Visits New York City frequently on business, takes the family to Keokuk for a family reunion, and spends summer in Elmira with family.

✛ 1887 ✛

Travels only between Hartford and Elmira this year.

Webster & Co. begins its seven-year decline toward bankruptcy.

Writes a dramatic adaptation entitled *Colonel Sellers as a Scientist.*

✛ 1888 ✛

Publishes *Mark Twain's Library of Humor.*

Makes Fred J. Hall manager of Webster & Co.; Webster withdraws from his contract as the relationship with Twain deteriorates.

Visits Thomas A. Edison's lab and receives an honorary Master of Arts degree from Yale.

✛ 1889 ✛

A Connecticut Yankee in King Arthur's Court is published in December.

Even after Paige delays public demonstrations of his typesetting device, Twain agrees to maintain financial support of the inventor.

A dramatic adaptation of *The Prince and the Pauper* opens in Philadelphia December 24.

✛ 1890 ✛

The Prince and the Pauper opens in New York January 20, goes on tour March 1; one of its stops is in London April 12.

Lives in Hartford, but vacations with the family July to September at Onteora in the Catskills; visits his mother, Jane Lampton Clemens, in Keokuk in August.

Is busy with the Paige Compositor, to which he buys all the rights.

Jane Lampton Clemens dies October 27; attends his mother's funeral in Hannibal. In November, his mother-in-law, Olivia L. Langdon, dies; attends her funeral in Elmira. That same month, his daughter Jane Clemens experiences her first epileptic seizure.

✛ 1891 ✛

Markets Mark Twain's Memory Builder, based on a history game he developed, promoting it as "a way to make history dates stick."

Rheumatism forces him to write temporarily with his left hand (he was right-handed).

Stops payments on the Paige Compositor.

Ends residence in Hartford, closing the house June 6–14. Takes the family to Europe, visiting European health spas along the way. They go to France, then boating down the Rhône in Germany, and to Switzerland and Berlin.

November to March 1892, publishes six travel sketches in the *New York Sun*.

✤ 1892 ✤

Twain and family continue their European sojourn: Menton, France, with Livy only, and Italy; settles in Bad Nauheim, Germany, in June. Returns alone to New York from mid-June to early July. Moves family near Florence, Italy, where they live until June 1893.

Publishes *The American Claimant* in May.

Writes "Those Extraordinary Twins," which becomes the basis for *Pudd'nhead Wilson*.

✤ 1893 ✤

With the family in Florence, Twain travels frequently to Chicago and Elmira on business through March, April, and May.

Resettles family in Berlin June 28.

Sails to New York with Clara in August.

Rooms in New York City September–March 1894. During this time, he makes many public appearances, earning him the sobriquet "Belle of New York."

Meets Henry H. Rogers and, with his help, negotiates with Paige over the compositor after almost giving up on the investment.

✤ 1894 ✤

Gives frequent speeches and readings in New York City until March, when he returns to family, now in France.

Gives power of attorney to H. H. Rogers, who assigns his copyrights to Livy.

Webster & Co. goes into bankruptcy in April.

Publishes *Tom Sawyer Abroad* and *Pudd'nhead Wilson*.

Paige Compositor is tested at the *Chicago Herald,* where it proves impractical as a commercial device.

✤ 1895 ✤

Abandons all interest in the Paige Compositor.

Travels frequently this year. His family is in France the first half of the year; in May they move back to Elmira. Twain travels to Paris, London, and New York alone and with his family.

Pudd'nhead Wilson opens in Hartford as a play April 8. April 15 moves to New York City.

Contracts with R. S. Smythe, a well-known lecture agent, to do a round-the-world tour.

In July, undertakes the tour by going overland from Elmira to British Columbia with Livy, Clara, and James B. Pond. Sails to Vancouver in August, anchors off Honolulu, stops in Fiji, Australia, and New Zealand, and returns to Australia until January 5.

✤ 1896 ✤

Continues his round-the-world tour. Sails from Australia to Ceylon, then Bombay and other Indian stops, crosses the Indian Ocean, and rests in Mauritius. Sails to South Africa, stops at Lourenço Marques, Mozambique; then from South Africa to England until July 1897.

Publishes *Joan of Arc*.

On August 15, after hearing of Susy's failing health, Livy and Clara sail for home from England. Susy dies in Hartford August 18, before they arrive. Twain receives the news in England.

Livy, Clara, and Jean rejoin Twain in England September 9.

Reaches a new agreement with the American Publishing Co. to issue a uniform edition of his books.

✤ 1897 ✤

In London January to July, then Switzerland July to September; from September to May 1898, lives in Vienna's Hotel Metropole.

Following the Equator is published.

Rejects James B. Pond's offer of $50,000 for 125 lectures in America.

Writes about growing tensions in central Europe in his essay "Stirring Times in Austria," published in *Harper's* magazine.

✢ 1898 ✢

Stays in Vienna January to May. Clara Clemens studies music and meets Ossip Gabrilowitsch, her first husband, in Vienna.

In March, learns from H. H. Rogers that his creditors are paid off.

✢ 1899 ✢

Begins issuing the collected *Writings of Mark Twain* in January.

Goes to London June to July. In London, speaks frequently and meets Booker T. Washington July 4.

Beginning in October, lives in London for a year.

✢ 1900 ✢

In June, publishes *The Man That Corrupted Hadleyburg, and Other Stories and Essays.*

In October, sails to New York City, where he lives at 14 West Tenth Street and lectures frequently through December.

Introduces Winston Churchill to his first American lecture audience in New York December 12.

✢ 1901 ✢

Lives in New York City and speaks often there.

Publishes "To the Person Sitting in Darkness" and "Extracts from Adam's Diary."

In March, with Livy, attempts to communicate with Susy through a spiritualist.

✢ 1902 ✢

Invests in American Plasmon, a pharmaceutical company of which he will become acting president. In 1907, a bankruptcy petition would be filed against the company, bringing huge losses to Twain.

Publishes "A Double-Barreled Detective Story."

Buys a house in Tarrytown, New York, and puts the Hartford house on the market.

In May and June, visits Hannibal, Springfield, and St. Louis, Missouri. Is photographed outside his boyhood home in Hannibal May 30.

Spends time at York Harbor, Minnesota, with family June to October, after which he returns to Riverdale, New York.

August to December, Livy becomes seriously ill and spends long periods in isolation and apart from Twain.

Hires Isabel Lyon as his secretary.

✢ 1903 ✢

Lives in Riverdale January–July. Lives in Elmira with family early July to October. Is allowed to see Livy briefly as her illness worsens.

Beginning in April, spends five weeks in bed with bronchitis.

Publishes *My Debut as a Literary Person, with Other Essays and Stories* and "A Dog's Tale."

In May, finally sells the Hartford home.

Negotiates a contract making Harper & Bros. his exclusive publisher.

Takes his family to Italy in October; they live in a Florentine villa November–June 1904.

✢ 1904 ✢

In Florence, begins dictating his autobiography.

Publishes "Italian Without a Master" and "Extracts from Adam's Diary."

In April, is forbidden to see Livy, as doctors think that might overexcite her.

Livy dies in Florence June 5. Twain sails from Naples to New York with his daughters and Livy's body June 28–July 13. The family buries Livy in Elmira's Woodlawn Cemetery July 14.

Jean Clemens resumes epileptic seizures and Clara has a nervous breakdown; in July, Clara enters a sanitarium.

Lives in Lee, Massachusetts, until September. Jean is injured in a horseback-riding accident July 31.

Moves to 21 Fifth Avenue, New York City, where he will live September–June 1908. Publishes "The $30,000 Bequest."

✤ 1905 ✤

Lives in New York City, staying in Dublin, New Hampshire, late May to October 21.

Publishes "A Monument to Adam," *King Leopold's Soliloquy,* and "Eve's Diary."

Clara Clemens has an appendectomy May 10. He sees Clara in August for the first time in a year.

Jean Clemens tries to kill Katy Leary, family maid, during an epileptic seizure.

Twain dines at the White House with President Theodore Roosevelt.

Is honored with a seventieth-birthday banquet at Delmonico's in New York City December 5.

✤ 1906 ✤

Continues to live in New York City, where he frequently speaks at public gatherings. A. B. Paine joins Twain's household to write his biography.

Visits Washington, DC, in December, and addresses congressional committees on copyright protection, wearing a white suit. It becomes his trademark public outfit.

Once again, Jean attempts to kill Katy Leary during an epileptic attack. Jean enters a private institution in Katonah, New York.

Twain buys land near Redding, Connecticut, for a new home.

Publishes "Chapters from My Autobiography," a serial that runs from September to December 1907.

✤ 1907 ✤

June to July, makes his last transatlantic trip to England, with Ralph Ashcroft. Receives honorary degree from Oxford University and speaks in London.

On July 22, H. H. Rogers has a stroke.

Meets Dorothy Quick aboard the SS *Minnetonka* during return voyage. She visits him at Tuxedo Park in August.

✤ 1908 ✤

In Bermuda January–early February and February 24–April 11. While there, plays golf and socializes with future president Woodrow Wilson.

Officially organizes the Angelfish Club of young girls, briefly calling his residence Innocence at Home. Moves into this home, his last, at Redding, Connecticut. Angelfish girls are guests there June–September.

Begins revising *Life on the Mississippi* for a new edition but never completes the job.

Burglars break into his residence on September 18. Some Angelfish are visiting, but none are hurt. Afterward, gives a few interviews on how he confronted the burglars with a gun, demonstrating for photographers.

Jean Clemens goes to Germany to be treated for epilepsy September 26 to January 1909.

Twain begins calling Redding home Stormfield on October 7.

Gives Ralph Ashcroft and Isabel Lyon power of attorney over his business affairs, a decision that costs him dearly.

✤ 1909 ✤

Lives at Stormfield. Jean lives in sanitariums January to April.

Isabel Lyon marries Ralph Ashcroft March 18.

Fires Isabel Lyon in April; severs ties with her and Ralph Ashcroft in September, accusing them of mismanaging his money.

Jean moves into Stormfield April 26.

Publishes *Is Shakespeare Dead?*

Delivers his last public speech at Angelfish. Frances Nunnally's graduation from St. Timothy's School, in Catonsville, Maryland, June 9.

In July, is diagnosed with heart disease. Later that month, makes A. B. Paine his business manager.

Clara is married at Stormfield, October 6.

Publishes *Extract from Captain Stormfield's Visit to Heaven.*

In December, the collapse of Plasmon Company, a producer of dried milk biscuits that Twain said improved health, wipes out Twain's investment in the company.

Jean drowns in the bathtub during a seizure at Stormfield December 24.

Writes "The Death of Jean" in late December.

✦ 1910 ✦

Lives at Stormfield.

On January 5, before leaving for Bermuda, sees William Dean Howells for the last time. Bermuda is his last trip outside the United States, January 5–April 14.

In February, publishes "The Turning Point in My Life" and in March, Thomas Edison releases the film *A Mountain Blizzard,* a dramatic adaptation of *Roughing It.*

Clara returns to Stormfield April 17. Twain's only grandchild, Nina Gabrilowitsch, is born at Redding, Connecticut, April 18.

The night of April 20, Halley's Comet streaks across the sky as it did two weeks before Twain's birth. Twain dies at sunset at Stormfield April 21.

Joseph Twichell conducts funeral service in New York City for his friend April 23.

Twain is buried April 24 in Elmira's Woodlawn Cemetery.

THE AUTHOR'S MEMORIES.

CHAPTER ONE

River of Dreams

In 1835, the year Sam Clemens was born, rivers powered the nation's commerce, transportation, and communications, serving as highways for freight and passengers. Roads and railways were few and far between. While Henry Clay and other politicians advocated for "internal improvements" to ease travel, open new markets, and move people, ideas, and products, speculators invested in local and regional waterways to attract development. Steamboats, barges, rafts, and riverboats delivered news and goods across the nation, linking rural homesteads and city parlors.

For Clemens and many of his compatriots, rivers also represented the allure of exploration and escape. Unknown vistas and untold opportunities lay around the next bend. During the 1820s, 1830s, and 1840s, American artists and writers in the East found inspiration in the remote regions of the Hudson River, producing landscapes, poems, and novels portraying the Hudson River Valley as wild, picturesque, mysterious, and a sublime metaphor for the human spirit. Thomas Cole's allegorical visions of wilderness and empire fueled the Hudson River School; Asher B. Durand went deep into the Catskills to immortalize Cole and poet William Cullen Bryant as kindred spirits, finding in nature a common source of spiritual knowledge and strength.

City of Washington from Beyond the Navy Yard. Aquatint engraving by William Bennett after George Cooke painted by G. Cooke, engraved by W. J. Bennett, ca. 1833.

This elegant etching, an aquatint mimicking the effects of watercolor, depicts the rural character of pre-industrial Washington, DC, a new capital rising from fields and swamps at the confluence of the Anacostia and Potomac rivers. By the time Sam Clemens first saw the capital, in the 1850s, a growing population of legislators, lawyers, and lobbyists, and their aides, clerks, and assistants, had helped swell the population and transform the city.

Suspension Bridge, Grand March, Cincinnati, Ohio. Lithograph, Strobridge and Co., ca. 1867.

This pictorial sheet music cover celebrates John Roebling's new bridge in Cincinnati spanning the Ohio River. The city was a hub of commerce, from the west, and cotton, from the south; it was also an early center for commercial art and lithography, from small trade cards and pictorial covers like this one, to outsized advertising posters for theaters, circuses, and sporting events.

Transcendentalist writers, led by Ralph Waldo Emerson and Henry David Thoreau, further extolled wilderness as an expression of free will and a source of enlightenment. James Fenimore Cooper's popular novels conferred natural nobility on the backwoodsmen, trappers, soldiers, settlers, and Native Americans who lived and died in the pristine forests.

This early generation of artists and writers treated wilderness as an abstract concept, an escape valve for the soul. They were educated intellectuals searching for truth and finding its essence beyond the boundaries of civilized society. Thoreau lived alone for two years in the woods by Walden Pond in Concord, Massachusetts, twenty miles west of Boston, and found virtue in the simple, self-reliant, rustic life.

Contemporaries of Thoreau's, including Herman Melville and Walt Whitman, described scenes they had witnessed firsthand and people they had met in their travels. Melville's sea stories and Whitman's rural rambles drew as much from memory and observation as from their imagination; they were both working journalists and brought to American literature a raw new realism. Artists traveled farther afield as well; Frederic Church journeyed to the Andes, while George Caleb Bingham produced a portfolio of western scenes—citizens gathering to vote, flatboatmen expressing joy atop their river barges.

Rivers fueled Samuel Clemens's earliest memories, restless ambitions, and lifelong travel lust, bringing mystery, romance, danger, opportunity, and adventure to his life and carrying along many of the people and stories that appeared in his work. In *Life on the Mississippi*, he acknowledged the river's influence on his education and career, maintaining contact throughout his life with people he knew from his early days:

> *During the two or two and a half years of my apprenticeship, I served under many pilots, and had experience of many kinds of steamboatmen and many varieties of steamboats.... I am to this day profiting somewhat by that experience; for in that brief, sharp schooling, I got personally and familiarly acquainted with about all the different types of human nature that are to be found in fiction, biography, or history.... When I say I am still profiting by this thing, I do not mean that it has constituted me a judge of men—no, it has not done that; for judges of men are born, not made. My profit is various in kind and degree; but the*

THE JUNCTION OF THE SACANDAGA AND HUDSON RIVERS.

N.º 2 of the Hudson River Port Folio

Published by H.I.Megarey & W.B.Gilley, New York & John Mill, Charleston S.C. and transferd to

The Junction of the Sacandaga and Hudson Rivers, Aquatint by I. Hill after W. G. Wall. New York: published by Henry I. Megarey & W. B. Gilley; Charleston, S. C.: John Mill [between 1821 and 1825].

The landmark Hudson River Portfolio of prints after William Wall's original paintings from the early 1820s portrays the western edge of civilization, a remote region in which cultivated fields border densely forested wilderness.

feature of it which I value most is the zest which that early experience has given to my later reading. When I find a well-drawn character in fiction or biography, I generally take a warm personal interest in him, for the reason that I have known him before—met him on the river.

By the mid-nineteenth century, internal improvements and growing industry had created jobs and a population of young men and women possessing income and free time. They were educated in newly built public schools and libraries, or through the study of modern instructional readers, which replaced the *New-England Primer.* Noah Webster's *American Dictionary of the English Language* had first appeared in 1828.

Economically, however, there were growing pains: As expansion outstripped available capital, the

The Jolly Flat Boat Men. Mezzotint by George Caleb Bingham, engraved by T. Doney; printed by Powell & Co., ca. 1847.

"The river's earliest commerce was in great barges.... They floated and sailed from the upper rivers to New Orleans, changed cargoes there, and were tediously warped and poled back by hand. A voyage down and back sometimes occupied nine months. In time this commerce increased until it gave employment to hordes of rough and hardy men; rude, uneducated, brave, suffering terrific hardships with sailor-like stoicism; heavy drinkers, coarse frolickers in moral sties like the Natchez-under-the-hill of that day, heavy fighters, reckless fellows, every one, elephantinely jolly, foul-witted, profane; prodigal of their money, bankrupt at the end of the trip, fond of barbaric finery, prodigious braggarts; yet, in the main, honest, trustworthy, faithful to promises and duty, and often picturesquely magnanimous." (*Life on the Mississippi*)

The Times. Lithograph by Edward Williams Clay, New York: printed & published by H. R. Robinson, 1837.

Responding to the financial Panic of 1837, comic artist Edward W. Clay attacked President Andrew Jackson's Treasury policies with this Hogarthian portrayal of New York City in the throes of depression. Beneath an ironic flag proudly proclaiming the sixty-first anniversary of American Independence, desperate citizens storm the Mechanics Bank, while the Custom House is deserted; the city square boasts a pawnbroker's shop and a liquor store; beyond lie an almshouse and a debtors' prison. Clay's sad street people include a penniless sailor, an idle soldier, a widow and child begging from a venal landlord, and a drunken Bowery thug accosting a destitute mother with an infant by her side.

nation's citizens suffered from excessive credit and periodic recessions. The Panic of 1837, for example, stifled the flow of settlers west and proved disastrous for John Marshall Clemens, Sam's father—known as Marshall—who had invested heavily in unsettled Tennessee land.

During the 1830s and 1840s, English and American travel writers who preceded Mark Twain journeyed through the United States and its territories describing incidents and inhabitants they encountered, offering vivid descriptions and often an outsider's perspective. British authors Charles Dickens and Frances Trollope scandalized the nation with their critical comments about the former colonies, while in the 1850s native Pennsylvanian Bayard Taylor enchanted his readers with eloquent descriptions of the goldfields and Spanish missions he found in California.

Taylor anticipated Twain's career, starting out as a printer's apprentice, poet, and newspaper

Saint Louis, MO., in 1855. Lithograph by Leopold Gast & Brother, ca.1855.

While cotton remained king in the prewar South and settlers set off from the city for the West, the wharves of St. Louis were crowded with steamboats, as passengers, teamsters, merchants, and boatmen streamed along the busy quays.

correspondent. He traveled the world, tramping through Europe, journeying to the Holy Land, up the Nile in Egypt, and throughout the Far East; he also chronicled his experiences among miners in the American West. His travel books found an audience eager for descriptions and views of foreign lands and newly explored regions closer to home.

When Taylor made his way to California in 1849 for the gold rush, he traveled by ship from New York to San Francisco via the Nicaraguan isthmus. However, for most, the inland rivers fueled the nation's westward movement. Pioneers, miners, farmers, laborers, and entrepreneurs traveled with their families by boat, barge, stagecoach, and covered wagon across the prairies and Rocky Mountains to Nevada and California. The opening of the Oregon and Santa Fe trails made the journey possible, if still fraught with danger. St. Louis had become a staging area for westward travel. Lewis and Clark embarked on their epic journey from the city in 1804 and returned there two years later upon completion of their expedition. The introduction of steamboats in 1818 opened the Mississippi and Missouri rivers to further commerce, expanding southern travel downriver to New Orleans and to cities and markets back east. Travelers heading west from St. Louis found information, guides, transportation, equipment,

and provisions for their journey. The city grew rapidly on the dreams and ambitions of westward expansion.

Samuel Clemens was born thirty miles west of Hannibal, in the small settlement of Florida, Missouri. A hundred miles northwest of St. Louis, Florida boasted the Salt River but offered few amenities. The family lived there in a two-room cabin. Sam's mother, Jane Lampton Clemens, had two older sons, Orion and Henry, and two daughters, Pamela and Margaret. Another boy, Pleasant, died in childbirth.

The family had come to Missouri the year of Sam's birth, following a period of economic struggle, as John Clemens sought to acquire land and build a fortune. Trained as a lawyer in Kentucky and named for the country's first Chief Justice of the Supreme Court, he served in Fentress County, Tennessee, as clerk, circuit judge, and attorney general, but he poured his earnings into speculative land purchases. He opened a general store as well, but any profits went into real estate acquisitions. Huge grants of land in Tennessee were available at cheap prices and Clemens bought in, yet the land would have no value unless settlers appeared who wished to buy it. They never did, and although his large holdings made John Clemens feel like landed gentry, the debts he incurred brought him only financial ruin. Starting fresh in 1835, John Clemens moved his family to Florida, where his wife's sister made her home with her husband, John Quarles.

Although the Clemens family maintained their own household, Jane and the children spent a great

American Progress; or, Westward the course of destiny. Chromolithograph by George A. Crofutt (after 1872 painting of the same name by John Gast), ca. 1873.

This lithograph, printed in color after John Gast's popular painting, expresses the spirit of Manifest Destiny, a political notion from the expansionist 1840s which suggested that God favored the nation's westward push. Columbia, the spirit of America, holds a book of learning in one hand while laying telegraph cable with the other as she guides settlers across the Great Plains, sweeping away dark clouds of ignorance obscuring the horizon. Below her, a parade of pioneers traveling on foot and horseback, by stagecoach, locomotive, and covered wagon, chase Native Americans from their path to the Pacific.

Clemens home, Florida, Missouri. Photograph by E. B. and C. M. Lasley, ca. 1890.

This vintage photograph, erroneously identified as the Mark Twain birthplace, documents the third house, in Florida, Missouri, purchased by John Marshall Clemens to house his family. Sam Clemens was born in a nearby cabin that the family had rented.

Salt River Navigation. Advertisement, 1838.

Sam Clemens's father joined the Salt River Company in Florida, Missouri, to develop the waterway for commercial traffic. The riverbed proved too shallow for modern cargo vessels, and the venture became just another failed enterprise for John Marshall Clemens, hastening the family's move to Hannibal.

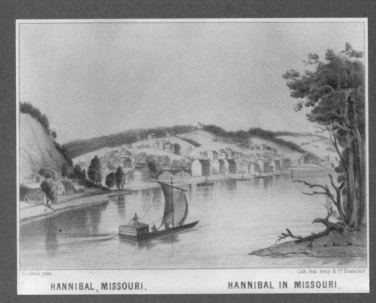

HANNIBAL, MISSOURI.   HANNIBAL IN MISSOURI.

Hannibal, Missouri. Lithograph, Jnst. Arnst & Co., after drawing by H. Lewis, ca. 1857.

Bluffs of drift near the Plank and Rail-Roads West of Hannibal in Marion County. Lithograph by Schaerff & Brother, St. Louis, after R. B. Price, 1855.

By the 1850s, as the cotton trade powered American commerce and industry, riverfront cities and towns, including St. Louis and Hannibal, flourished with the waterborne trade. Southern culture intrigued overseas readers, and European writers and their publishers produced beautifully illustrated views from journeys and accounts of the region.

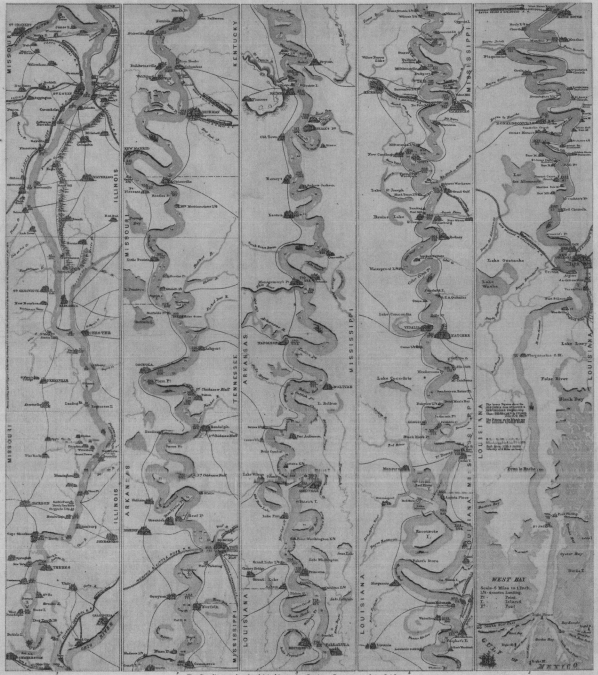

THE MISSISSIPPI, [ALTON TO THE GULF OF MEXICO] AS SEEN FROM THE HURRICANE DECK.

CONSTRUCTED FROM RELIABLE SOURCES.

These five slips may be cut, and joined in one piece, forming a Panorama nearly ten feet long.

Published by SCHÖNBERG & CO., New York 1861.

The Mississippi, Alton to the Gulf of Mexico, as Seen from the Hurricane Deck. Color lithograph, Schönberg & Co., 1861.

The convoluted course of the Mississippi River, and the obstacles to navigation it presented, is revealed in this extraordinary, extended map from 1861, designed as a souvenir for passengers on a Mississippi River steamboat.

deal of time at the nearby Quarles Farm. Filled with loving family and friends, the household offered young Sam a stimulating and nurturing haven at a time when his health was precarious and his family's finances were uncertain. Sam made some of his earliest friends among the slaves at the farm, absorbing their words, wit, and wisdom.

John Clemens's dreams never materialized in the rustic river hamlet of Florida, either. He found support among family and the community but no success, and his Tennessee land represented long-term debt, not profits. He was appointed to a commission to promote the Salt River for commercial traffic, but the river proved too shallow to accommodate the deeper draft of newer steamboats and larger cargo vessels.

By 1839 he saw promise in Hannibal, a growing town forty miles east, on the banks of the Mississippi, and relocated his family there. Hannibal, with a population of about fifteen hundred people, represented a potential step up, a larger house, and seemingly more opportunity.

Sam's health improved, and he immersed himself in the life of Hannibal. He went to school and found friends in the neighborhood: Tom Blankenship, the model for Huck Finn, and Laura Hawkins–who became Sam's own childhood sweetheart, later serving as a model for Tom Sawyer's love interest, Becky Thatcher. His boisterous spirit, skeptical nature, and natural confidence and curiosity led him to the riverfront, where teamsters, pilots, trappers, and merchants brought news and accounts from around the nation and the world.

Amid the slaves at Quarles Farm during his frequent visits, and among his family, friends, neighbors, and the people he encountered by the riverfront, Sam Clemens heard stories and found characters enough for a lifetime of creativity. Mark Twain would write in 1895, "The art of telling a humorous story–understand, I mean by word of mouth, not print–was created in America, and has remained at home."

Samuel L. Clemens. 1851.

This was the year young Sam began working for his older brother Orion as a printer, occasionally running Orion's newspaper, the *Hannibal Journal,* when he was away on other business.

His mother, Jane, brought domestic stability, humor, and a "perky stoicism" to the young Sam's life in a household of hardship and despair. He recalled her constant good humor and contentment, her love of novelties and pageantry. Religious in her Christian piety, she was good-humored, loving, and tolerant. Her household was lively, and Sam was a major contributor. She was a source of faith and fun, while his father remained stern and aloof, fixated on his commercial ventures. John Clemens failed in his efforts to generate income: opening a general store, offering his legal services as circuit judge and commissioner, and investing in speculative ventures. When he died in 1847, mired in debt, Sam, then twelve, went to work as an apprentice typesetter, also known as a printer's devil, supporting the family and embarking on a career that transformed his life and the nation's.

During the 1840s, small-town newspaper publishers were limited by technology; urban publishers could afford the new steam presses, but in rural areas type was still laboriously set one letter at a time on manual presses. Journals remained small, eight pages or less, and local news and stories made up most of the content. Rival publishers vied with one another to increase circulation and advertising revenue. Editors and reporters augmented their newsworthy coverage with attacks on their local colleagues in an effort to create drama and interest readers. Journalists contributed short ditties, tall tales, public hoaxes, and jokes to supplement the hard news and enliven the papers. They often used pen names to maintain anonymity and protect themselves from offended readers and potential libel charges. Like Joel Chandler Harris's Br'er Rabbit in the briar patch, Sam Clemens jumped right in, reveling in the rough, raucous arena of frontier journalism.

He entered the arena at age twelve, apprenticing initially at the *Hannibal Gazette* and then under Joseph Ament, editor of the *Hannibal Courier*. Almost sixty years later, Clemens recalled, "Surreptitiously and uninvited, I helped to edit the paper when no one was watching; therefore I was a journalist. I have never been wholly disconnected from journalism since."

In 1851 Sam left the *Courier* to join his brother Orion, who now operated the competing *Hannibal Journal*. During the next two years Sam worked under his older brother, along with younger brother Henry, supporting production of the newspaper and adding his own original poems and comic sketches.

First national essay, *Boston Carpet-Bag*, 1852.

After publishing several short pieces in the local Hannibal paper, Sam Clemens sent off to a Boston paper this sketch, which marked his debut on a national stage. Dated May 1, 1852, the byline coyly consists only of his initials.

THE CARPET-BAG.

Written for the Carpet-Bag.

The Dandy Frightening the Squatter.

BY S. L. C.

About thirteen years ago, when the now flourishing young city of Hannibal, on the Mississippi River, was but a "wood-yard," surrounded by a few huts, belonging to some hardy "*squatters*," and such a thing as a steamboat was considered quite a sight, the following incident occurred:

A tall, brawny woodsman stood leaning against a tree which stood upon the bank of the river, gazing at some approaching object, which our readers would easily have discovered to be a steamboat.

About half an hour elapsed, and the boat was moored, and the hands busily engaged in taking on wood.

Now among the many passengers on this boat, both male and female, was a spruce young dandy, with a killing moustache, &c., who seemed bent on making an impression upon the hearts of the young ladies on board, and to do this, he thought he must perform some heroic deed. Observing our squatter friend, he imagined this to be a fine opportunity to bring himself into notice; so, stepping into the cabin, he said:

"Ladies, if you wish to enjoy a good laugh, step out on the guards. I intend to frighten that gentleman into fits who stands on the bank."

The ladies complied with the request, and our dandy drew from his bosom a formidable looking bowie-knife, and thrust it into his belt; then, taking a large horse-pistol in each hand, he seemed satisfied that all was right. Thus equipped, he strode on shore, with an air which seemed to say—"The hopes of a nation depend on me." Marching up to the woodsman, he exclaimed:

"Found you at last, have I! You are the very man I've been looking for these three weeks! Say your prayers!" he continued, presenting his pistols, "you'll make a capital barn door, and I shall drill the key-hole myself!"

The squatter calmly surveyed him a moment, and then, drawing back a step, he planted his huge fist directly between the eyes of his astonished antagonist, who, in a moment, was floundering in the turbid waters of the Mississippi.

Every passenger on the boat had by this time collected on the guards, and the shout that now went up from the crowd speedily restored the crest-fallen hero to his senses, and, as he was sneaking off towards the boat, was thus accosted by his conqueror:

"I say, yeou, next time yeou come around drillin' key-holes, don't forget yer old acquaintances!"

The ladies unanimously voted the knife and pistols to the victor.

He ran the paper when Orion was away, made his first mark and drew his first blood, experimented with pen names, and slipped unauthorized contributions into his brother's editorials. In one instance, with Orion out of town, he responded to a mild attack on his brother by a rival editor with a series of derisive letters accompanied by crude satirical wood engravings. Orion stopped the feud upon his return, while the confident Sam went on to bigger, better things. He sent contributions to eastern publishers he knew about from perusing the journals and magazines that came through the print shop, and in May 1852 he published his first sketch and earned his first byline, under the initials "S.L.C.," in the weekly Boston *Carpet-Bag*.

Sam chafed under Orion's control and aspired to see the world beyond Hannibal, the wider world described by people he met along the waterfront and in the journals arriving in Orion's shop. Always restless, at age ten he stowed away on a steamboat for a short trip before returning home. In June 1853, however, confident in his abilities and eager to strike out on his own, after informing Orion and his mother just days before his departure, he abruptly left Hannibal on a riverboat, "disappeared one night and fled to St. Louis," according to biographer Ron Powers.

The river took him first to St. Louis, where he found temporary work as a printer. He quickly moved

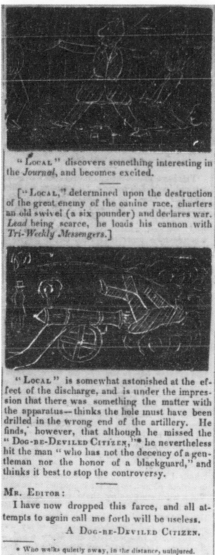

"LOCAL" discovers something interesting in the *Journal*, and becomes excited.

["LOCAL," determined upon the destruction of the great enemy of the canine race, charters an old swivel (a six pounder) and declares war. Lead being scarce, he loads his cannon with *Tri-Weekly Messengers*.]

"LOCAL" is somewhat astonished at the effect of the discharge, and is under the impression that there was something the matter with the apparatus—thinks the hole must have been drilled in the wrong end of the artillery. He finds, however, that although he missed the "Dog-be-Deviled Citizen," he nevertheless hit the man "who has not the decency of a gentleman nor the honor of a blackguard," and thinks it best to stop the controversy.

Mr. Editor:
I have now dropped this farce, and all attempts to again call me forth will be useless.
A Dog-be-Deviled Citizen.

* Who walks quietly away, in the distance, uninjured.

"LOCAL" RESOLVES TO COMMIT SUICIDE.

'LOCAL,' disconsolate from receiving no further notice from 'A Dog-be-Deviled Citizen,' contemplates Suicide. His 'pocket-pistol' (i. e. the *bottle*,) failing in the patriotic work of ridding the country of a nuisance, he resolves to 'extinguish his chunk' by feeding his carcass to the fishes of Bear Creek, while friend and foe are wrapt in sleep. Fearing, however, that he may get out of his depth, he *sounds the stream with his walking-stick*.

Woodcuts in *Hannibal Journal* by Samuel Clemens, September 23, 1852.

Sam Clemens created these crude caricatures to publicly punish Josiah Hinton, a rival editor who published an offensive remark regarding Sam's older brother Orion. Because Orion, who edited the paper, was away at the time, Sam struck back with this graphic sally and a series of scathing comments. Mark Twain doodled and sketched all his life, noting in *A Tramp Abroad* that while in Europe, he took art classes and learned to paint.

on to similar jobs in New York City and Philadelphia and then visited Washington, DC, before returning to St. Louis in 1855.

During the two years that he was away, Sam contributed travel pieces and comic sketches, including three letters under the pen name Thomas Jefferson Snodgrass, to newspapers Orion now published in Iowa. Returning to Hannibal and Florida for family visits, Sam kindled his dream of life on the river.

He tried unsuccessfully in the summer of 1855 to secure a position aboard a steamboat. Finally, in 1857, during a journey from Cincinnati to New Orleans, he

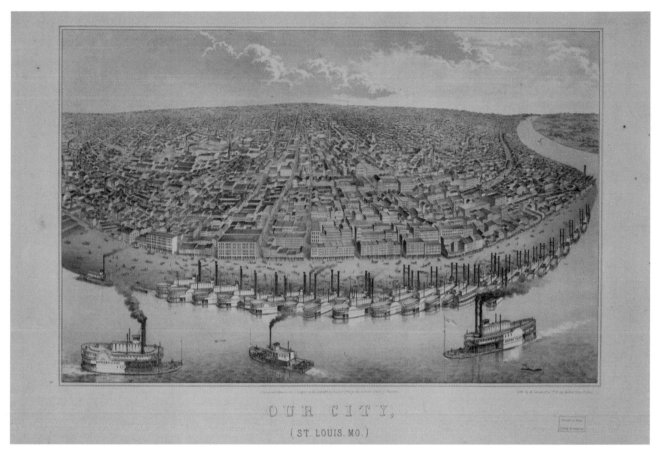

Our City (St. Louis, MO). Color lithograph by A. Janicke & Co., published by Hagen & Pfau at the Anzeiger des Westens, ca. 1859.

Before the Civil War stopped commercial traffic on the Mississippi River, St. Louis became the principal gateway and staging depot for travelers to the west.

persuaded veteran pilot Horace Bixby to take him on as an apprentice. Bixby showed Clemens the ropes and taught him lessons from the river. Twain would recall gratefully years later, in *Life on the Mississippi:*

> *The face of the water, in time, became a wonderful book—a book that was a dead language to the uneducated passenger, but which told its mind to me without reserve, delivering its most cherished secrets as clearly as if it uttered them with a voice. And it was not a book to be read once and thrown aside, for it had a new story to tell every day.*

There never was so wonderful a book written by man; never one whose interest was so absorbing, so unflagging, so sparklingly renewed with every reperusal. The passenger who could not read it was charmed with a peculiar sort of faint dimple on its surface (on the rare occasions when he did not overlook it altogether); but to the pilot that was an italicized passage; indeed, it was more than that, it was a legend of the largest capitals, with a string of shouting exclamation points at the end of it, for it meant that a wreck or a rock was buried there that could tear the life out of the strongest vessel that ever floated. It is the faintest and simplest expression the water ever makes, and the most hideous to a pilot's eye. In truth, the passenger who could not read this book saw nothing but all manner of pretty pictures in it, painted by the sun and shaded by the clouds, whereas to the trained

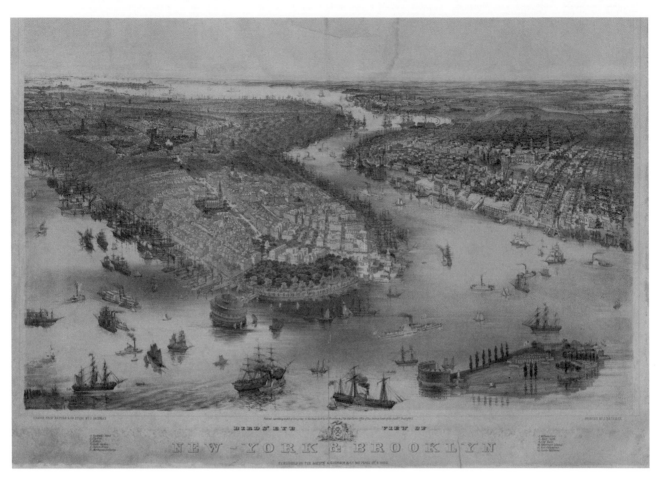

Birds' Eye View of New-York & Brooklyn. Lithograph, published by A. Guerber & Co., printed by J. Bachmann, ca. 1851.

In 1853, Sam Clemens first saw New York City, taking in the bustle of Broadway while working as a printer preparing type for books and periodicals.

eye these were not pictures at all, but the grimmest and most dread-earnest of reading matter.

On the river, Clemens felt in control and independent. In a letter written to his former Hannibal cohort Will Bowen in 1866, he explained,

…all men—kings & serfs alike—are slaves to other men & to circumstance—save alone, the pilot—who comes at no man's beck and call, obeys no man's orders & scorns all men's suggestions. The king would do this thing, & would do that:

but a cramped treasury overmasters him in the one case & a seditious people in the other. The Senator must hob-nob with canaille whom he despises, & banker, priest & statesman trim their actions by the breeze of the world's will & the world's opinion. It is a strange study,—a singular phenomenon, if you please, that the only real, independent & genuine gentlemen in the world go quietly up and down the Mississippi river, asking no homage of any one, seeking no popularity, no notoriety, & not caring a damn whether school keeps or not.

In becoming a pilot Clemens realized his ultimate childhood goal, riding the river free of society's shackles and obligations, in charge of his own destiny and the destiny of those who depended upon him

Sam Clemens as a pilot. Photograph, 1858.

Sam served as a cub pilot this year on several different boats, including the ill-fated *Pennsylvania.*

Birds' Eye View of New-Orleans. Tinted lithograph, published by A. Guerber & Co., printed by J. Bachmann, New York, ca. 1851.

Sam Clemens achieved his goal of becoming a Mississippi River pilot during a steamboat trip south from Cincinnati to New Orleans, the center for international commerce in the South.

for their safety and lives. Steering his own course, literally and figuratively, Clemens would eventually find that authority brings responsibility, robbing the river of much of its romance and tarnishing the idealized dreams of youth. If life on the river came to represent Clemens's lifelong search for independence and recognition, lessons learned as a pilot shaped his later response to difficult relationships, money problems, irritating editors, pirate publishers, and the vagaries of the literary marketplace.

The river gave but it also took away. In 1858 tragedy struck when Sam's brother Henry died following an explosion aboard the *Pennsylvania,* a ship Sam had left only days before, following a knockdown fight with the pilot. Sam had encouraged his brother to take a job with him on the steamboat and blamed himself for his brother's untimely death. Despite the hazards and the loss of Henry, Sam

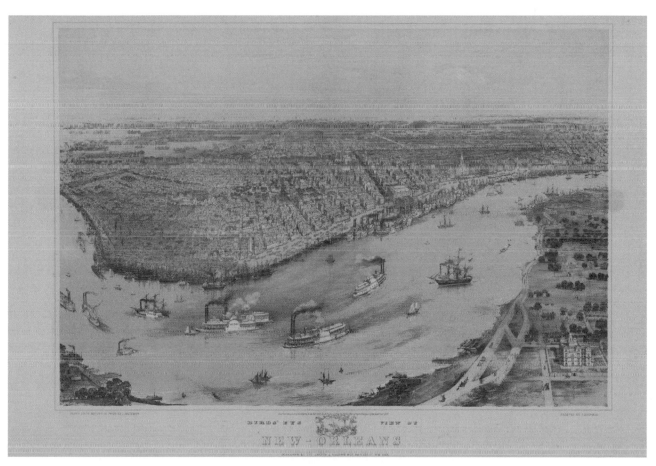

Samuel Clemens's pilot's certificate, 1859.

Sam's official license to pilot steamboats, preserved in the Mariners' Museum in Newport News, Virginia.

Henry Clemens, Sam's younger brother. Daguerreotype, ca. 1851.

In 1858, Sam persuaded his brother to join him as a lowly worker on the *Pennsylvania,* a boat on which Sam was a cub pilot. They made six trips together, but after a disagreement with the ship's pilot, Sam was put off the vessel and agreed to meet his brother later. Shortly thereafter, the *Pennsylvania*'s boilers exploded, and Henry was fatally injured. Sam blamed himself for not being there to save him.

stayed on the river, learning the trade of riverboat pilot. He received his pilot's license in 1859 and continued piloting a series of vessels up and down the Mississippi while contributing occasional sketches drawn from observations made from the wheelhouse.

In *Life on the Mississippi* he recalls,

In due course I got my license. I was a pilot now, full fledged. I dropped into casual employments; no misfortunes resulting, intermittent work gave place to steady and protracted engagements. Time drifted smoothly and prosperously on, and I supposed—and hoped—that I was going to follow the river the rest of my days, and die at the wheel when my mission was ended. But by and by the war came, commerce was suspended, my occupation was gone.

The outbreak of the Civil War in spring 1861 stopped commercial riverboat traffic on the Mississippi, ending Sam Clemens's career as a pilot. With his occupation went his hard-won, long-sought-after sense of freedom and independence. Fleeing the fight, Clemens, according to Powers, "was not interested in war." His head lay with the Union, his heart with his fellow rebels. Following the attack by Confederate batteries on federal Fort

Sumter off Charleston, South Carolina, in mid-April 1861, he briefly followed his heart. While troops from both sides massed around Washington, DC, in the weeks before First Manassas, or the First Battle of Bull Run, Clemens signed on as lieutenant in a local Missouri militia composed of Hannibal men and created to protect the town and its citizens from Northern depredations. The activities of Lieutenant Clemens and the Ralls County Rangers, as the company was called, seem comic in retrospect, as described in several accounts, yet they gave him enough of a taste of battle and military discipline to convince him there was no place for him and his personal aspirations in the wartime South.

Torn between his belief in the Union and his sympathies for the South, driven by his ambitions, he avoided the conflict entirely, accompanying Orion

Awful Conflagration of the Steam Boat Lexington *in Long Island Sound on Monday Eveᵍ, Janʸ. 13th 1840 by which melancholy occurrence, over 100 Persons Perished.* Hand-colored lithograph by N. Currier after W. K. Hewitt, New York; published by Currier & Ives, ca. 1840.

Henry Clemens's death was not uncommon. The *Lexington* was a luxury steamer, built by Cornelius Vanderbilt, that plied Long Island Sound. In mid-January 1840, carrying a large cargo of cotton, along with 143 passengers and crew, the ship caught fire and the bales burned quickly, sending 139 souls to their death in the frigid winter waters. Nathaniel Currier produced this lurid lithograph of the burning steamboat just days after the event, creating a sensation and signaling a growing demand for timely, newsworthy pictures of current events.

Passage down the Ohio of Gen. Negley's Penn. brigade consisting of 77th, 78th, and 79th regiments. Drawing by Frank Schell, ca. October 1861.

Before the Civil War, scenes like this view of Mississippi riverboats steaming side by side evoked the romance of a race and the familiar roaring cadence of commerce on the river. With the war, steamboats and smaller craft were converted by both sides to military purposes. In fall 1861, artist Frank Schell, following the Union army on assignment for Frank Leslie's *Illustrated Newspaper,* captured this sketch of new troop transports carrying soldiers toward the front.

upriver to Iowa and then setting out by stage to Nevada, and eventually California, opening a new chapter in his life that led to unprecedented literary fame and celebrity. Silver and gold discoveries had been luring people west since 1848, and while Clemens was no prospector, he surely understood that opportunities abounded in the newly created towns on the frontier.

In his mind, however, Sam Clemens never left the river and the world he knew as a youth in Hannibal on the banks of the Mississippi. Throughout his life, the South and the river returned in his books and letters, defining his identity and symbolizing his remarkable journey to fame and fortune. Sam Clemens chose Mark Twain's path carefully. Not only did he have a deep passion for and broad knowledge of the river, but he was aware of its potential as a largely untapped creative vehicle. Later, in 1895, when asked by an interviewer whether he considered the Mississippi his "real field of work," Twain responded,

Yes, and the reason is plain. By a series of events–accidents–I was the only one who wrote about old times on the Mississippi...the Mississippi was a

The Levee at Vicksburg, Miss., February, 1864. Stereograph by William Redish Pywell, Hartford, Conn.: The War Photograph & Exhibition Co., ca. 1864.

Union gunboats and river craft crowded the levee at Vicksburg, Mississippi, after the city surrendered to Ulysses S. Grant's combined assault from May to July 1863.

virgin field. No one could write that life but a pilot entered into the spirit of it. But the pilots were the last men in the world to write its history.... Every pilot had to carry in his head thousands of details of the great river. Details, moreover, that were always changing, and in order to have nothing to confuse those details they entered into a compact never to read anything. Thus if they had thought of writing, they would have no connected style, no power of describing anything; and, moreover, they were so engrossed in the river that there was nothing in the life unusual to them. Here then was my chance, and I used it.

However, for ten years, from 1863, when Clemens wrote his first story under the pen name Mark Twain, until 1873, when he began work on his autobiographical novel *The Adventures of Tom Sawyer,* the river featured little in his work, as he left the Mississippi and the South for further adventures out West, back East, and abroad.

He became a national sensation upon the 1865 publication of "Jim Smiley and His Jumping Frog" (collected two years later in the book *The Celebrated Jumping Frog of Calaveras County*), a story he first heard in a California gold mining camp. He followed that success with *The Innocents Abroad* (1869),

chronicling his adventures on a Holy Land tour, and *Roughing It* (1872), a memoir of his experiences in the goldfields of California and Nevada. Taking to the lecture circuit, he gained further fame and income.

He married Olivia Langdon (Livy) in 1870, and by 1873 they were living in Elmira, New York, far removed from his Mississippi roots. He would return to the river in his writing, working from memory, notes, and correspondence. The Mississippi appeared initially as a backdrop in his first novel, undertaken in collaboration with author Charles Dudley Warner. *The Gilded Age,* a satiric look at rampant speculation and corruption, gave its name to the era, a chimera of gold adorning base metal. Twain contributed the book's opening chapters, drawing from recollections of his father's quest for wealth and the family's attempts to rise out of poverty. He follows the fictional family of Squire Hawkins, a figure based on John Clemens, as they relocate south to Missouri seeking success and security. Drawing from memories of Quarles Farm, the family and slaves who lived there, and his own youthful experiences, Twain re-creates the river of his childhood and imagines the first impressions of the newcomers as they encounter it. Investing his description with mystery, romance, race, religion, and the supernatural, Twain offers glimpses of great works yet to come:

"Uncle Dan'l" (colored,) aged 40; his wife, "aunt Jinny," aged 30, "Young Miss" Emily Hawkins, "Young Mars" Washington Hawkins and "Young Mars" Clay, the new member of the family, ranged themselves on a log, after supper, and contemplated the marvelous river and discussed it. The moon rose and sailed aloft through a maze of shredded cloud-wreaths; the sombre river just perceptibly brightened under the veiled light; a deep silence pervaded the air and was emphasized, at intervals, rather than broken, by the hooting of an owl, the baying of a dog, or the muffled crash of a carving bank in the distance.

The little company assembled on the log were all children (at least in simplicity and broad and comprehensive ignorance,) and the remarks they made about the river were in keeping with the character; and so awed were they by the grandeur and the solemnity of the scene before them, and by their belief that the air was filled with invisible spirits and that the faint zephyrs were caused by their passing wings, that all their talk took to itself a tinge of the supernatural, and their voices were subdued to a low and reverent tone.

An approaching steamboat breaks their reverie.

A deep coughing sound troubled the stillness, way toward a wooded cape that jetted into the stream a mile distant. All in an instant a fierce eye of fire shot out from behind the cape and sent a long brilliant pathway quivering athwart the dusky water. The coughing grew louder and louder, the glaring eye grew larger and still larger, glared wilder and still wilder. A huge shape developed itself out of the gloom, and from its tall duplicate horns dense volumes of smoke, starred and spangled with sparks, poured out and went tumbling away into the farther darkness. Nearer and nearer the thing came, till its long sides began to glow with spots of light which mirrored

themselves in the river and attended the monster like a torchlight procession.

"What is it! Oh, what is it, Uncle Dan'l!"

With deep solemnity the answer came:

"It's de Almighty! Git down on yo' knees!"

The success of *The Gilded Age*, which also generated a theatrical production, expanded Twain's literary celebrity, and he went back to work on the autobiographical novel about his childhood along the river that was to become *Tom Sawyer*. Before he got very far, however, he received an offer from his friend William Dean Howells enticing him to take his recollections of the Mississippi in another direction. The result was *Old Times on the Mississippi*, a series of memory pieces published in 1875 in the *Atlantic Monthly*, a Boston journal edited by Howells, who first brought Clemens to the attention of the city's exalted literati. Paid handsomely for the essays, Clemens delayed work on *Tom Sawyer*. Eight years later, the pieces Clemens wrote for Howells were incorporated into *Life on the Mississippi*.

In *Old Times on the Mississippi*, Clemens recounted his days as a steamboat pilot, and the river took center stage. Based largely on recollections, the essays memorialize the river as it was before the war. Later, tugboats and barges, railroads and new road coaches, would leave the steamboats–and the men who piloted them–forever behind in their wake.

Nonetheless, Clemens knew from experience that the knowledge he gleaned from working on the river could teach lessons and provide answers found nowhere else: "By going into the minutiae of the science of piloting," he "sought to carry the reader step by step to a comprehension of what the science consists of; and at the same time I have tried to show him that it is a very curious and wonderful science, too, and very worthy of his attention." Along with the science of piloting, Clemens infused his stories with the sense of wonder, romance, and adventure he had found along the river:

A Steamboat Race on the Mississippi (between the Baltic & Diana***).*** Colored lithograph after George T. Fuller by Weingartner, 1859.

"In the 'flush times' of steamboating, a race between two notoriously fleet steamers was an event of vast importance. The date was set for it several weeks in advance, and from that time forward, the whole Mississippi Valley was in a state of consuming excitement. Politics and the weather were dropped, and people talked only of the coming race. As the time approached, the two steamers 'stripped' and got ready. Every incumbrance that added weight, or exposed a resisting surface to wind or water, was removed, if the boat could possibly do without it.... When the Eclipse and the A. L. Shotwell ran their great race twenty-two years ago, it was said that pains were taken to scrape the gilding off the fanciful device which hung between the Eclipse's chimneys, and that for that one trip the captain left off his kid gloves and had his head shaved. But I always doubted these things." (*Life on the Mississippi*)

When I was a boy, there was but one permanent ambition among my comrades in our village on the west bank of the Mississippi River. That was, to be a steamboatman. We had transient ambitions of other sorts, but they were only transient. When a circus came and went, it left us all burning to become clowns; the first negro minstrel show that came to our section left us all suffering to try that kind of life; now and then we had a hope that if we lived and were good, God would permit us to be pirates. These ambitions faded out, each in its turn; but the ambition to be a steamboatman always remained.

The Adventures of Tom Sawyer. Frontispiece from first edition by True Williams, 1876.

Williams's vision of Tom is an odd blend of formality (the buttoned jacket and hat) and casualness (the bare feet). But he's clearly in his element: outdoors and ready for mischief.

Joining their ranks, first as an apprentice and finally as a captain, he had come to appreciate the challenges they faced and portrayed his fellow pilots as extraordinary men with extreme skills:

One cannot easily realize what a tremendous thing it is to know every trivial detail of twelve hundred miles of river and know it with absolute exactness. If you will take the longest street in New York, and travel up and down it, scanning its features patiently until you know every house and window and door and lamp-post and big and little sign by heart, and know them so accurately that you can instantly name the one you are abreast of when you are set down at random in that street in the middle of an inky black night, you will then have a tolerable notion of the amount and the exactness of a pilot's knowledge who carries the Mississippi River in his head.

With all that knowledge comes an appreciation for the dangers of hidden bars, sunken logs, and exploding steam boilers. In the eyes of veteran pilots, romance soon gives way to reality. Responsibility for the boat, its passengers, and freight took away from Clemens's delight in his professional position, elevating the mundane and diminishing the sublime.

Having written his Mississippi River memory pieces for Howells, Twain turned back to finishing *Tom Sawyer*, published in the national centennial year 1876. In the book, Twain transformed the river of his youth. Hannibal becomes the fictional St. Petersburg, a garden of good and evil for Tom and his mates: murder and mayhem offset by natural beauty and splendid isolation. He rendered descriptions with loving attention, lavishly evoking the town, its citizens, and the rhythm of life along the river:

Saturday morning was come, and all the summer world was bright and fresh, and brimming with life. There was a song in every heart; and if the heart

"SHOWING OFF."

TOM DREAMS.

was young the music issued at the lips. There was cheer in every face and a spring in every step. The locust-trees were in bloom and the fragrance of the blossoms filled the air. Cardiff Hill, beyond the village and above it, was green with vegetation and it lay just far enough away to seem a Delectable Land, dreamy, reposeful, and inviting.

At a time when Americans were celebrating a century of independence, immigrants crowded growing cities, and the nation's frontiers were shrinking rapidly, Twain reaffirmed the country's shared rural roots, its refugees and rogues, pillars and pretenders, with intimate knowledge and powerful familiarity.

He created a setting and cast of characters firmly embedded in contemporary life yet instantly bearing a patina of age and innocence. Like Washington Irving's earlier stories, "Rip Van Winkle" and "The Legend of Sleepy Hollow," horror, humor, fantasy, and reality proved a potent and popular mix.

The river itself became a romantic refuge for Tom, a safe, quiet place away from the demands of school and family, responsibilities and relationships:

He wandered far from the accustomed haunts of boys, and sought desolate places that were in harmony with his spirit. A log raft in the river invited him, and he seated himself on its outer edge and contemplated the dreary vastness of the stream, wishing, the while, that he could only be drowned, all at once and unconsciously, without undergoing the uncomfortable routine devised by nature.

The river represented adventure, too, as Tom Sawyer and his pals Joe Harper and Huckleberry Finn imagined themselves as renegades beyond the reach of the law, played at pirates, and bemoaned the expectations imposed on them by civilized society. Tom and Joe "said they would rather be outlaws a year in Sherwood Forest than President of the United States forever."

Finding shelter on the islands and woods near St. Petersburg, they plotted and schemed, living free of social restraints. Proclaiming themselves villains with horrible names, they terrorized woodland creatures and each other. In Clemens's deft hands, a grown-up aura of horror and mystery hangs over the truant youths, giving added life to their childish fears:

On Board Their First Prize. Illustration by True Williams, *The Adventures of Tom Sawyer.*

Clemens's prodigious memory and Dickensian love of detail inform numerous passages throughout his river novels. In *Tom Sawyer* his description of the boys' first "prize," a raft they appropriate from the riverbank, defines a scene full of sensuous delights: "They came back to camp wonderfully refreshed, glad-hearted, and ravenous; and they soon had the camp-fire blazing up again. Huck found a spring of clear cold water close by, and the boys made cups of broad oak or hickory leaves, and felt that water, sweetened with such a wildwood charm as that, would be a good enough substitute for coffee. While Joe was slicing bacon for breakfast, Tom and Huck asked him to hold on a minute; they stepped to a promising nook in the river-bank and threw in their lines; almost immediately they had reward. Joe had not had time to get impatient before they were back again with some handsome bass, a couple of sun-perch and a small catfish—provisions enough for quite a family. They fried the fish with the bacon, and were astonished; for no fish had ever seemed so delicious before. They did not know that the quicker a fresh-water fish is on the fire after he is caught the better he is; and they reflected little upon what a sauce open-air sleeping, open-air exercise, bathing, and a large ingredient of hunger make, too."

About midnight Tom arrived with a boiled ham and a few trifles, and stopped in a dense undergrowth on a small bluff overlooking the meeting-place. It was starlight, and very still. The mighty river lay like an ocean at rest. Tom listened a moment, but no sound disturbed the quiet. Then he gave a low, distinct whistle. It was answered from under the bluff. Tom whistled twice more; these signals were answered in the same way. Then a guarded voice said:

"Who goes there?"

"Tom Sawyer, the Black Avenger of the Spanish Main. Name your names."

"Huck Finn the Red-Handed, and Joe Harper the Terror of the Seas." Tom had furnished these titles, from his favorite literature.

"'Tis well. Give the countersign."

Two hoarse whispers delivered the same awful word simultaneously to the brooding night:

"BLOOD!"

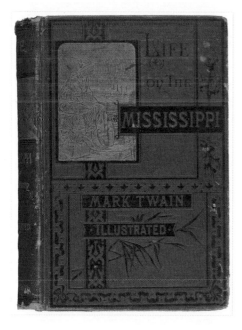

far left: *Life on the Mississippi.* Cover by Daniel Carter Beard.

left: *Life on the Mississippi.* Sketch for title page by Daniel Carter Beard.

The cover promises a nostalgic cruise down the river, and there's that, but it wouldn't be Mark Twain if there weren't also shafts of darkness and doubt, undercurrents of misery and sorrow.

Tom Sawyer became a bestseller, solidifying Twain's literary reputation. A household name, he built a dream house for himself and Livy and their growing family. The wonderfully eccentric Shingle-style home is located in Hartford, Connecticut, halfway between Boston and New York City, where many of his publishers and editors lived and worked.

Twain wrote *Tom Sawyer* and *Old Times on the Mississippi* from memory and imagination, re-creating a world he knew intimately yet hadn't visited for many years. In 1882, after publishing the European travel book *A Tramp Abroad* (1880) and the historical novel *The Prince and the Pauper,* also set in Europe, he returned to the river in person. He journeyed up the Mississippi from New Orleans to Minneapolis in pursuit of fresh material for *Life on the Mississippi* (1883) and *Adventures of Huckleberry Finn* (1884). He stopped at Hannibal, renewing his acquaintance with the scenery, former friends, and neighbors.

His observations and reminiscences from this trip added depth to his new work. Although his romantic notions of the region maintained their hold and his love of the river remained, Clemens came away disappointed and disillusioned by the changes he found, especially the lack of steamboats and absence of life along the waterfront. The vanity fair he had come to associate with crowded city levees and busy town wharves no longer existed. The South appeared to him charmed as ever by its timeless graces, lost in its own rhetorical past and its persistent, though outmoded, myths of heroism and chivalry.

In *Life on the Mississippi* and *Adventures of Huckleberry Finn,* Twain strips the river of its innocence; the poverty, racism, ignorance, and intolerance he found upon his return diminished the region and its people in his eyes. He found the lack of river trade "depressing," a shadow of the waterway's former brilliance:

> *The loneliness of this solemn, stupendous flood is impressive—and depressing. League after league, and still league after league, it pours its chocolate tide along, between its solid forest walls, its almost untenanted shores, with seldom a sail or a moving object of any kind to disturb the surface and break the monotony of the blank, watery solitude."*

In St. Louis, he noted the quiet wharves:

*The pavements along the river-front were bad:
the sidewalks were rather out of repair; there was
a rich abundance of mud. All this was familiar
and satisfying; but the ancient armies of drays,
and struggling throngs of men, and mountains of
freight, were gone; and Sabbath reigned in their
stead. The immemorial mile of cheap foul doggeries
remained, but business was dull with them;
the multitudes of poison-swilling Irishmen had
departed, and in their places were a few scattering
handfuls of ragged negroes, some drinking, some
drunk, some nodding, others asleep. St. Louis is a
great and prosperous and advancing city; but the
river-edge of it seems dead past resurrection.*

His affection for the South of his youth never
waned, but he expressed dismay at the region's slow
cultural progress. Clemens chastised his fellow
Southerners for "pretending to be what they are not,"
taking too seriously the outmoded medieval influence
of novelist Sir Walter Scott, whose "grotesque

'chivalry' doings and romantic juvenilities" appeared
absurd to Clemens "in an atmosphere in which is
already perceptible the wholesome and practical
nineteenth-century smell of cotton-factories and
locomotives." Clemens came to recognize that the
same solidarity along old-fashioned lines that fueled
the Southern war effort had calcified its society,
inhibiting modern ways of thinking and the growth
of the region and its people.

At the same time, Hannibal's depressed economy
had perhaps saved the town some innocence, and the
return visit spiked Clemens's enthusiasm for the past.
In *Life on the Mississippi*, he lovingly described the
Hannibal of his boyhood and the excitement created
by arriving steamboats:

*Once a day a cheap, gaudy packet arrived upward
from St. Louis, and another downward from
Keokuk. Before these events, the day was glorious
with expectancy; after them, the day was a dead
and empty thing. Not only the boys, but the whole*

The Sunny South.
Chromolithograph, Calvert
Lithograph and Engraving Co.,
ca. 1883.

The imposition of Democratic rule
and the rise of Jim Crow laws in the
South following Reconstruction
spurred nostalgia for the ideals
of antebellum life, with productive
plantations worked by healthy,
humanely treated slaves.

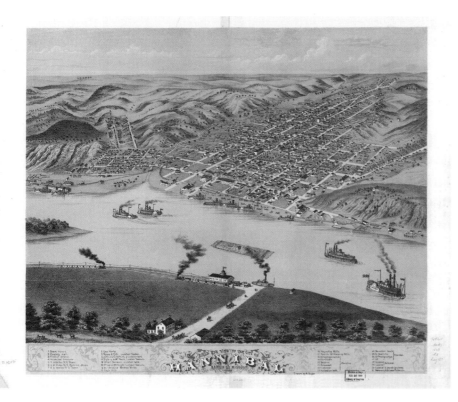

Bird's Eye View of the city of Hannibal, Marion Co., Missouri.
Color lithograph by A. Ruger, 1869.

Hannibal changed little in the decades following Sam Clemens's departure in 1861, due to the depressing effects of war and a decline in Mississippi River traffic.

village, felt this. After all these years I can picture that old time to myself now, just as it was then: the white town drowsing in the sunshine of a summer's morning; the streets empty, or pretty nearly so; one or two clerks sitting in front of the Water Street stores, with their splint-bottomed chairs tilted back against the wall, chins on breasts, hats slouched over their faces, asleep—with shingle-shavings enough around to show what broke them down; a sow and a litter of pigs loafing along the sidewalk, doing a good business in watermelon rinds and seeds; two or three lonely little freight piles scattered about the "levee"; a pile of "skids" on the slope of the stone-paved wharf, and the fragrant town drunkard asleep in the shadow of them; two or three wood flats at the head of the wharf, but nobody to listen to the peaceful lapping of the wavelets against them; the great Mississippi, the majestic, the magnificent Mississippi, rolling its mile-wide tide along, shining in the sun; the dense forest away on the other side, the "point" above

the town, and the "point" below, bounding the river-glimpse and turning it into a sort of sea, and withal a very still and brilliant and lonely one.

The power of the past and of his memories did not diminish Clemens's sense of irony. He could not help but record his thoughts on the current residents of his boyhood home:

On my way through town to the hotel, I saw the house which was my home when I was a boy. At present rates, the people who now occupy it are of no more value than I am; but in my time they would have been worth not less than five hundred dollars apiece. They are colored folk.

Clemens quickly followed the publication of *Life on the Mississippi* with the novel *Adventures of Huckleberry Finn*. As if the dust of years and longing had been washed from his eyes, he sees and portrays the region as it actually was and not as he would

43

have liked it to be, with its awesome natural beauty, impoverished populace, and terrible social conflicts. The river itself becomes a constant, brooding presence, an active participant in the drama, as Huck befriends the fugitive slave Jim and they embark on their epic journey down the Mississippi.

The runaway slave and truant schoolboy flee civilization's shackles along the watery corridor with few witnesses:

> We had mountains on the Missouri shore and heavy timber on the Illinois side, and the channel was down the Missouri shore at that place, so we warn't afraid of anybody running across us. We laid there all day, and watched the rafts and steamboats spin down the Missouri shore, and up-bound steamboats fight the big river in the middle....
>
> Every night we passed towns, some of them away up on black hillsides, nothing but just a shiny bed of lights; not a house could you see. The fifth night we passed St. Louis, and it was like the whole world lit up. In St. Petersburg they used to say there was twenty or thirty thousand people in St. Louis, but I never believed it till I see that wonderful spread of lights at two o'clock that still night. There warn't a sound there; everybody was asleep.

Huck described the river as a living thing, dominating the landscape and imposing its will on the towns and cities along its banks:

> On the riverfront some of the houses was sticking out over the bank, and they was bowed and bent, and about ready to tumble in, the people had moved out of them. The bank was caved away under one corner of some others, and that corner was hanging over. People lived in them yet, but it was dangersome, because sometimes a strip of land as wide as a house caves in at a time. Sometimes

> a belt of land a quarter of a mile deep will start in and cave along and cave along till it all caves into the river in one summer. Such a town as that has to be always moving back, and back, and back, because the river's always gnawing at it.

For Huck and his companions, the river provided passage and provisions. It also fueled Huck's ruminations over social responsibility and the rights of all men and women, no matter their color or social station, to live freely. Moving along the river, Huck described his onshore foraging and the ethical dilemma it posed:

> Mornings before daylight I slipped into cornfields and borrowed a watermelon, or a mushmelon, or a punkin, or some new corn, or things of that kind. Pap always said it warn't no harm to borrow things if you was meaning to pay them back some time; but the widow said it warn't anything but a soft name for stealing, and no decent body would do it. Jim said he reckoned the widow was partly right and pap was partly right; so the best way would be for us to pick out two or three things from the list and say we wouldn't borrow them any more—then he reckoned it wouldn't be no harm to borrow the others. So we talked it over all one night, drifting along down the river, trying to make up our minds whether to drop the watermelons, or the cantelopes, or the mushmelons, or what. But towards daylight we got it all settled satisfactory, and concluded to drop crabapples and p'simmons. We warn't feeling just right before that, but it was all comfortable now. I was glad the way it come out, too, because crabapples ain't ever good, and the p'simmons wouldn't be ripe for two or three months yet.

Although Tom Sawyer and Huck Finn brought Sam Clemens financial success and international renown, by the early 1890s he was broke and

Mark Twain was hugely popular with British publishers and their readers. Some of his writings, including *The Adventures of Huckleberry Finn,* appeared first in England.

right: *The Adventures of Huckleberry Finn.* Frontispiece by E. W. Kemble, 1884.

In contrast to Tom Sawyer, Huck appears entirely self-reliant, a legacy of his deadbeat dad, wearing shabby clothes, armed with a hunting rifle, and bearing a trophy for his dinner.

HUCKLEBERRY FINN

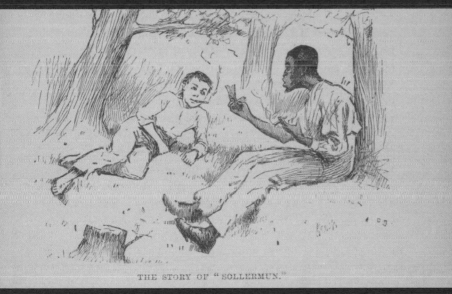

THE STORY OF "SOLLERMUN."

The Story of "Sollermun."
Illustration by E. W. Kemble in *The Adventures of Huckleberry Finn.*

The natural companionship of Huck Finn and the runaway slave Jim, sharing a smoke while discussing life's dilemmas in light of lessons from the Bible, offered a groundbreaking literary view of race relations.

Mississippi River, Keokuk, IA. Panoramic photographic by Frederick J. Bandholtz, ca. 1907.

This panoramic photograph captures the quiet commerce on the Mississippi River after the turn of the century. In the foreground are the railroad tracks that doomed river shipping.

Samuel Clemens and Laura Frazier/Becky Thatcher. Photograph, 1902.

Mark Twain's boyhood friends. Photograph, 1922.

Mrs. Laura Frazier, better known as Tom Sawyer's love interest, Becky Thatcher, was among the old friends on hand to greet Mark Twain upon his final return to Hannibal in 1902. Twelve years after his death, Frazier assembled with several of Sam Clemens's old pals for a group photo.

bankrupt, his wealth, and some of his wife's, lost in bad investments and huge debts. Saved by the intervention and support of financier H. H. Rogers, who loaned him money and took over his business matters, and a highly successful worldwide lecture tour, Clemens recouped his losses and regained his fortune.

In May 1902, eight years before his death, and almost fifty years since he had first left town, Clemens made a final return to Hannibal. Although worries over Livy's frail health haunted the trip, he did find comfort in the embrace of the townspeople, and he spent a few enjoyable days catching up with his former schoolmates, including Mrs. Laura Frazier. He visited his family gravesite, where his parents, Orion, and Henry lay buried. He was feted by the town; a reporter accompanying Clemens wrote, "Today Hannibal is full of Huck Finns, Tom Sawyers,

and Beckys." It was a satisfying yet bittersweet experience. He acknowledged the visit as his last, saying, "I realize that this must be my last visit to Hannibal, and in bidding you hail I also bid you farewell." Saying good-bye to Hannibal and the riverfront that had fired his imagination and that symbolized his achievements, Clemens soon returned to his family and the challenges to come as his life and career came to a close.

Mark Twain standing in doorway of his boyhood home on Hill Street, Hannibal, Missouri. Photograph, 1902.

Mark Twain bid a final farewell to Hannibal in 1902, surrounded by former friends and neighbors and a town filled with "Tom Sawyers and Huck Finns."

CHAPTER TWO

Western Swing

Before railroad magnate Leland Stanford hammered home the golden spike in May 1869 at Promontory Point, Utah, uniting the nation by train from coast to coast; before newspaper publisher Horace Greeley was quoted telling young men to "go west" to find their fortune, Sam Clemens had already been there, done that, and returned east, having discovered a commodity more valuable than silver or gold: the unique literary voice that would bring him great wealth and international acclaim.

In July 1861, when Clemens lit out for the territories, stagecoaches ruled the few existing rutted roads and the Pony Express ran mail to far-flung outposts during its brief heyday. Only twenty years before, the explorer and future presidential hopeful John C. Frémont, nicknamed The Pathfinder after James Fenimore Cooper's pioneering character Natty Bumppo in the Leatherstocking Tales, had helped map the way across the Rocky Mountains. He helped codify the route to the Pacific Northwest that, during the 1840s, became known as the Oregon Trail. Before Frémont, hunters and trappers rode the rivers, climbed the mountains, and walked the forest floors. Before them, Lewis and Clark's epic explorations made known to the public the majestic landscapes far west of civilized settlements. By the time Clemens departed from California for New York as Mark Twain in December 1866, the West had been transformed as much as he had, the vast empty frontier

Butte City. Watercolor by George Henry Burgess, ca. 1854.

Not to be confused with Butte, Montana, the city transformed later in the nineteenth century by copper mines, Butte City, California, was a quiet settlement in 1854, when artist George Henry Burgess painted its portrait. Burgess and his brother were among the miners who settled there.

left: *The Independent Gold Hunter on His Way to California: I Neither Borrow nor Lend.* Hand-colored lithograph by Currier & Ives, New York: published by N. Currier, ca. 1849.

below: *The Way They Go to California.* Lithograph by Currier & Ives, Spruce, N.Y.: published by N. Currier, ca. 1849.

The mania that attended the mass migration of fortune seekers to California and other points west starting in 1848 inspired artists to lampoon the would-be prospectors, their gear, and their various modes of transportation. Though Sam Clemens's avowed motive for going west was to assist his brother Orion in administering the Nevada Territory, he inevitably fell in with the get-rich-quick crowd. From those experiences he would derive little real capital but a wealth of material for his budding career as a writer.

THE WAY THEY GO TO CALIFORNIA.

Col. Frémont Planting the American Standard on the Rocky Mountains. Wood engraving with letterpress, New York: Baker & Godwin, ca. 1856.

John C. Frémont, pioneer and politician, celebrated for his exploring exploits and prominent role in California's early days, first as military governor, later as one of its first two U.S. senators. Cultivating his renown as "The Pathfinder," a modern Natty Bumppo, James Fenimore Cooper's buckskin backwoodsman Western Division, he became the nation's first Republican Party presidential candidate in 1856, losing to Democrat James Buchanan in the election.

Study for "Westward Ho!" showing figures with wagon train from "Westward the course of empire takes its way." Drawing, pencil and ink wash by Emanuel Leutze, ca 1861.

German American artist Emanuel Leutze produced two of the era's most popular and patriotic paintings. His renowned portrait of *Washington Crossing the Delaware* now hangs in Boston's Museum of Fine Arts, while the U.S. Capitol is home to his mural "Westward the Course of Empire Takes Its Way," for which this detailed sketch is a preparatory study.

now dotted with cities and settlements linked by telegraph poles and railroad lines. There were still plenty of empty spaces, but they were easier to get to and communicate with.

Most Americans only dreamed of celebrity, while Clemens achieved it with his own brand of pluck, initiative, and Victorian stick-to-itiveness. He had gone West at least in part to escape service in the Civil War, to see a part of the country unknown to him, and perhaps to strike it rich. In the West he found a bounty of material fit for a budding young comic writer: pioneers and prospectors, cutthroats and cardsharps, entrepreneurs and evangelists, peopled a society that was inventing itself and thus not only welcomed but rewarded his provocative blend of fact, fiction, and outright falsehoods. He not only took on the twin professions of writer and lecturer in company with contemporary humorists,

but he also adopted the euphonious pen name that forever defined his public identity. Well before Clemens headed back East, having hit literary pay dirt in 1865 with the mining-camp tall tale "The Celebrated Jumping Frog of Calaveras County," his pseudonym and alter ego Mark Twain was a household name in the American West.

The frontier provided Clemens with a freedom he had never known, even during his piloting days on the river. In *Beyond the Mississippi,* Clemens's contemporary, roving reporter Albert D. Richardson, described the allure of the West for those who wished to find a fortune or reinvent themselves:

Territory of Nevada, U.S. of A., 1861. Engraved seal, attributed to Orion Clemens, ca. 1861.

In 1861, as Union and Confederate troops mustered for war, Sam Clemens took a stagecoach west with his brother Orion, who had received a patronage appointment as secretary of the newly organized Nevada Territory. Orion designed the official seal representing the region.

In exhaustlessness and variety of resources, no other country on the globe equals ours beyond the Mississippi.... Its air invites the invalid, healing the system wounded by ruder climates. Its society welcomes the immigrant, offering high interest upon his investment of money, brains or skill; and if need be, generous obliviousness of errors past—a clean page to begin anew the record of his life.

Had he stayed in Missouri in 1861, Sam Clemens would have faced shame as a deserter or death as a soldier. The war had terminated his career as riverboat pilot—the only traffic on the river now was military-related—and his brief sojourn in a band of Confederate irregulars was enough to convince him that life in uniform in wartime was not to his liking. When his brother Orion, a stalwart Lincoln recruiter, was appointed in March through his friendship with fellow Missourian and Lincoln's attorney general, Edward Bates, as assistant secretary of the Nevada Territory, Sam jumped at the opportunity to join him out West. Sam even offered to pay travel expenses in return for an unofficial position as personal secretary to the assistant secretary. He had no intention of being left behind in a war zone as his brother hit the jackpot with his new posting.

Mark Twain would publish his account of his time on the frontier, *Roughing It,* in February 1872. Drawn in part from his own dispatches and writings during his sojourns in Nevada, California, and Hawaii, it remains one of the most vivid accounts of daily life way out West. In its opening pages, he writes of his departure with the gleeful anticipation of a young boy awaiting the arrival of Christmas morning.

Pretty soon he would be hundreds and hundreds of miles away on the great plains and deserts, and among the mountains of the Far West, and would see buffaloes and Indians, and prairie dogs, and antelopes, and have all kinds of adventures, and maybe get hanged or scalped, and have ever such a fine time, and write home and tell us all about it, and be a hero. And he would see the gold mines and the silver mines, and maybe go about of an afternoon when his work was done, and pick up two or three pailfuls of shining slugs, and nuggets of gold and silver on the hillside. And by and by he would become very rich, and return home by sea, and be able to talk as calmly about San Francisco and the ocean, and "the isthmus" as if it was nothing of any consequence to have seen those marvels face to face.

At the time, neither brother had any idea that Orion's appointment would be his last real job, or that wayward young Sam would soon be responsible for the family's fortunes. Sam's goals in going west were in fact modest, as he wrote:

I only proposed to stay in Nevada three months—I had no thought of staying longer than that. I meant to see all I could that was new and strange, and then hurry home to business. I little thought that I would not see the end of that three-month pleasure excursion for six or seven uncommonly long years!

Although *Roughing It* appeared in print ten years after his departure from Hannibal, Clemens infused his writing with a sense of history and nostalgia, as if he knew even then that the frontier was a moving target that time and civilization might soon erase. His Nevada and California frontier scenes have lingered far less vividly in the popular imagination than those perpetuated in Western fiction and, especially, movies. There are no characters in *Roughing It* to approach the enduring mythos of Wyatt Earp, Billy the Kid, Sitting Bull, Geronimo, or Calamity Jane. No set pieces like Custer's Last Stand, Wild Bill Hickok drawing a dead man's hand, or the gunfight at the O.K. Corral. Miners and prospectors figure far less frequently in our view of the Old West than do cowboys and Indians. Nonetheless, Mark Twain's accounts record with authenticity and wide variety the raw and risky lives led by the thousands who made their hazardous way to the region's gold and silver mines.

The journey began in July 1861, about the time Confederate troops chased the Union army back to Washington in the First Battle of Bull Run. The brothers embarked at St. Louis on a steamboat traveling upriver to St. Joseph, Missouri; they transferred to a stagecoach bound for the silver-mining settlements rapidly expanding in Nevada. For most of the trip, the two men reclined on mailbags and smoked pipes, watching the unfamiliar landscape unfold as the miles went by. Clemens made notes and later recalled the journey in *Roughing It*:

The stage whirled along at a spanking gait, the breeze flapping curtains and suspended coats in a most exhilarating way; the cradle swayed and swung luxuriously, the pattering of the horses' hoofs, the cracking of the driver's whip, and his

Innocent Dreams. Illustration in *Roughing It.*

In Twain's second book, his account of his adventures way out West, he is happy to depict himself as the ultimate dude, with totally unrealistic expectations of his journey and what he would find.

"Hi-yi! g'lang!" were music; the spinning ground and the waltzing trees appeared to give us a mute hurrah as we went by, and then slack up and look after us with interest, or envy, or something; and as we lay and smoked the pipe of peace and compared all this luxury with the years of tiresome city life that had gone before it, we felt that there was only one complete and satisfying happiness in the world, and we had found it.

Jolting over rough roads through sparsely populated terrain was uncomfortable, but Clemens embraced the experience, enjoying himself immensely. His cares seemed to dissolve, and a new world spread before him as the coach rolled west. Rooted to the river his entire life, he now appeared to have limitless horizons.

He marveled at the region's flora and fauna—"jackass rabbits," sagebrush, "cayotes"—made conversation with a notorious gunslinger, and drank slumgullion, a beverage of uncertain merits.

Ironically, in the midst of a hostile wilderness–*Roughing It* notes the keen eyes the coach's occupants kept out for unfriendly Indians–Clemens's main nemesis appears to have been the six-pound dictionary Orion had brought along: "Every time we avalanched from one end of the stage to the other, the Unabridged Dictionary would come too; and every time it came it damaged somebody."

Clemens noted similarities between the steamboat captains and crews he had known on the Mississippi and the men responsible for driving and maintaining the stages and the routes they followed. At the depots along the way he met a new set of characters unlike any he'd encountered on the river. These rest stops offered few amenities. With few established western routes available and limited competition, depots offered a take-it-or-leave-it proposition to travelers. Unsavory hosts and miserable meals created with questionable ingredients were the usual fare. In *Roughing It*, Clemens described one particularly despicable dinner thus:

> He had no sugar and no milk–not even a spoon to stir the ingredients with.... We could not eat the bread or the meat, nor drink the "slumgullion." And when I looked at that melancholy vinegar-cruet, I thought of the anecdote (a very, very old one, even at that day) of the traveler who sat down to a table which had nothing on it but a mackerel and a pot of mustard. He asked the landlord if this was all. The landlord said:
>
> "All! Why, thunder and lightning, I should think there was mackerel enough there for six."
>
> "But I don't like mackerel."
>
> "Oh–then help yourself to the mustard."
>
> In other days I had considered it a good, a very good, anecdote, but there was a dismal plausibility about it, here, that took all the humor out of it.

Despite crude fare and lodgings, Sam and Orion Clemens were more fortunate than most western

Drinking Slumgullion. Illustration in *Roughing It.*

Western travelers often confronted crude lodgings and poor fare. Slumgullion referred to a souplike stew comprising often indeterminate ingredients.

travelers who did not have the means to travel in such relative style. Sam had paid three hundred dollars for two tickets. Most who headed west traveled in large wagon trains, sharing the cost, while those beginning on the East Coast journeyed by sail from New York to San Francisco via the Nicaraguan isthmus. Stagecoaches traveled much more quickly than wagon trains, and Clemens's enchantment grew as his coach moved speedily west. His exultation was amplified one day by the appearance of a Pony

opposite: *The Persuit [Pursuit].* Hand-colored lithograph by J. H. Bufford, ca. 1861.

Mark Twain's rousing eyewitness description in *Roughing It* of a Pony Express messenger in full flight thrilled the nation and helped shape the popular image of a courageous lone rider braving harsh, hostile terrain, uniting the continent while providing a crucial overland connection with California. A private enterprise, the delivery service stretched westward from St. Joseph, Missouri, to Sacramento, California. Created in spring 1860, the service shut down in fall 1861, disrupted by the Civil War and expansion of the telegraph.

Express rider hell-bent for leather, inspiring this passage from *Roughing It*:

"HERE HE COMES!"

Every neck is stretched further, and every eye strained wider. Away across the endless dead level of the prairie a black speck appears against the sky, and it is plain that it moves. Well, I should think so!

In a second or two it becomes a horse and rider, rising and falling, rising and falling–sweeping toward us nearer and nearer–growing more and more distinct, more and more sharply defined– nearer and still nearer, and the flutter of the hoofs comes faintly to the ear–another instant a whoop and a hurrah from our upper deck, a wave of the rider's hand, but no reply, and man and horse burst past our excited faces, and go winging away like a belated fragment of a storm!

So sudden is it all, and so like a flash of unreal fancy, that but for the flake of white foam left quivering and perishing on a mail-sack after the vision had flashed by and disappeared, we might have doubted whether we had seen any actual horse and man at all, maybe.

The Pony Express would cease operations that October, replaced by the telegraph, but this thrilling description, published ten years after the service's demise, laid the foundation for a romantic view of one short-lived aspect of the history of the West. For all of Twain's vivid descriptions of the good, the bad, and the ugly during his years on the frontier, his portrait of the lone rider crossing the plains, courageous and self-reliant, remains one of our most enduring images.

"Whirling high above the common world," the stagecoach took the brothers over the Rocky Mountains, through South Pass in Dakota Territory (now southern Wyoming), one of the Oregon Trail's most famous sights. For the first time, Sam saw summertime snow. In *Roughing It*, he wrote, "We

The South Pass. Illustration in *Roughing It.*

The means by which many a traveler could traverse the Rocky Mountains most easily was found in what is now south-central Wyoming. Sam and Orion Clemens made the crossing in the summer of 1861, on their way to the Nevada Territory.

were in such an airy elevation above the creeping populations of the earth, that now and then when the obstructing crags stood out of the way it seemed that we could look around and abroad and contemplate the whole great globe, with its dissolving views of mountains, seas and continents stretching away through the mystery of the summer haze." The thin air and natural majesty made him giddy. Views like this simply didn't exist back in Missouri.

The stage turned south and made an extended stopover in Salt Lake City, which Sam described as "an extremely healthy city. They declared there was only one physician in the place and he was arrested every week regularly and held to answer under the vagrant act for having 'no visible means of support.'"

He found the Mormons and their leader Brigham Young fascinating and ripe for ridicule, their pompous hierarchy and bigamous households unfathomable. The Mormon religion had been developed by New York native Joseph Smith in the 1820s. An inspiring and evangelical leader, Smith led his followers west to avoid clashing with authorities and others who reviled their beliefs. In June 1844 Smith and his brother Hyrum were killed by an angry mob in Carthage, Illinois. Brigham Young took over

leadership of the Mormons and moved his people westward into the sparsely settled Utah Territory, where, in 1847, they, like the lost tribes of Israel, found their Zion and built a city and society in splendid isolation.

In a new homeland well removed from their persecutors, the Mormons became defensive, turning inward to protect their settlement and its citizens. The constant encroachment of non-Mormon settlers into Utah led to conflict: In September 1857 a Mormon militia, along with sympathetic Paiute Indians, attacked an emigrant train at Mountain Meadows, 320 miles southwest of Salt Lake City. After several days of battles, the Mormons and Indians offered a truce and then turned on the defenseless settlers and slaughtered about one hundred and twenty men, women, and children, leaving only a few younger children alive.

News of the Mountain Meadows Massacre, as it came to be called, was still fresh when Sam Clemens arrived in Salt Lake City, but he seemed more interested in the orthodoxy of the church and its strange social practices. He devoted one paragraph to the tragedy in *Roughing It,* claiming not to know who was at fault–the Indians alone, the Indians and the Mormons, or the Mormons alone–and allowing as how the truth would have to come out at another time. Instead, the book is filled with comic descriptions of Mormon activities and attitudes, reinforcing their alien identity to readers outside Utah. For Twain, Mormonism was a wilderness cult more fascinating than frightening, The Book of Mormon "merely a prosy detail of imaginary history, with the Old Testament for a model; followed by a tedious plagiarism of the New Testament." With tongue in cheek, he revealed his desire to reform Mormon ways and liberate their wives from servitude in polygamy:

I had the will to do it. With the gushing self-sufficiency of youth I was feverish to plunge in

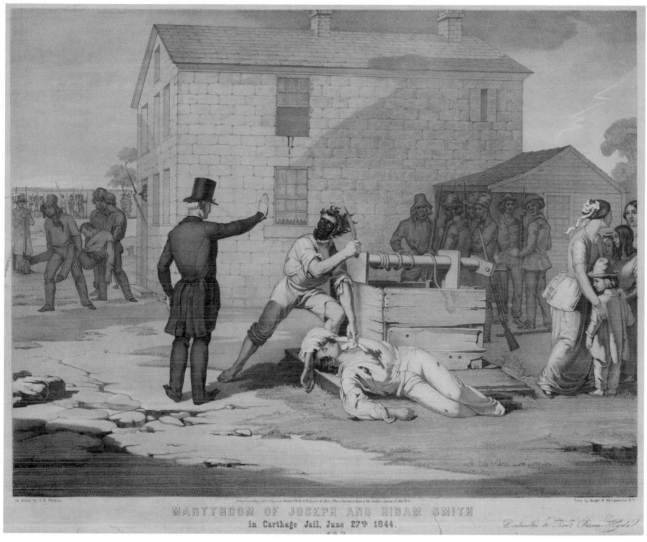

MARTYRDOM OF JOSEPH AND HIRAM SMITH
in Carthage Jail, June 27th 1844.

Martyrdom of Joseph and Hiram Smith in Carthage Jail, June 27th, 1844. Tinted lithograph after G. W. Fasel on stone by C. G. Crehen; print by Nagel & Weingaertner, N.Y., ca. 1851.

Not everyone emigrating westward was seeking gold or silver. The Church of Jesus Christ of Latter-Day Saints, or the Mormons, was founded in New York State by Joseph Smith in 1830. After he met resistance from mainstream Protestants and moved farther west to escape persecution, he and his brother met their demise at the hands of a lynch mob outside an Illinois jail in 1844. Their followers would decamp more than 1,000 miles westward, to the sparsely settled Utah Territory.

headlong and achieve a great reform here—until I saw the Mormon women. Then I was touched. My heart was wiser than my head. It warmed toward these poor, ungainly and pathetically "homely" creatures, and as I turned to hide the generous moisture in my eyes, I said, "No—the man that marries one of them has done an act of Christian charity which entitles him to the kindly applause of mankind, not their harsh censure—and the man that marries sixty of them has done a deed of open-handed generosity so sublime that the nations should stand uncovered in his presence and worship in silence."

His first recorded encounter with Indians, 250 miles west of Salt Lake City, elicited a much

Wells Fargo & Co.'s Express Office, C Street, Virginia City.
Photograph by Lawrence & Houseworth, ca. 1866.

Lawrence & Houseworth, Opticians, of Montgomery Street, San Francisco, offered catalogs filled with their own published photographs of western scenery and points of interest, including the Wells Fargo stage depot in Virginia City, Nevada, where Sam would begin his writing career.

tribe he has only found Goshoots more or less modified by circumstances and surroundings—but Goshoots, after all. They deserve pity, poor creatures; and they can have mine—at this distance. Nearer by, they never get anybody's.

This is the only extended description of Indians in *Roughing It.* Clemens had little to do with any tribe during his years on the frontier. The Indians offered no obstacle to his prospecting ambitions. They simply weren't much of a presence wherever he chose to live. In some sense they were simply part of the scenery, but the distance between his preconceived notion of their nature and the ugly reality he saw clearly upset him. His views of Native Americans would eventually change as he matured and better understood their plight. But for many others on the frontier, Indians were to be feared, despised, and considered a major impediment to peaceful settlement.

Twenty days out of St. Joseph, the stage finally pulled into Carson City, Nevada, which Clemens described as a "wooden" town of two thousand inhabitants. Its main street consisted of "four or five blocks of little white frame stores which were too high to sit down on, but not too high for various other purposes; in fact, hardly high enough." The sidewalk boards "inclined to rattle when walked upon." In the middle of town was a plaza, "which is native to all towns beyond the Rocky Mountains—a large, unfenced, level vacancy, with a liberty pole in it, and very useful as a place for public auctions, horse trades, and mass meetings, and likewise for teamsters to camp in." The rest of Carson City was "pretty scattering."

In fact, in August 1861, the newly formed Nevada Territory was "pretty scattering." The 1860 official census count in Nevada totaled barely seven thousand souls. (Ten years later, fueled by the discoveries of gold and silver, it had grown to over 42,000.) When Sam and Orion Clemens arrived, there were no railroad lines linking the new towns

more complex set of emotions. Like many whites accustomed to literary descriptions of the "noble savage," he was unprepared for the impoverished and dissipated state of the Gosiute (which he spelled "Goshoot") tribe, living in subsistence along the stage route and outside settlements. Wanting to believe in their natural nobility, feeling cheated by their diminished appearance, he unleashed an angry rant:

I say that the nausea which the Goshoots gave me, an Indian worshipper, set me to examining authorities, to see if perchance I had been over-estimating the Red Man while viewing him through the mellow moonshine of romance. The revelations that came were disenchanting. It was curious to see how quickly the paint and tinsel fell away from him and left him treacherous, filthy and repulsive—and how quickly the evidences accumulated that wherever one finds an Indian growing around mines, along trade routes, or abutting the few rivers and lakes that served the region. Limited transportation, a harsh climate, and lack of water all helped shape communities in the desert. Those inhabitants without means routinely walked from camp to camp, or town to town. When local resources ran out, miners moved on and communities became ghost towns.

Carson City was located in western Nevada, in Eagle Valley, near the Carson River; both river and town were named after the explorer Kit Carson. It would be designated Nevada's state capital when the territory became a state in 1864. But in 1861, towns like Carson City offered rudimentary facilities: "I would have been more or less than human if I had not gone mad like the rest," Clemens wrote in *Roughing It*. "Cart-loads of solid silver bricks, as large as pigs of lead, were arriving from the mills every day, and such sights as that gave substance to the wild talk about me. I succumbed and grew as frenzied as the craziest." The writer's lifelong quest for riches had begun.

With no usable skill other than flourishing his pen and no grubstake with which to set up a business, Sam Clemens had few options out West other than to make a go of it as a miner. It was a harsh life, under primitive, mostly lawless conditions, and few reaped rewards. Life could be cheaper than a spurious claim; outright murder was all too common. More often than not, miners found little profit and big disappointment. Existence on the frontier was dangerous, arbitrary, and cruel, a far cry from the romantic descriptions flowing back East.

The Miner's Ten Commandments. Wood engraving and letterpress on blue paper by Anthony & Baker after Harrison Eastman, San Francisco, ca. 1853.

On the frontier, as society re-formed in new configurations under new conditions, miners came up with their own codes of conduct to maintain a sense of civilization and decorum.

Nonetheless, Clemens kept reaching for that big payoff. One classic misadventure occurred in August 1861, soon after his arrival, during a lull in his new "duties" allegedly working for Orion, as described in *Roughing It*:

I had become an officer of the government, but that was for mere sublimity. The office was a unique

*sinecure. I had nothing to do and no salary. I was
private Secretary to his majesty the Secretary
and there was not yet writing enough for two
of us. So Johnny K— and I devoted our time to
amusement. He was the young son of an Ohio
nabob and was out there for recreation. He got it.
We had heard a world of talk about the marvelous
beauty of Lake Tahoe, and finally curiosity drove
us thither to see it.... We strapped a couple of
blankets on our shoulders and took an axe apiece
and started—for we intended to take up a wood
ranch or so ourselves and become wealthy. We were
on foot. The reader will find it advantageous to
go horseback.*

For several weeks Clemens and his companion
felled yellow pines, dreams of a timber empire
softening their sleep under cover of riverbank
boulders.

One evening, upon their return from a restocking
trip to Carson City, Clemens lit a fire for dinner and
went off to retrieve the frying pan. The untended
flames spread to the carpet of dry pine needles,
and fire soon consumed the campsite. Clemens
and Johnny escaped in their skiff and waited out
the inferno before retreating to Carson City, soot-
covered, exhausted, their dreams gone, literally, up
in smoke.

Back at the mines, Clemens and his new
companions took up various claims, started digging
shafts and tunnels on them, "but never finished any
of them."

He lived in a miner's cabin, and he and Orion
poured money into supplies, equipment, and
speculative purchases of mining stock, measured
in tunnel "feet" and traded like cigarettes in a
penitentiary.

He did learn the ways of the miner—how you had
to work a claim at least one day in three to keep it. A
claim left alone for too long would go wanting, and
another man could stake it. In the society that sprang
up around the camps and the small towns, order was
important, in the absence of any real government-
backed authority. Crimes were dealt with quickly
by an ad-hoc court of judge, jury, prosecutor, and
defender. Twain wrote in *Roughing It*:

*It was the strangest phase of life one can imagine.
It was a beggars' revel. There was nothing
doing in the district—no mining—no milling—no
productive effort—no income—and not enough
money in the entire camp to buy a corner lot in an
eastern village, hardly; and yet a stranger would
have supposed he was walking among bloated
millionaires. Prospecting parties swarmed out of
town with the first flush of dawn, and swarmed in
again at nightfall laden with spoil—rocks. Nothing
but rocks. Every man's pockets were full of them;
the floor of his cabin was littered with them; they
were disposed in labeled rows on his shelves.*

Sam's only real job during his first year in
Nevada was a two-month assignment clerking for
the territorial legislature. After bumping around
several locations, he finally got a break: an offer
in the fall of 1862 of a job with a Virginia City
newspaper to report on the territorial legislature.
His regular correspondence had laid the groundwork.
Nonetheless, the offer came as a surprise:

*Now in pleasanter days I had amused myself with
writing letters to the chief paper of the Territory,
the* Virginia Daily Territorial Enterprise, *and
had always been surprised when they appeared in
print. My good opinion of the editors had steadily
declined; for it seemed to me that they might have
found something better to fill up with than my*

The Miner's Dream. Shurtleff illustration in ***Roughing It.***

Among miners, ambitious dreams of fortune and fame
often gave way to simpler wishes for a comfortable bed and
appetizing meals.

THE MINER'S DREAM.

Virginia City, Nevada Territory, 1861. Lithograph by Charles Conrad Kuchel after Grafton T. Brown, Britton & Co., San Francisco, 1861.

Publishers in Western cities seeking settlers produced handsome views to lure prospective citizens. A San Francisco publisher printed this bird's-eye view of the mining community at Virginia City, Nevada, surrounded by vignettes of local merchants who helped fund the print in return for advertising their services.

literature. I had found a letter in the post office as I came home from the hill side, and finally I opened it. Eureka! [I never did know what Eureka meant, but it seems to be as proper a word to heave in as any when no other that sounds pretty offers.] It was a deliberate offer to me of Twenty-Five Dollars a week to come up to Virginia and be city editor of the Enterprise.

His hire at the *Enterprise* transformed his life. Instead of prospecting full-time and writing part-time,

he could focus on his real talents and get paid for it while pursuing his speculative schemes on the side.

Virginia City was even younger than Carson City, all of three years old, having sprung up in the fall of 1859 around silver mines that centered on the legendary Comstock Lode. Following the contours of its site, like other Western communities, the town spread itself along a mountainside punctured by shafts and tunnels leading to the ore. As Clemens recalled in *Roughing It,*

The "city" of Virginia roosted royally midway up the steep side of Mount Davidson, seven thousand two hundred feet above the level of the sea, and in the clear Nevada atmosphere was visible from a distance of fifty miles! It claimed a population of fifteen thousand to eighteen thousand, and all day long half of this little army swarmed the streets like

above: Virginia [City], Nevada. Photograph by Timothy O'Sullivan, 1867, plate 93 from Geological Exploration of the Fortieth Parallel, United States Army Corps of Engineers, ca. 1871.

Famed Civil War photographer Timothy O'Sullivan followed the army west after the war as part of a governmental expedition led by geologist Clarence King. The United States Geological Survey hired artists and photographers including O'Sullivan, A. J. Russell, and Thomas Moran to document the landscape, natural landmarks, and newly built mining settlements developing in the region.

right: *Mining on the Comstock, Nevada.* Lithograph drawn by T. L. Dawes, engraved and printed by Le Count Bros., San Francisco. published by J. B. Marshall, 1876.

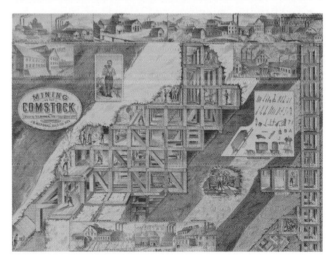

The Comstock Lode, discovered in the late 1850s, extended deep beneath the community of Virginia City. Mark Twain described the hidden maze of tunnels and shafts in *Roughing It:* "Virginia was a busy city of streets and houses above ground. Under it was another busy city, down in the bowels of the earth, where a great population of men thronged in and out among an intricate maze of tunnels and drifts, flitting hither and thither under a winking sparkle of lights, and over their heads towered a vast web of interlocking timbers that held the walls of the gutted Comstock apart. These timbers were as large as a man's body, and the framework stretched upward so far that no eye could pierce to its top through the closing gloom. It was like peering up through the clean-picked ribs and bones of some colossal skeleton. Imagine such a framework two miles long, sixty feet wide, and higher than any church spire in America. Imagine this stately lattice-work stretching down Broadway, from the St. Nicholas to Wall street, and a Fourth of July procession, reduced to pigmies, parading on top of it and flaunting their flags, high above the pinnacle of Trinity steeple."

Six mile canyon from C Street, Virginia City. Photograph by Lawrence and Houseworth, 1866.

The town of Virginia City was born in 1859 and seven years later sported a respectable skyline amid the hills of western Nevada.

Quartz mining works at Gold Hill. Photograph by Lawrence and Houseworth, 1866.

Sam Clemens reached a low point in his life on the frontier while working in a Virginia City quartz mine for "ten dollars a week and board." He lasted a week before giving notice. As a reporter, Mark Twain soon earned forty dollars per week.

bees and the other half swarmed among the drifts and tunnels of the "Comstock," hundreds of feet down in the earth directly under those same streets. Often we felt our chairs jar, and heard the faint boom of a blast down in the bowels of the earth under the office.

The Comstock Lode lay directly beneath the town, and miners worked the claims in shifts, providing twenty-four-hour production, with laborers earning between four and six dollars per day. The Lode had attracted many disappointed miners away from the played-out California goldfields and provided the West with its first eastward migration. The city itself grew by leaps and bounds, eventually becoming, as historian Russell Elliott wrote in *The New Encyclopedia of the American West,* "an important political, financial, and social hub," without equal in the history of the far western states. For an ambitious young man of twenty-seven, Sam Clemens could do

no better than to be living here with a full-time job that did not involve descending into a mine shaft seven days a week.

Journalism in the West attracted a rough crowd, and Clemens fit right in. Although he discarded his mining clothes–blue wool shirt, canvas pants stuffed in his boots–he did keep a navy revolver at the belt of his city duds, explaining, "I had never had occasion to kill anybody, nor ever felt a desire to do so, but had worn the thing in deference to popular sentiment, and in order that I might not, by its absence, be offensively conspicuous, and a subject of remark. But the other editors, and all the printers, carried revolvers." (Historian Roy Morris Jr. points out that Clemens scarcely knew how to handle a firearm without shooting himself in the foot.) Life was tough both in the mines and in the streets, and arguments turned quickly into killings. Public feuds between rival editors and reporters were commonplace and duels not uncommon. Occasionally, though, rivalries were staged for publicity, as was the case with Clemens's extended satirical correspondence with Clement Rice, his counterpart at the *Virginia City Union*. Clemens, signing his libelous letters "The Reliable," kept up a vigorous exchange with Rice, dubbed "The Unreliable." In truth, Clemens and Rice were great friends and traveling companions.

Clemens settled into his surroundings, found his way around town, enjoying camaraderie with his new colleagues and the varied population of the city. He looked for hard news and compelling human interest stories. When he could not find any, in the tradition of wildcat journalism he created one. Hoaxes and sensationally fraudulent stories were fresh meat to reporters in the West. Papers existed as much to provide entertainment as hard information. Within a few weeks of starting his job, Clemens filed a fictitious account of the local discovery of a perfectly preserved "petrified man"; the story spread widely, only careful readers noticing that the ancient corpse was thumbing his nose at them.

In the office he ate noodles prepared by a Chinese cook; Clemens admired the Chinese population, and toured their neighborhood of restaurants and opium dens. He commented on the Chinese population in *Roughing It*.

> *They are a harmless race when white men either let them alone or treat them no worse than dogs; in fact they are almost entirely harmless anyhow, for they seldom think of resenting the vilest insults or the cruelest injuries. They are quiet, peaceable, tractable, free from drunkenness, and they are as industrious as the day is long. A disorderly Chinaman is rare, and a lazy one does not exist. So long as a Chinaman has strength to use his hands he needs no support from anybody; white men often complain of want of work, but a Chinaman offers no such complaint; he always manages to find something to do. He is a great convenience to everybody—even to the worst class of white men, for he bears the most of their sins, suffering fines for their petty thefts, imprisonment for their robberies, and death for their murders. Any white man can swear a Chinaman's life away in the courts, but no Chinaman can testify against a white man. Ours is the "land of the free"—nobody denies that—nobody challenges it. [Maybe it is because we won't let other people testify.]*

Three of the suspected men still in confinement at Aurora.
Photograph, cabinet card, unattributed, 1864.

Mark Twain made his first public appearances while reporting on the newly established Nevada Territorial legislature. He is flanked here by Rep. William H. Clagett and Speaker A. J. Simmons.

top: *Celestial Empire in California: Miners, Gamblers.* Pictorial letter sheet, lithograph on blue paper, published by Britton & Rey, San Francisco, ca. 1850–53.

Asians looking to settle in the West after the Civil War, whether building railroads or working a claim, were subject to resentment, ridicule, and immigration restrictions following the 1882 Chinese Exclusion Act, the opening salvo in an eighty-year era of legislative limitations that were finally lifted in 1965.

bottom: Chinamen sluicing. Stereograph by William H. Jackson, United States Geological Survey, Washington, DC, 1871.

William Henry Jackson advanced the cause of conservation in the United States with his magnificent early views of the Yellowstone River and Rocky Mountains, which led to the creation of Yellowstone, the country's first national park. Jackson produced promotional scenic views on behalf of the Union Pacific Railroad before joining the United States Geological Survey expedition led by Ferdinand Hayden in 1870. Along with majestic scenery, Jackson captured the mundane lives of frontier workers. In *Roughing It,* Mark Twain extolled the Chinese: "They are a kindly disposed, well-meaning race, and are respected and well treated by the upper classes, all over the Pacific coast. No Californian gentleman or lady ever abuses or oppresses a Chinaman, under any circumstances, an explanation that seems to be much needed in the East. Only the scum of the population do it—they and their children; they, and, naturally and consistently, the policemen and politicians, likewise, for these are the dust-licking pimps and slaves of the scum, there as well as elsewhere in America."

Chinese laborers vied with Irish immigrants and other settlers for jobs and resources. Clemens's evident empathy for the Chinese workers and their families was unusual. Like blacks and Indians, they were commonly vilified and satirized in the press for their foreign ways.

Life on the frontier was fluid and people were transient, moving from mine to mine and job to job, ever seeking their fortune. Clemens moved as quickly and often as any of them, exhibiting a lifelong restlessness and love of travel, which in turn served to inform his views. Back East, men worked in settled communities flush with trade and commerce. In the West, the quest for riches took precedence and men traveled the region seeking opportunities.

On February 2, 1863, Clemens first signed his letters with the pen name Mark Twain, recalling his days on the river when mates announced river soundings by the "mark." "Mark Twain" meant two fathoms, or twelve feet of water, providing a safe threshold for steamboats below the hull. Under the new moniker he became a local celebrity, participating in the social life surrounding Orion and his wife, Mollie, who had joined her husband in nearby Carson City. He took up public speaking, quickly gaining a reputation as a wit and raconteur and a bit of a rake. Yet such was his wanderlust and seemingly short attention span that, as his social life became more exciting, Clemens grew bored at work, tired of reporting on "the proceedings of the legislature once a year, and horse-races and pumpkin-shows once in three months.... I wanted to see San Francisco. I wanted to go somewhere. I wanted–I did not know what I wanted. I had the 'spring fever' and wanted a change."

Change came soon, and not on his timetable. In early 1864 his editor, Joe Goodman, took two months off from the paper, leaving Clemens and his veteran colleague and good friend Dan De Quille (a pen name for William Wright) in charge. According to Dan, "We went merrily along, laughing and joking, and

never feeling the weight of the work we were doing in the whirl and excitement of the times." De Quille and Twain shared a small apartment and a devil-may-care attitude. They smoked, read, ate oysters, sparred for exercise in a nearby boxing gym, shared a bottle and, of necessity in close quarters, a bed.

The drinking bouts and Goodman's absence added up to trouble. Under the influence, Clemens concocted a little hoax of a story implicating his sister-in-law Mollie in a nonexistent scheme to divert funds from the U.S. Sanitary Commission to a miscegenation society. The published item, which Clemens would claim was only a private joke between him and De Quille, never meant to be printed, caused a cruel scandal for Mollie just weeks after the death of Jennie, her daughter and Sam's niece. In playing the race card and accusing the women of Carson City of embezzlement, Sam became a pariah in Virginia City. Challenges from the husbands of the women involved scared Sam straight and precipitated his departure for San Francisco. A rival paper, the Gold Hill *News,* crowed in his wake, "He has vamoosed, cut stick, absquatulated; and among the pine forests of the sierras, or amid the purlieus of the city of earthquakes, he will tarry awhile, and the office of the *Enterprise* will become purified." Even the Wild West had its limits, and Clemens was learning them on the job.

He jumped a stage for San Francisco, spending May and June there. At first sight, he was unimpressed with the town, finding that "many streets are made up of decaying, smoke-grimed, wooden houses, and the barren sand-hills toward the outskirts obtrude themselves too prominently." In fact, at the time San Francisco was the epicenter of commerce and culture in the West and rapidly widening its influence. Following the discovery in 1848 of gold at Sutter's Mill on the American River north of Sacramento, the city became the primary port for travelers and goods from the East Coast, serving the Nevada mining communities to the east

San Francisco. Chromolithograph by M. & N. Hanhart after S. Frank Marryat, London: M. & N. Hanhart, ca. 1850.

San Francisco from Russian Hill, looking down Vallejo Street. Photograph by Lawrence and Houseworth, ca. 1866.

San Francisco, California—Mission Street wharf. Photograph by Lawrence and Houseworth, ca.1866.

A trio of views of San Francisco, the cultural, political, and social capital of the West Coast for decades after the onset of the gold rush. Twain first visited in 1863 and enjoyed several sojourns in the next three years. He was drawn back to the goldfields several times, only to return to the city, which offered better opportunities not only for his writing but, for a bachelor crossing the threshold of thirty, general carousing.

Occidental Hotel, Montgomery Street, from the Russ House.
Photograph by Lawrence and Houseworth, San Francisco,
ca. 1866.

In San Francisco Twain patronized the Occidental Hotel, a favorite
haunt and watering hole he called Heaven on the Half Shell.

published author and an acclaimed
speaker; his rise to stardom under
an assumed name and comic persona
made tangible Clemens's own
aspirations.

He settled for a time in San
Francisco in 1864, earning twelve
dollars weekly for the *Golden
Era,* edited by Harte, and sending
letters back east. But even the
cosmopolitan and bustling city
on the bay couldn't hold Twain's
attention for long. Restless once
more, he began spending time in
the mining camps of California, in
search of a jackpot while observing
his fellow prospectors and hearing
their tales. The attraction of the
California goldfields for many men
was that gold generally lay in veins
and pockets close to the surface; it could be sluiced
from a riverbed and separated from the surrounding
soil. Silver in Nevada lay below the earth, demanding
extensive tunneling, with more expense and
danger involved.

Twain didn't just write about mining; he was
an active participant and intimate with the details
of camp life. He understood the miners' motives
and their aspirations because he shared them.
Undaunted by his own failures, he continued to
write and publish even as he persisted in the miner's
dream. Get-rich-quick schemes infected his thinking
and would not abate for most of his adult life; he
hungered after wealth and the comforts it would
bring. In that sense, he was like his father, who was
always chasing the dream of financial stability. As
with any prospector, true fortune always seemed
tantalizingly close, even as few actually found
real treasure.

For Clemens, life in the mining camps was
irresistible material for illustrating the best and worst

as well. It boomed with new buildings and modern-
day amenities. Clemens frequented the bar at the
opulent Occidental Hotel.

Over the next few years he came to love the
city, returning again and again. He began writing
for San Francisco papers, working under author and
editor Bret Harte. Born in New York in 1836 and
a Californian since 1853, Harte was in 1864 still
four years away from national literary fame with
his editorship of *Overland Monthly* and publication
of the story "The Luck of Roaring Camp." He and
humorist Artemus Ward, whom Clemens had met in
Virginia City while Ward was touring the West as
a lecturer, became role models for the career Clemens
hoped to build. Born Charles Farrar Browne in
1834 in Waterford, Maine, Ward had been both a

of humankind. It was a single-minded society with its own codes and mores. He recalled in *Roughing It*,

> But they were rough in those times! They fairly reveled in gold, whisky, fights, and fandangoes, and were unspeakably happy. The honest miner raked from a hundred to a thousand dollars out of his claim a day, and what with the gambling dens and the other entertainments, he hadn't a cent the next morning, if he had any sort of luck. They cooked their own bacon and beans, sewed on their own buttons, washed their own shirts—blue woolen ones; and if a man wanted a fight on his hands without any annoying delay, all he had to do was to appear in public in a white shirt or a stove-pipe hat, and he would be accommodated. For those people hated aristocrats. They had a particular and malignant animosity toward what they called a "biled shirt."

In the goldfields and camps, women were scarce and highly prized. "In those days," he wrote in *Roughing It*, "miners would flock in crowds to catch a glimpse of that rare and blessed spectacle, a woman!" He heard a story about a camp where news got out early one morning that a woman had arrived overnight. Someone had seen a calico dress hanging outside a wagon, a "sign of emigrants from over the great plains." Everybody assembled at the site, and a male emigrant soon appeared. The miners cried, "Fetch her out!"

> He said: "It is my wife, gentlemen—she is sick—we have been robbed of money, provisions, everything, by the Indians—we want to rest."
> "Fetch her out! We've got to see her!"
> "But, gentlemen, the poor thing, she—"
> "FETCH HER OUT!"

Gold miners, El Dorado, California. Photograph, unattributed, between ca. 1848 and ca. 1853.

El Dorado (Spanish for "the gilded one") was ground zero for the California gold rush, when precious nuggets were discovered near the town now known as Coloma, about thirty-six miles north of Sacramento.

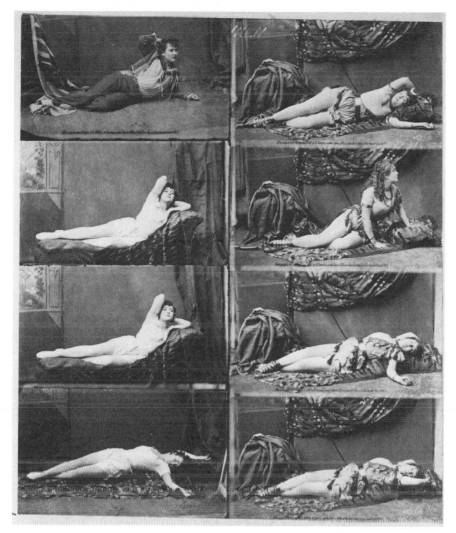

Adah Isaacs Menken, 1835—1868, in 8 seductive reclining poses. Photographic contact sheet by N. Sarony, ca. 1866.

Adah Isaacs Menken was one of the notorious characters of the era, an actress whose gimmick was to appear on stage in a flesh-colored body stocking. Twain saw her perform in San Francisco and wrote about her, at first favorably, but later with disdain, when he perceived her as a woman more interested in celebrity than real accomplishment.

He "fetched her out," and they swung their hats and sent up three rousing cheers . . . ; and they crowded around and gazed at her, and touched her dress, and listened to her voice with the look of men who listened to a memory rather than a present reality—and then they collected twenty-five hundred dollars in gold and gave it to the man, and swung their hats again and gave three more cheers, and went home satisfied.

Beautiful, talented, independent women were truly rare and cherished on the frontier, where men dominated social and commercial circles. Among the women Twain came across, none was more intriguing than Adah Isaacs Menken, a stage star and a national sensation. On a trip to San Francisco in late 1863, Twain caught her in her most famous play, *Mazeppa,* whose lead character appeared to be nude and bound to a real horse onstage in the final scene. Sam described the performance: "They said she was dressed from head to foot in flesh-colored 'tights,' but I had no opera-glass, and I couldn't see it, to use the language of the inelegant rabble." A dark-haired beauty who shed husbands like costumes, Menken actually came looking one night for Clemens and his fellow bohemians, treating them to a dinner, marred by the unhappy appearance of her cuckold husband. "The Menken," as she was known, gave

Shasta, Shasta County, Cal. Hand-colored lithograph drawn by Kuchel & Dresel, print by Britton & Rey, ca. 1856.

The discovery of gold in 1849, one year after the original strike at Sutter's Mill, south of Shasta, created instant settlements in sight of Mt. Shasta, one of California's tallest mountains.

Clemens a vivid lesson in showmanship and building a public persona.

Clemens, growing into his new identity as Mark Twain, took to the California goldfields north and east of Sacramento during the winter of 1864–65. Passing through Sacramento, the closest city to the fields, he made acute observations about its male-dominated populace. Sacramento was nearly as busy as San Francisco, but mostly from commerce. There wasn't the fragrant stew of many ethnic groups, the sophisticated culture, and the heady views that made San Francisco unique among all frontier settlements. Still, Twain found a certain vigor there that captivated him. Even five years into his frontier sojourn, he could

still be intoxicated by the spirit of the West.

In early 1865 Twain spent a few months in the Tuolumne County gold diggings at Jackass Hill and Angels Camp. He lived in a small cabin on a hillside overlooking the now largely abandoned goldfields and captured the downside of the West's boom-or-bust mentality:

> *When the mines gave out, the town fell into decay,*
> *and in a few years wholly disappeared—streets,*
> *dwellings, shops, everything—and left no sign.*
> *The grassy slopes were as green and smooth and*
> *desolate of life as if they had never been disturbed.*
> *The mere handful of miners still remaining, had*

Placer Mining, Columbia, Tuolumne County, The Reservoirs. Photograph by Lawrence and Houseworth, 1866.

Placer (rhymes with "passer") was miner argot for a deposit of sand, dirt, or clay, usually in a streambed, that contained fine particles of gold or silver. Miners obtained their find by washing to reveal the precious minerals. Tuolumne County would eventually contain the northern portion of Yosemite National Park.

Miner's cabin, Sierra Nevada. Photograph by Lawrence and Houseworth, 1866.

Considering the risks and temporary nature of the work, miners were capable of erecting substantial, if modest, cabins.

Up Jackass Hill in Tuolumne County in the California Sierras. Photograph by Caroline Highsmith, ca. 1980–2000.

This is a reproduction, though the chimney and fireplace are original, of a cabin where Mark Twain lived in 1864 and 1865.

Exterior, general view of cabin showing entrance and original stone chimney after restoration—Mark Twain Cabin, Sonora, Tuolumne County, California. Photocopy of photograph, unattributed, ca. 1923.

Two views of a partial re-creation of the cabin in which Twain resided while prospecting from 1864 to 1865. During that rainy winter, with nothing but each other for amusement, he and fellow miners swapped stories, supplying the writer with plenty of material.

Washington Street, Sonora, Tuolumne County, California.
Photograph by Lawrence and Houseworth, 1866.

What passed for civilization some miles from Twain's cabin.

seen the town spring up spread, grow and flourish
in its pride; and they had seen it sicken and die,
and pass away like a dream. With it their hopes
had died, and their zest of life. They had long
ago resigned themselves to their exile, and ceased
to correspond with their distant friends or turn
longing eyes toward their early homes. They had
accepted banishment, forgotten the world and
been forgotten of the world. They were far from
telegraphs and railroads, and they stood, as it
were, in a living grave, dead to the events that
stirred the globe's great populations, dead to the
common interests of men, isolated and outcast
from brotherhood with their kind.

He was now resigned to working the fields as
a reporter, not a miner, taking in the stories heard
among the men and around the campfires. They were
his gold. Thanks to his highly praised contributions
to New York papers, Mark Twain was gathering a
following in the East. His keen ear for dialect and

Sacramento City, CA from the Foot of J. Street, Showing
I., J., & K. St^s with the Sierra Nevada in the Distance.
Lithograph printed in colors on stone by Charles Parsons, drawn
Dec. 20, 1849, by G. V. Cooper; William Endicott & Co., New York;
published by Stringer & Townsend, ca. 1850.

"It was a driving, vigorous, restless population in those days. It
was a curious population. It was the only population of the kind
that the world has ever seen gathered together, and it is not
likely that the world will ever see its like again. For observe, it
was an assemblage of two hundred thousand young men—not
simpering, dainty, kid-gloved weaklings, but stalwart, muscular,
dauntless young braves, brimful of push and energy, and royally

endowed with every attribute that goes to make up a peerless and magnificent manhood—the very pick and choice of the world's glorious ones. No women, no children, no gray and stooping veterans,—none but erect, bright-eyed, quick-moving, strong-handed young giants—the strangest population, the finest population, the most gallant host that ever trooped down the startled solitudes of an unpeopled land. And where are they now? Scattered to the ends of the earth—or prematurely aged and decrepit—or shot or stabbed in street affrays—or dead of disappointed hopes and broken hearts—all gone, or nearly all victims devoted upon the altar of the golden calf—the noblest holocaust that ever wafted its sacrificial incense heavenward. It is pitiful to think upon.

"It was a splendid population—for all the slow, sleepy, sluggish-brained sloths staid at home—you never find that sort of people among pioneers—you cannot build pioneers out of that sort of material. It was that population that gave to California a name for getting up astounding enterprises and rushing them through with a magnificent dash and daring and a recklessness of cost or consequences, which she bears unto this day—and when she projects a new surprise, the grave world smiles as usual, and says "Well, that's California all over." (*Roughing It*)

*The Mammoth Trees (*Sequoia gigantea*), California (Calaveras County).* Lithograph printed in color, Middleton, Strobridge & Co., Cincinnati, Ohio, published by A. J. Campbell, ca. 1860.

In Calaveras County, California, in the Sierra Nevada beyond Sacramento, miners shared the region's natural resources with loggers attracted by stands of gigantic old-growth sequoias.

ability to embellish a story with comic timing and telling details set him apart and made his tales seem fresh and completely believable.

In February 1865, Twain received a request from New York and his friend Artemus Ward for a comic sketch to be included in a forthcoming book. He furnished Ward with a story about a jumping frog contest, told to him during his stay at Angels Camp. Although the story arrived too late for publication in Ward's work, the editor of the *New York Sunday Press* ran it under the title "Jim Smiley and His Jumping

Frog." Readers loved the colorful language, bald-faced lies, and outrageous humor embedded in the piece. The New York correspondent for the San Francisco-based *Alta California* declared it "the best thing of the day."

Still, true financial rewards for his growing reputation were in the future, and there remained one last western adventure. Twain returned from the goldfields to San Francisco in the spring of 1866 penniless. His prolonged exile from Virginia City had allowed for a reconciliation, and he was taken

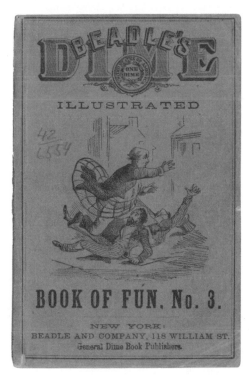

Beadle's Illustrated Book of Fun, No. 3, General Dime Book Publishers, 1866.

Mark Twain's backwoods tall tale recounting the peculiar circumstances surrounding a jumping-frog contest catapulted him to international fame. Twain first heard the story of one swindler swindling another in a hotel at Angels Camp in the Sierra Nevada. The sketch appeared initially in newspapers, soon making the leap to dime novels for young readers and published anthologies for more mature minds.

on again by the *Territorial Enterprise* as their San Francisco correspondent. Then, another break: the *Sacramento Union,* in his words "an excellent journal and liberal with employees," offered to finance a trip to the Hawaiian Islands for a series of reports from this tropical paradise.

Restless again for new locals and locales, Twain sailed for Hawaii in March 1866. There were no mines on the islands, no opportunities for income beyond his skills as a writer. He was forced to focus solely on words, without the crutch of prospecting. Sobered by that experience, for the first time he began to assess and acknowledge his talents. Just as his first job with the Virginia City paper had rescued him from life as a feckless prospector, Twain's all-expenses-paid trip to the Hawaiian Islands proved a

watershed in his career. Freed from the desperation of the goldfields, he could delight in the tropical climate and the plants and animals he found. Other writers had described the islands in earlier works, but most Americans knew Hawaii as a land of hula-hula dancers, gentle breezes, violent volcanic eruptions, and the site of the celebrated English explorer Captain James Cook's violent end in 1779 at the hands of natives.

Twain offered a more nuanced portrait. On a walk through Honolulu, for instance, he described a multitude of cats, all quite different, and all enjoying a nap. In *Roughing It,* he noted the women with their "comely features" and strange headgear:

> *The further I traveled through the town the better I liked it.... I saw cats—Tom-cats, Mary Ann cats, long-tailed cats, bob-tailed cats, blind cats, one-eyed cats, wall-eyed cats, cross-eyed cats, gray cats, black cats, white cats, yellow cats, striped cats, spotted cats, tame cats, wild cats, singed cats, individual cats, groups of cats, platoons of cats, companies of cats, regiments of cats, armies of cats, multitudes of cats, millions of cats, and all of them sleek, fat, lazy and sound asleep. I looked on a multitude of people, some white, in white coats, vests, pantaloons, even white cloth shoes, made snowy with chalk duly laid on every morning; but the majority of the people were almost as dark as negroes—women with comely features, fine black eyes, rounded forms, inclining to the voluptuous, clad in a single bright red or white garment that fell free and unconfined from shoulder to heel, long black hair falling loose, gypsy hats, encircled with wreaths of natural flowers of a brilliant carmine tint, plenty of dark men in various costumes, and some with nothing on but a battered stove-pipe hat tilted on the nose, and a very scant breech-clout;—certain smoke-dried children were clothed in nothing but sunshine—a very neat fitting and picturesque apparel indeed.*

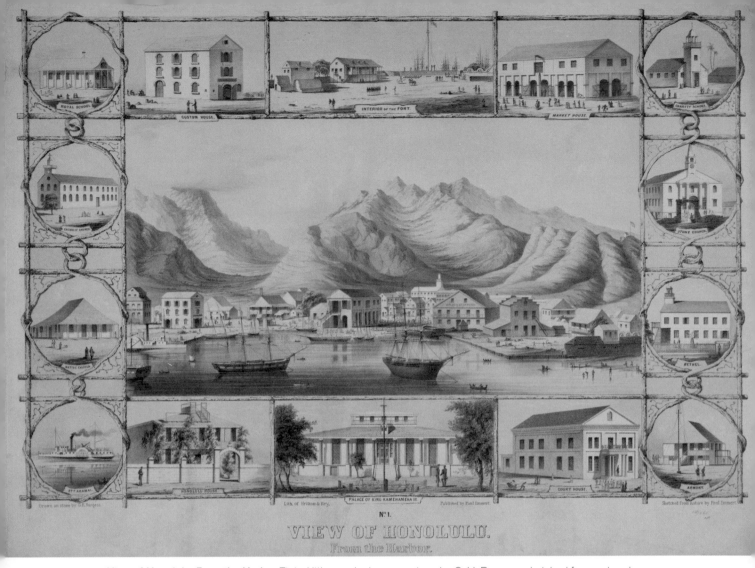

VIEW OF HONOLULU.
From the Harbor.

View of Honolulu. From the Harbor. Tinted lithograph, drawn on stone by G. H. Burgess, sketched from nature by Paul Emmert, Britton & Rey, San Francisco, ca. 1854.

In 1866, the *Sacramento Union* paid Twain's way to Hawaii in return for descriptive accounts of the trip. Twain described the Pacific archipelago as "the loveliest fleet of islands," home to lush landscapes, brilliant birds, and unusual plants and animals, and peopled by transient sailors, temporary tourists, mercenary missionaries, and a native population proud of its heritage and customs. Twain remarked on their odd habits and customs, their strange clothing, and particularly the hula-hula girls and athletic young men surfing the waves.

Completely entranced by this strange paradise, Twain rode horseback around the islands, witnessed lava flowing from Kilauea on the big island of Hawaii, and threw stones into the dormant crater of Haleakala on Maui. He particularly commented, in *Roughing It*, on the dress of the men and women, who wore what struck him as an often bizarre and usually revealing blend of loincloths and nonnative garb.

The girls put on all the finery they can on Saturday afternoon—fine black silk robes; flowing red ones that nearly put your eyes out; others as white as snow; still others that discount the rainbow; and they wear their hair in nets, and trim their jaunty hats with fresh flowers, and encircle their dusky throats with home-made necklaces of the brilliant vermillion-tinted blossom of the ohia; and they fill the markets and the adjacent street

*with their bright presences, and smell like a rag
factory on fire with their offensive cocoanut oil.*

He also remarked on the routine nakedness
exhibited by the locals. Encountering a group
of young women bathing naked in a stream, he
described his gallant efforts to protect the clothes
they shed on the bank and coax them all from the
water. He recorded young men surfing on their crude
wooden boards and noted that he fell headlong into
the surf in his first and only attempt.

He visited the site of Captain Cook's savage end,
revealing an anti-imperial attitude with the comment,
in *Roughing It,* that "Small blame should attach to
the natives for the killing of Cook. They treated
him well. In return, he abused them. He and his men
inflicted bodily injury upon many of them at different
times, and killed at least three of them before they
offered any proportionate retaliation."

Back in San Francisco, Twain developed a
public lecture on his recent excursion, producing
a poster that promised: "Doors open at 7 1/2. The
trouble will begin at 8." This was an age when many
writers, including Artemus Ward and Bret Harte,
supplemented their income by taking to the stage.
Public speakers were highly valued at a time when a
large percentage of the population could not read and
no electronic media existed to amuse and entertain.
Lecturers offered a window into other lives and
exotic places that few would ever experience for
themselves. Twain's Hawaiian Islands talk in San
Francisco was well attended and a complete success,
and he knew he had entered a new phase of his life.
He was known now across the country as Mark
Twain, writer and public personality, and it was time
to cash in. His comic account of the frog-jumping
contest had gone the nineteenth-century version of
viral, reprinted in journals across the country.

Sensing opportunity, he embarked on December
15, 1866, on a ship bound for New York City, the
nation's publishing center, via the Nicaraguan

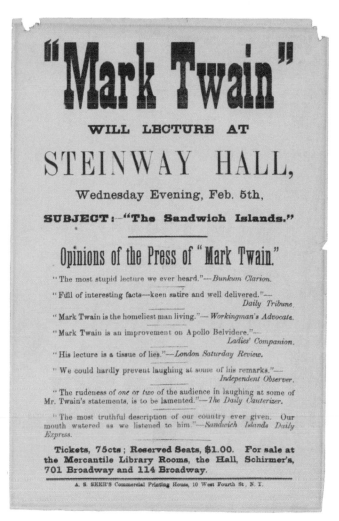

Mark Twain Sandwich Islands lecture, Steinway Hall, New York,
1873. Poster.

Twain would deliver his lecture on his experiences in the Sandwich
Islands, or Hawaii, over a hundred times, and as the blurbs on this
poster indicate, his promoters were not above contributing to the
levity of the occasion.

isthmus. Shipboard cholera killed numerous
passengers during the trip, but Twain arrived intact,
if sobered by the passage. He might have felt upon
arrival in New York like the prodigal returning
home. Five and a half years before, he had impulsively
set out for the West with no real plans other than
avoiding the war. Now, with the war over and
America rebuilding and reuniting, he had a national
reputation and a blueprint for a successful career.

CHAPTER 3

Trade Mark

The two decades following the Civil War were flush times for Mark Twain. They witnessed his rise from roustabout reporter to commentator on the world stage, from the Wild Humorist of the Pacific Slope to the People's Author. During Reconstruction, a period marked by continued political and social strife, Clemens's wit and Mark Twain's influence helped heal and bind the nation's self-inflicted wounds.

He created literary masterpieces, traveled the world, and indulged his inventive and entrepreneurial instincts, for better or worse. He brought light and laughter to homes darkened by death of young and old from war and disease, a condition made manifest by the display of memento mori–hair ornaments and deathbed photographs recalling family and friends. Twain's engaging humor allowed people to laugh again, at themselves and others; comedy was a scarce commodity in the years after the war, when Ambrose Bierce's blood-stained stories and Herman Melville's *Battle Pieces and Aspects of the War* (1866) made grim, if topical, reading.

Politically, the country remained divided, as Northerners "waved the bloody shirt," evoking the Union war dead, while undaunted Southerners acted to protect their political and property interests from politicians who took over their legislatures in an effort to reform their customs and institutions. African Americans looked for traction in local communities and the workplace. Ethnic tensions continued to plague the nation, as a burgeoning wave of immigrants and freed slaves competed for jobs and housing.

"Mark Twain," America's Best Humorist. Chromolithograph by Joseph Keppler, New York: published by Keppler & Schwarzmann, *Puck,* Dec. 16, 1885, p. 256.

THE FIFTEENTH AMENDMENT.

CELEBRATED MAY 19th 1870.

The Fifteenth Amendment. Celebrated May 19th 1870. Hand-colored lithograph after James C. Beard, New York: published by Thomas Kelly, ca. 1870.

The Reconstruction era reached its height in 1870 with ratification of the Fifteenth Amendment, giving black men the vote, a big win for Northern Radical Republicans. The backlash against the Fifteenth featured a resurgent Democratic Party, Jim Crow laws, and intimidation by white vigilantes to keep African Americans from the polls.

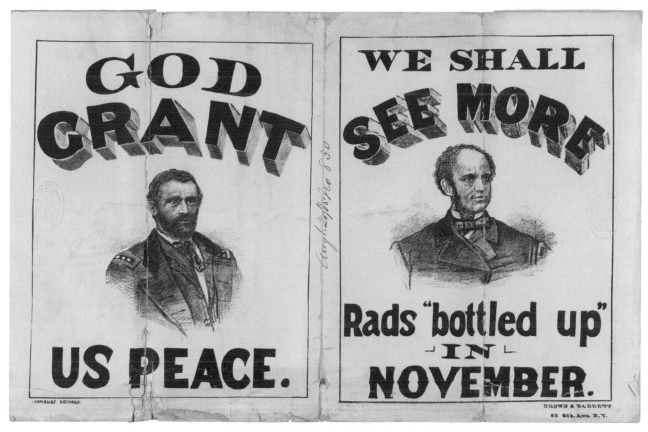

God Grant Us Peace. We Shall See More Rads "Bottled Up" in November. Lithograph, Brown & Barrett, New York, ca. 1868.

Mark Twain admired President U.S. Grant. He won election in 1868 on the strength of his military success during the Civil War and his political distance from the Northern radicals in his Republican party, who sought a more punitive policy during Reconstruction. His opponent, Horatio Seymour, is pictured at right.

Women advanced in the marketplace and in politics, boosted by their contributions during the war and the increasingly industrial nature of society. Women also worked in factories and mills, owned shops, became authors and doctors and politicians. In 1849, Elizabeth Blackwell became the first officially recognized female physician in America, and within a generation, Victoria Woodhull, Susan B. Anthony, and others were openly advocating for women's suffrage and running for president.

More children were educated than ever before, though they still died prematurely and often worked long hours in terrible conditions for small, supplemental wages. The frontier was closing fast.

Native Americans fought a losing battle for their homelands and vanishing way of life, although Indian schools were created in an attempt to educate and assimilate young warriors and their siblings.

Enterprise and entertainment helped fill the void left by war. The industrial revolution had brought leisure time and income to families. Advances in transportation and communications enabled authors, athletes, actors, and politicians to reach new audiences and expand their influence. Writers, performers, boxers, and baseball players became overnight sensations, as media outlets all over the country proclaimed their exploits. Within a few

Grand Caricaturama: The massacre at New Orleans. Oil on canvas by Thomas Nast, 1867.

Largely forgotten among Thomas Nast's achievements as an editorial cartoonist is his Caricaturama, a series of huge painted commentaries on contemporary political life designed for exhibition on a performance stage. This one illustrates the race riot of July 1866, in which whites and blacks clashed over the disenfranchisement of black citizens. A crowned President Andrew Johnson is depicted hiding while black delegates to a Radical Republican convention are slaughtered by local police.

"TREASON IS A CRIME"
"TRAITORS MUST
MY POLICY
THE TIME
WILL COME
WHO IS
BEST FRIEN

Going home to lunch! Two boys from Singer Manufacturing Co., South Bend, Indiana. Photograph by Lewis Wickes Hine, October 1908.

Throughout the nineteenth century, American boys and girls worked long hours for minimal pay in mills and factories, supplementing their family's income and the nation's workforce with their youthful energy. Lewis Hine brought the plight of young workers to Congress and the nation, forcing reform with his monumental archive of photographs documenting child labor in the United States.

Occupational portrait of a woman working at a sewing machine. Hand-colored daguerreotype, ca. 1853.

The advent of commercial photography in the form of daguerreotypes, ambrotypes, tintypes, cartes-de-visite, and cabinet cards opened the world of portraiture to unprecedented subjects. Carpenters, clergymen, seamstresses, and salesmen sat for photographers, promoting their wares, skills, and services, presenting a new public face for working and professional men and women.

years of Clemens's arrival in New York in the winter of 1867, Mark Twain became a household name, an American brand. His Western sketches, which captured the spirit of the frontier and his readers' imaginations, introduced him to an eager public. The sketches were a breath of fresh air to Americans clamoring for entertainment to help them forget the war and fill the emotional vacuum it had created. His words brought hilarity and even profanity to staid Victorian parlors more familiar with Bible readings and pious stories. Readers in America and abroad were charmed by his command of dialects and his affecting descriptions.

Next, he set out on a landmark cruise to Europe and the Holy Land, acting not as simply a reporter chronicling his fellow passengers and exotic locales but as a more-than-skeptical observer, a writer who was as often amused and appalled by what he saw as he was awed and amazed. His 1869 account of the trip, *The Innocents Abroad*, was a travel book unlike any published before, offering passages that alternated between rueful humor and genuine wonder. That the book was such a huge bestseller attested both to Twain's talent for description and

Graphic Statues, No. 17—"The Woman Who Dared [Susan B. Anthony]." Wood engraving by Thomas Wust, *Daily Graphic,* New York, June 5, 1873.

During the 1870s, the *[New York] Daily Graphic* published full front-page editorial cartoons, including this satirical send-up of women's rights activist and presidential candidate Susan B. Anthony.

The Eighth Wonder of the World. The Atlantic Cable. Color lithograph, New York: Kimmel & Forster, 1866.

The laying of the transatlantic cable, connecting Britain on the left (as a lion) and the United States on the right (as an eagle) and blessed in the middle by Neptune, god of the seas, and Cyrus Field, the American who arranged the financing, was accomplished in 1866. The world became a bit smaller that day, as telegraphic communications between two continents were established.

Taken from Steamer "Patrol", 28 October, 1886. Copyright 1887, H. O'Neil, 31 Union Square, New York

"LIBERTY ENLIGHTENING THE WORLD"
INAUGURATION OF THE BARTHOLDI STATUE, HARBOR OF NEW YORK.
MILITARY AND NAVAL SALUTE, THE PRESIDENT'S ARRIVAL AT LIBERTY ISLAND.

"Liberty Enlightening the World." Inauguration of the Bartholdi Statue, Harbor of New York. Military and Naval Salute, the President's Arrival at Liberty Island. Photograph, copyright by H. O'Neil, New York, ca. 1887.

The dedication of the Statue of Liberty in New York Harbor in October 1886 was the cause for great celebration of America's open-arms policy toward immigrants. The clouds in this photograph are smoke from the shipboard military guns fired off as part of the festivities.

to a new sensibility among American readers, less impressionable after surviving the conflict that nearly tore their country apart.

Times were changing, a new era was at hand with seemingly unlimited possibilities for those with intellect and initiative. In *The Gilded Age* Twain and Warner not only named the era but did so almost as soon as it had begun, creating a composite portrait of contemporary characters pursuing their dreams: an incorrigible speculator, a female lobbyist, a female doctor. In the process, they delineated the way we lived and thought, the vicissitudes of daily life in modern America. They captured the huge contrasts of the times, noting the cataclysmic impact of the war: "The eight years in America from 1860 to 1868 uprooted institutions that were centuries

MONOPOLY IN HADES.
How the Place will be Run, Two Years after Jay Gould's

Monopoly in Hades.
How the Place Will Be
Run, Two Years After
Jay Gould's Arrival.
Chromolithograph by
Frederick Opper. New York:
published by Keppler &
Schwarzmann in *Puck,*
Sept. 19, 1883.

Frederick Opper enjoyed a
long career as an editorial
cartoonist and creator
of Happy Hooligan,
Alphonse and Gaston, and
other memorable comic
characters. The weekly
illustrated satirical journal
Puck printed cartoons in
full color, splashing potent
political commentary
on vivid covers and in
centerfolds.

old, changed the politics of a people, transformed the social life of half the country, and wrought so profoundly upon the entire national character that the influence cannot be measured short of two or three generations."

Within this volatile social climate there were economic changes as well. The country experienced booms and busts throughout the Gilded Age, as wealthy capitalists forged steel, built railways moving goods and people, and amassed vast fortunes, while creating monopolies for the fortunate few. William K. Vanderbilt and Jay Gould were among the most notorious, Vanderbilt publicly damning the people and Gould becoming the poster boy for corporate greed. In his *Autobiography*, Twain commented, "The people had *desired* money before

above: *"The Public Be —!" caricature of William Henry Vanderbilt, 1821–1885.* Wood engraving in the *[New York] Daily Graphic* title page, October 12, 1882.

W. H. Vanderbilt delighted cartoonists when he was questioned by a reporter about his running an express train between New York and Chicago at a loss, only because the rail line insisted. "But don't you run it for the public benefit?" he was asked. "The public be damned," replied Vanderbilt, claiming "I don't take any stock in this silly nonsense about working for anybody's good but our own, because we are not." His brutal honesty in the form of an uncensored utterance became a derisive rallying cry for reformers.

right: *Our Robber Barons.* Chromolithograph by Bernhard Gillam. New York: published by Keppler & Schwarzmann in *Puck,* June 14, 1882, centerfold.

Jay Gould (labeled "R[ail] Road Monopoly"), W. H. Vanderbilt ("Corporations"), and Cyrus Field ("Telegraph Monopoly") were among the poster boys for Gilded Age avarice, publicly criticized and satirized for their apparent disregard of the public interest.

[Jay Gould's] day, but *he* taught them to fall down and worship it.... In my youth there was nothing resembling a worship of money or of its possessor, in our region. And in our region no well-to-do man was ever charged with having acquired his money by shady methods." Shady methods and outright intimidation were part and parcel of doing business, often hand in glove with unscrupulous politicians who facilitated their schemes and provided legal sanction for their activities. The presidential administrations of Ulysses S. Grant (1869–1877), in spite of his efforts at civil reform, were rife with scandals and misdeeds.

The Gilded Age also witnessed the rise of the working classes, as farmers, factory workers, miners, and laborers began to act collectively, forming unions.

I Feed You All! Milwaukee, Wisconsin, Lithograph by American Oleograph Co., Milwaukee, ca. 1875.

While capitalists built business empires, workers began to organize. The Granger movement promoted the rights of farmers and their crucial contributions to the nation.

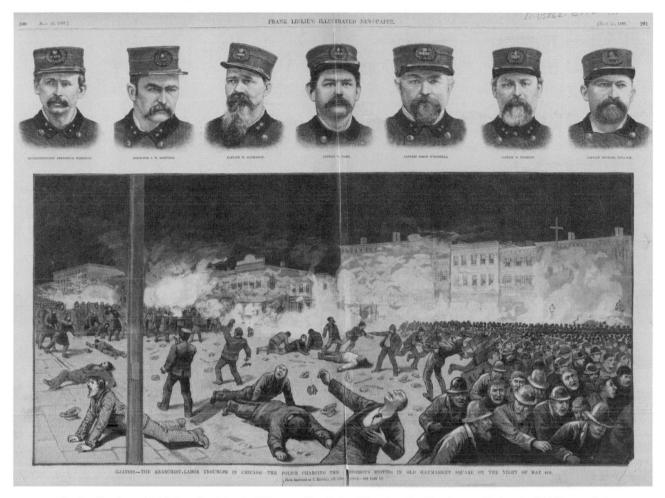

Illinois—the Anarchist-Labor Troubles in Chicago—The Police Charging the Murderous Rioters in Old Haymarket Square on the Night of May 4th. Engraving from sketches by C. Bunnell and Chas Upham, May 15, 1886, *Frank Leslie's Illustrated Newspaper,* pp 200–201

Eight anarchist leaders were convicted for inciting the Haymarket incident. Four were hanged, one committed suicide, and the three others were pardoned in 1893 after public opinion shifted and questions about the 1886 trial emerged.

Corporations fought back, often with violence, breaking strikes and heads with seeming impunity. Racism remained rampant, even as the Fifteenth Amendment allowed black men to vote for the first time.

Against this turbulent backdrop, Twain worked tirelessly to promote himself. His comic sketches appeared everywhere, in newspapers and journals. His second nonfiction book, *Roughing It* (1872), an account of his adventures in Nevada, California, and Hawaii, joined *Innocents* and *Gilded Age* on the bestseller list, along with a bound compilation of comic sketches featuring the Jumping Frog story. He was a favorite of photographers and cartoonists, his flowing mane of red hair and bushy mustache instantly recognizable.

People read his works aloud; his ear for the vernacular and his eye for loving detail contributed to the work's authenticity, its truthful scenarios artfully arranged under layers of humor and misdirection. He seemed to know what people wanted, stating famously, "High and fine literature

"The First Dynamite Bomb Thrown in America," May 4th 1886. The Personnel of the Great Anarchist Trial at Chicago. Begun Monday June 21st 1886. Ended Friday, August 20th 1886. Published by the Inter Ocean Co., 1886.

On May 3, 1886, a strike at Chicago's McCormick Reaper Company turned deadly with the killing of a protester by the police. Radical labor leaders called for a protest the next day in Haymarket Square, issuing provocative broadsides published in English and German—"Working Men Arm Yourselves and Appear in Full Force!"—signed by the "Executive Committee." During the May 4 rally, an unknown assailant threw an incendiary, inciting a riot that caused multiple deaths and injuries to police and protesters alike.

is wine, and mine is only water; but everybody likes water." Twain made people smile: "Against the assault of laughter nothing can stand." Jessie Conrad, widow of the celebrated novelist Joseph Conrad, spoke for many when she recalled, "I have known my late husband reading and re-reading [Twain's] books. It was *The Innocents Abroad* that was one of the first that he read aloud to me.... He would stop reading aloud and continue reading to himself, chuckling and laughing for every so many pages, and then turn back the leaves and read aloud one more." In 1867, upon his arrival in New York, he was not a known figure on the East Coast, although the New York papers had featured his work. He commented on the anonymity the city's crowded streets provided, setting out instead to see and be seen. He attended plays, visited P. T. Barnum's rebuilt museum, and attended services at the Plymouth Congregational Church led by the charismatic Reverend Henry Ward Beecher.

That spring, he made a quick trip back to Hannibal, St. Louis, and Keokuk, presenting his Hawaiian Islands lecture. It was a sobering homecoming. "I found home a dreary place after my long absence; for half the children I had known were now wearing whiskers or waterfalls, and few of the grown people I had been acquainted with remained at their hearthstones prosperous and happy—some of them had wandered to other scenes, some were in jail, and the rest had been hanged." Twain would live in many places before he died, but never again in Missouri or the South. May saw the publication of his first book, *The Celebrated Jumping Frog of Calaveras County, and Other Sketches.* On May 6, he gave his first New York lecture, playing to a full, appreciative house at the prestigious Cooper Union, where presidential hopeful Abraham Lincoln had first introduced himself to the city in 1860. Ron Powers noted the significance of Twain's success in the face of competition from other public events occurring that night throughout the city. The man who would be seen now was.

Beecher's church was gathering travelers for a remarkable journey by luxury steamship through Europe and the Holy Land, a privilege previously available only to the very rich. The excursion on the *Quaker City* offered passage for any member of the public able to pay his or her way. It was a novel idea and irresistible to Twain, who could scarcely contain his excitement. In the event, the journey transformed his personal life as well as boosting the trajectory of his career. His shipboard friendship with Charles Langdon led him to meet and wed Langdon's sister Olivia, and his accounts of the journey produced his first full-length bestseller, *The Innocents Abroad: Or, the New Pilgrims' Progress,* published in 1869.

In June, he embarked with the *Quaker City* and its passengers, describing his keen anticipation for departure in his introduction to *Innocents Abroad:*

> *They were to sail for months over the breezy Atlantic and the sunny Mediterranean; they were to scamper about the decks by day, filling the ship with shouts and laughter—or read novels and poetry in the shade of the smokestacks, or watch for the jelly-fish and the nautilus over the side, and the shark, the whale, and other strange monsters of the deep; and at night they were to dance in the open air, on the upper deck, in the midst of a ballroom that stretched from horizon to horizon, and was domed by the bending heavens and lighted by no meaner lamps than the stars and the magnificent moon—dance, and promenade, and smoke, and sing, and make love, and search the skies for constellations that never associate with the "Big Dipper" they were so tired of; and they were to see the ships of twenty navies—the customs and costumes of twenty curious peoples—the great cities of half a world— they were to hob-nob with nobility and hold friendly converse with kings and princes, grand moguls, and the anointed lords of mighty empires!*

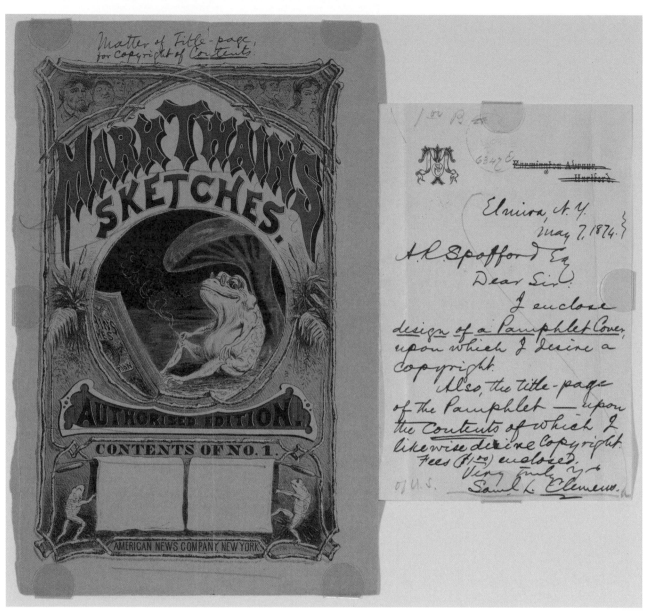

Pamphlet cover for which Samuel Clemens (Mark Twain) sought a copyright. Attributed to True Williams. Photograph by Carol Highsmith.

Mark Twain became synonymous with a jumping frog following the success of his 1865 short story. True Williams, who later illustrated *The Adventures of Tom Sawyer,* produced this colorful cover for a pamphlet announcing Mark Twain's first published compilation of comic sketches. The drawing was submitted by Samuel Clemens to the Copyright Office, now administered by the Library of Congress, with a handwritten note to Ainsworth Rand Spofford, the sixth Librarian of Congress.

It was a brave conception; it was the offspring of a most ingenious brain. It was well advertised, but it hardly needed it: the bold originality, the extraordinary character, the seductive nature, and the vastness of the enterprise provoked comment everywhere and advertised it in every household in the land.

The novelty and notoriety of the trip enabled Twain to recoup his hefty $1,250 fare through income earned from letters intended for publication in the *Alta California,* the San Francisco paper that brought him western fame, as well as the *New York Herald* and *Tribune.*

The *Quaker City* carried Twain and seventy fellow "pilgrims" on a five-month itinerary through twenty countries in Europe and the Middle East. In the course of the journey he attempted to explain his motivation for going:

What is it that confers the noblest delight? What is that which swells a man's breast with pride above that which any other experience can bring to him? Discovery! To know that you are walking where none others have walked; that you are beholding what human eye has not seen before; that you are breathing a virgin atmosphere. To give birth to an idea—to discover a great thought—an intellectual nugget, right under the dust of a field that many a brain-plow had gone over before. To find a new planet, to invent a new hinge, to find the way to make the lightnings carry your messages. To be the first—that is the idea. To do something, say something, see something, before any body else—these are the things that confer a pleasure compared with which other pleasures are tame and commonplace, other ecstasies cheap and trivial.

The *Quaker City* voyage highlighted Twain's ability and desire to mix with high society

Mark Twain. Photograph by Abdullah Frères, Istanbul, 1867.

Twain thought Istanbul beautiful from afar, but "Ashore, it was—well, it was an eternal circus. People were thicker than bees, in those narrow streets, and the men were dressed in all the outrageous, outlandish, idolatrous, extravagant, thunder-and-lightning costumes that ever a tailor with the delirium tremens and seven devils could conceive of. There was no freak in dress too crazy to be indulged in; no absurdity too absurd to be tolerated; no frenzy in ragged diabolism too fantastic to be attempted. No two men were dressed alike. It was a wild masquerade of all imaginable costumes—every struggling throng in every street was a dissolving view of stunning contrasts...; drifting noiselessly about are squads of Turkish women, draped from chin to feet in flowing robes, and with snowy veils bound about their heads, that disclose only the eyes and a vague, shadowy notion of their features. Seen moving about, far away in the dim, arched aisles of the Great Bazaar, they look as the shrouded dead must have looked when they walked forth from their graves amid the storms and thunders and earthquakes that burst upon Calvary that awful night of the Crucifixion. A stroll in Constantinople is a picture which one ought to see once—not oftener."

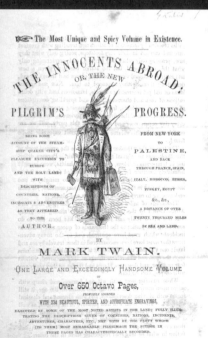

above: From the road leading to Bethany, April 9th 1839, Jerusalem. Illustration in *The Holy Land, Syria, Idumea, Arabia, Egypt and Nubia,* by David Roberts, from drawings made on the spot by David Roberts. Lithographed by Louis Haghe, London: F. G. Moon, 1842—1845.

Scottish artist David Roberts created brilliant portrayals in colored lithographs of The Holy Land and Middle East, meeting public demand for images from the region. In *Innocents Abroad,* Twain described a hair-raising escapade outside Jerusalem: "'Bedouins!' Every man shrunk up and disappeared in his clothes like a mud-turtle. My first impulse was to dash forward and destroy the Bedouins. My second was to dash to the rear to see if there were any coming in that direction. I acted on the latter impulse. So did all the others. If any Bedouins had approached us, then, from that point of the compass, they would have paid dearly for their rashness. We all remarked that, afterwards."

left: Twain's "Innocents Abroad," American Publishing Company broadside, ca. 1871.

Innocents Abroad was Mark Twain's first nonfiction book, developed from letters and notes he wrote while a passenger on the landmark *Quaker City* excursion, the country's first commercial tour through Europe and the Holy Land. The American Publishing Company sold the book by subscription, with salesmen taking the book door-to-door, promoting Mark Twain for the first time as "The People's Author."

while condemning capitalism and consumerism. He befriended his shipmates and made lasting friendships, joining in the smoking, drinking, reading, and evening entertainment that helped pass the time between ports. But there he drew the line, for most of the "Quakers" were sober citizens seriously devoted to their Holy Land pilgrimage. Having little in common with teetotaling pilgrims, he found their endless prayer meetings unendurable. Twain gave derisive nicknames to some of the passengers, referring to one as the Interrogationist for his incessant questions; others included the Doctor, the Oracle, and the Enthusiast. His group of close companions, self-proclaimed Nighthawks, included future brother-in-law Charles Langdon and Dan Slote. The latter recalled Twain with esteem and affection:

> *I know him from top to bottom. When we were out on the* Quaker City *expedition, he was the hardest-working man I ever saw. Why, out in Egypt, where the fleas were so thick you couldn't breathe without swallowing a thousand, that man used to sit up and write, write, half the night. I used to have to get my clothes off in a second and hustle into bed before any of the fleas had a chance to get between the sheets, and as I was vainly trying to get to sleep, I'd say to Clemens, "Sam, how the deuce can you stand it to write out there among the fleas?" "Oh, I'm all right," Sam would say. "They've got a railroad track eaten out around both ankles, and they keep in that pretty well, so I don't bother with them."*

Although the book contains descriptions of reverence and awe, *Innocents Abroad* in most respects overturned every existing convention in travel literature. Rather than passively observe new scenes and customs, Twain became an active participant. As narrator he converses with readers as the stories unfold, letting them in on secrets,

THE ASSAULT.

The Assault [on the Parthenon]. Illustration in *Innocents Abroad.*

On a cruise sponsored by a church and designed for Christian "pilgrims," as the author called his shipmates, Twain was among the small flock of black sheep who engaged in questionable behavior. In Athens, he and a few companions broke ship's quarantine, imposed by the port to deter cholera in the city, breaking into the Acropolis at night to enjoy the view.

sharing his surprises. In the preface he explained his goal:

> *This book is a record of a pleasure trip. If it were a record of a solemn scientific expedition, it would have about it that gravity, that profundity, and that impressive incomprehensibility which are so proper to works of that kind, and withal so attractive. Yet notwithstanding it is only a record of a picnic, it has a purpose, which is to suggest*

Street Cars of Damascus. Illustration in *Innocents Abroad*.

Among the witty illustrations for one edition of *Innocents* was this depiction of the most up-to-date transportation during the tour's stop in Syria.

to the reader how he would be likely to see Europe and the East if he looked at them with his own eyes instead of the eyes of those who traveled in those countries before him. I make small pretense of showing anyone how he ought to look at objects of interest beyond the sea—other books do that, and therefore, even if I were competent to do it, there is no need.

I offer no apologies for any departures from the usual style of travel-writing that may be charged against me—for I think I have seen with impartial eyes, and I am sure I have written at least honestly, whether wisely or not.

Readers appreciated his honesty and enjoyed his humorous descriptions of locations that usually inspired only serious writing. He was more companion than guide, witty and subversive, his accounts combining the sublime with the silly, jokes and personal stories punctuating his descriptive writing. As the ship passed through the Strait of Messina one night, Twain and his companions were on deck smoking and partying, waiting for a glimpse of the fabled landmarks Scylla and Charybdis.

Presently the Oracle stepped out with his eternal spy-glass and squared himself on the deck like another Colossus of Rhodes. It was a surprise to see him abroad at such an hour. Nobody supposed he cared anything about an old fable like that of Scylla and Charybdis. One of the boys said:

"Hello, doctor, what are you doing up here at this time of night?—What do you want to see this place for?"

"What do I want to see this place for? Young man, little do you know me, or you wouldn't ask such a question. I wish to see all the places that's mentioned in the Bible."

"Stuff—this place isn't mentioned in the Bible."

"It ain't mentioned in the Bible!—this place ain't—well now, what place is this, since you know so much about it?"

"Why it's Scylla and Charybdis."

"Scylla and Cha—confound it, I thought it was Sodom and Gomorrah!"

And he closed up his glass and went below.

Twain's accounts made lasting impressions on his readers. In Italy, he wrote, "'See Naples and die.' Well, I do not know that one would necessarily die after merely seeing it, but to attempt to live there might turn out a little differently. To see Naples as we saw it in the early dawn from far up on the side of Vesuvius, is to see a picture of wonderful beauty."

In 1906, an avid fan, a dying man, wrote to Twain:

Writing this letter is one of the pleasantest duties I have to perform before leaving for "Hell or Hadleyburg"—which the doctor tells me must be soon now.

In fact I'm living beyond my time,—because he said Oct 15 was my last day "on live"—The only reason I didn't die on that date was that I wanted to read your latest story in Harpers. Some people see Naples and die,—I prefer to read Mark Twain & die. I've never seen Naples,—and don't expect to. I've read almost everything you've written,—and when I finish your whole output I'll give up seeing Naples and die happily without that privilege.…

> *Yours gratefully*
> *Benj Ochiltree*

On the strength of such adoring testimony lies Twain's remarkable reputation. Most of his readers would never glimpse the sights he saw or experience his adventures, but they loved him for showing them worlds beyond their own with humor, empathy, and compassion.

In Athens, the ship was quarantined in the harbor for disease control, but Twain and his cohorts stole ashore, breaking into the closed-off Parthenon at night, a caper made more profound by the looming presence of the ancient marble edifice in the moonlight. In the Holy Land, he encountered marvelous scenes of antiquity, described in *Innocents Abroad* thus:

In the starlight, Galilee has no boundaries but the broad compass of the heavens, and is a theatre meet for great events; meet for the birth of a religion able to save a world; and meet for the stately Figure appointed to stand upon its stage and proclaim its high decrees. But in the sunlight, one says: Is it for the deeds which were done and the words which were spoken in this little acre of rocks and sand eighteen centuries gone, that the

bells are ringing to-day in the remote islands of the sea and far and wide over continents that clasp the circumference of the huge globe?

One can comprehend it only when night has hidden all incongruities and created a theatre proper for so grand a drama.

Views of the Holy Land were plentiful at the time. Artists such as David Roberts and photographers including Francis Frith and Abdullah Frères produced portfolios of views for sale and publication. As evocative as these views were, Twain added his own personal take on revered sites and relics, interpreting them in a way that made readers ponder heavy questions with a light heart. At the Church of the Holy Sepulcher, he genuflected before the grave of Adam, pondering the mysteries of humankind's past with characteristic good-humored skepticism:

It is a singular circumstance that right under the roof of this same great church, and not far away from that illustrious column, Adam himself, the father of the human race, lies buried. There is no question that he is actually buried in the grave which is pointed out as his—there can be none—because it has never yet been proven that that grave is not the grave in which he is buried.

The tomb of Adam! How touching it was, here in a land of strangers, far away from home, and friends, and all who cared for me, thus to discover the grave of a blood relation. True, a distant one, but still a relation. The unerring instinct of nature thrilled its recognition. The fountain of my filial affection was stirred to its profoundest depths, and I gave way to tumultuous emotion. I leaned upon a pillar and burst into tears. I deem it no shame to have wept over the grave of my poor dead relative. Let him who would sneer at my emotion close this volume here, for he will find little to his taste in my journeyings through the Holy Land.

THE GRAVE OF ADAM.

The Grave of Adam. Illustration in *Innocents Abroad.*

Cartoonists had a field day with Twain's account of his response to Adam's Tomb in the Church of the Holy Sepulcher, at Jerusalem's historic heart: "I leaned upon a pillar and burst into tears," wrote Twain. "I deem it no shame to have wept over the grave of my poor dead relative."

Closing his account of the Holy Sepulcher, Twain took a more reverent tone:

> With all its clap-trap side-shows and unseemly impostures of every kind, it is still grand, revered, venerable—for a god died there; for fifteen hundred years its shrines have been wet with the tears of pilgrims from the earth's remotest confines; for more than two hundred, the most gallant knights that ever wielded sword wasted their lives away in a struggle to seize it and hold it sacred from infidel pollution. Even in our own day a war, that cost millions of treasure and rivers of blood, was fought

because two rival nations claimed the sole right to put a new dome upon it. History is full of this old Church of the Holy Sepulchre—full of blood that was shed because of the respect and the veneration in which men held the last resting-place of the meek and lowly, the mild and gentle, Prince of Peace!

Lurching from the sublime to the ridiculous, in Syria he encountered recalcitrant donkeys and exhausted horses and spent miserable days in the desert sun. Humanely damning the treatment of the horses he and his fellow passengers rode unmercifully, Twain yet remained focused on the strange terrain and bizarre appearance of American tourists in the biblical landscape:

> But may be you can not see the wild extravagance of my panorama. You could if you were here. Here, you feel all the time just as if you were living about the year 1200 before Christ—or back to the patriarchs—or forward to the New Era. The scenery of the Bible is about you—the customs of the patriarchs are around you—the same people, in the same flowing robes, and in sandals, cross your path—the same long trains of stately camels go and come—the same impressive religious solemnity and silence rest upon the desert and the mountains that were upon them in the remote ages of antiquity, and behold, intruding upon a scene like this, comes this fantastic mob of green-spectacled Yanks, with their flapping elbows and bobbing umbrellas!

As the months-long journey progressed, he grew tired and frustrated with the enthusiasm of "the pilgrims" for even minor sites, complaining at their

Mark Twain at the Grave of Adam. Illustration by Frank Beard in *The American Publisher.*

Then as now, celebrity brought ridicule along with reverence. Cartoonist Frank Beard satirized Twain, even as he validated the young author's growing influence.

The American Publisher.

1872

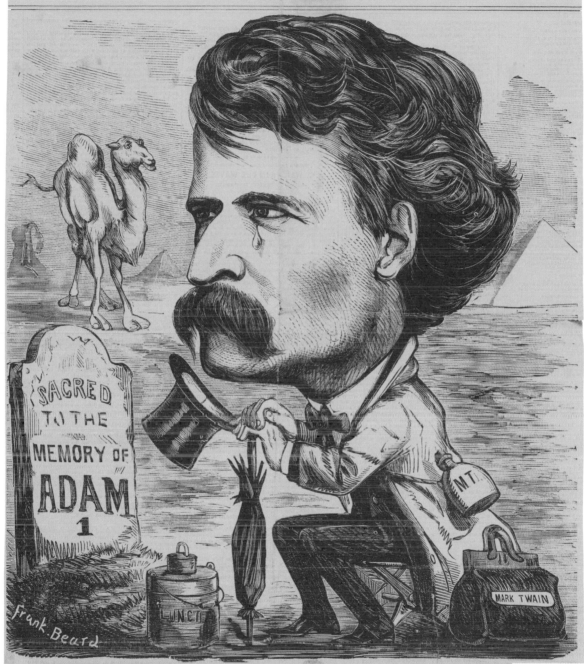

Frank Beard

SACRED TO THE MEMORY OF ADAM 1

LUNCH

MT.

MARK TWAIN

MARK TWAIN AT THE GRAVE OF ADAM.

Those of our readers who have perused the description given by the gifted author of the "Innocents Abroad," and "Roughing It," of his visit to the grave of our common ancestor, will, we are assured, read it again with pleasure here, given in connection with an illustration of the incident which our artist has most strikingly drawn; while those who have never read it (if such there be) will be enabled to do so for the first time, under the most favorable auspices, for a full realization of the situation and its surroundings. He says:

"The tomb of Adam! How touching it was, here in a land of strangers, far away from home, and friends, and all who cared for me, thus to discover the grave of a blood relation. True, a distant one, but still a relation. The unerring instinct of nature thrilled its recognition. The fountain of my filial affection was stirred to its profoundest depths, and I gave way to tumultuous emotion. I leaned upon a pillar and burst into tears. I deem it no shame to have wept over the grave of my poor dead relative.

Let him who would sneer at my emotion close this volume here, for he will find little to his taste in my journeyings through the Holy Land. Noble old man—he did not live to see me—he did not live to see his child. And I—I alas! I did not live to see him. Weighed down by sorrow and disappointment, he died before I was born—six thousand brief summers before I was born. But let us try to bear it with fortitude. Let us trust that he is better off, where he is. Let us take comfort in the thought that his loss is our eternal gain."

The Pirate Publisher—An International Burlesque That Has Had the Longest Run on Record. Chromolithograph by J. Keppler. New York: published by Keppler & Schwarzmann, *Puck,* centerfold, February 24, 1886.

From early in his career Twain tangled with publishers over copyrights to his work. In his *Autobiography* he recalled with venom his treatment by the *Alta California,* which delayed production of *Innocents Abroad:* "There were rights, it is true—such rights as the strong are able to acquire over the weak and the absent."

detour to the Fountain of Figia, where Balaam's Ass was said to have taken a drink. Twain did find some relief at the fountain, daring a quick dip in the icy cold water.

Returning to New York City in November 1867, Twain hit the ground running, writing to his mother, "Am pretty well known, now. Intend to be better known." By the end of the month he was in Washington, DC, serving as private secretary to Nevada senator William M. Stewart, architect of the final version of the Fifteenth Amendment. During Twain's stint with the Senate, he met leading legislators, recording the progress of President

Andrew Johnson's impeachment hearings for the senator and for papers in New York City. His personal life was helter-skelter, as described in Ron Powers's biography:

A visiting fellow journalist was fascinated by the wildness of his working scene: the floor littered with torn-up newspapers from which Sam had slashed out his letters, the "chaotic hovel foul with tobacco smoke," Sam himself stripped down to suspenders and pants, swearing and smoking and ripping up newsprint as he paced the floor.

Then, a break, similar to his hiring by the Virginia City newspaper that launched his writing career: Twain was approached by publisher Elisha Bliss with an offer to publish a humorous book of his letters from the *Quaker City* voyage. Bliss ran the American Publishing Company in Hartford, Connecticut, publishers of A. D. Richardson's *Beyond the Mississippi,* a popular travel book about a railroad trip from Sacramento to the Great Salt Lake on Leland Stanford's newly built Central Pacific Railroad. Unlike other large publishing houses, which produced and distributed their wares through urban booksellers, Bliss sold his books by subscription. His representatives reached readers beyond the traditional literary marketplace, going door-to-door in small towns and farming communities, pushing their publications like Bible or encyclopedia salesmen. Energized by the offer, Twain negotiated a 5 percent royalty on sales and set to work on filling six hundred pages of lavishly illustrated text for *Innocents Abroad.* He gathered letters from family, friends, and publishers, traveling to California to arrange for the rights to letters published by the *Alta California.* Successfully securing copyrights, he finished the manuscript while on a sojourn in San Francisco's Occidental Hotel, editing the pages during the sea voyage back to New York in July 1868.

As Twain's professional résumé took shape—*Innocents Abroad,* occasional letters and sketches, lecture tours—his personal life took a dramatic turn. He met fellow Nighthawk Charles Langdon's sister Livy and quickly fell in love. Livy's family had deep ties to progressive reform. Her father, Jervis Langdon, became wealthy selling coal during the Civil War, and he and his wife were staunch supporters of rights for women and abolitionists with ties to the Underground Railway. Langdon called Frederick Douglass a friend.

Livy herself grew up strong-minded but physically frail, a frequent invalid with a nervous disposition. A friend wrote that she "was rich, beautiful and

intellectual, but she could not see a joke, or anything to laugh at in the wittiest sayings unless explained in detail." She was well educated, literature-loving, beautiful, and intelligent—an appealing challenge for Twain, who longed for acceptance into the Eastern elite. He aspired to transcend his rough origins and be treated as a serious author and a respectable

Innocence Abroad (in Search of a Copyright). Wood engraving by Thomas Nast, *Harper's Weekly,* January 31, 1882.

Pirated editions of his works infuriated Twain, who went to great lengths, travelling to Canada and England, to ensure his copyright and protect his intellectual property. Nast lampooned his efforts following publication of *The Prince and the Pauper.* Twain told a reporter, "I am always protected in the matter of copyright on my books. I always take the trouble to step over in Canada and stand on English soil. Thus secure myself and receive money for my books sold in England."

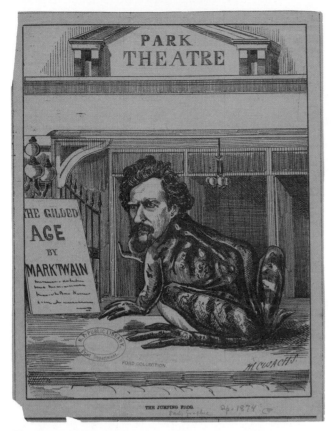

The Jumping Frog. Broadside by M. Cusachs, New York, ca. 1874.

During the 1870s and 1880s Twain was a familiar favorite on the lecture circuit, notable for his striking features, down home delivery, and signature jumping frog.

gentleman. Livy and the Langdon family offered validation for his achievements and connections with leading thinkers of the day. While pursuing an extended lecture tour, he courted her with letters, an estimated 189 missives all told.

In January 1869, Twain responded to a letter and enclosed photograph from Livy with an expressive outpouring of love and concern. He saw in her photograph "an angel beauty–something not of earth– something above the earth & its grossness.... Oh, it breaks my very heart to think of you suffering, even for an hour. You see I am wrought up, Livy–in fact I am in more distress than words can easily tell–& I find myself fettered hand-&-foot by this

lingering eternity of engagements." Livy represented the ideal Victorian woman, lovely and ethereal; she also suffered from melancholic spells and low self-esteem in the face of her formidable parents and their powerful friends. Nonetheless, she also proved strong and determined, a modern woman who longed to be active in the women's movement and prove her mettle. When she compared herself unfavorably to Anna Dickinson, one of the leading reformers of the day, Twain reassured her in a letter dated January 22, 1869:

> *Be content with the strength that God has given you, & the station He has given into your charge–& don't be discouraged & unsettled by Anna Dickinson's incendiary words. I like Anna Dickinson, & admire her grand character, & have often & over again made her detractors feel ashamed of themselves; but I am thankful that you are not the sort of woman that is her ideal, & grateful that you never can be, Livy, darling.*

She would become a steadying, supportive influence on Twain, complementing with dignified, quiet purpose his wayward, uncouth ways. But during the first months of courtship, Livy and her family had serious doubts about Twain's character. His *Quaker City* letters were unsettling, disturbingly sacrilegious to those who craved order and decorum in their lives; he seemed to belittle their faith, the underpinnings of their lives. Twain's publisher, Elisha Bliss, found himself forced to fight with reluctant board members who could not accept the manuscript's satirical, apparently irreligious tone. Upon publication in July 1869, the book proved a great success; according to Ron Powers, the book eventually earned $16,000 in royalties (about $200,000 today). Newspapers from all over the country praised the book for its humor and moral truths, while cartoonists began to caricature the provocative literary upstart.

left: The Lyceum Committeeman's Dream. Illustration in *Harper's Weekly,* November 15, 1873.

A cartoonist drew portraits of nineteen of the day's most celebrated public speakers, with Twain occupying front and center as a jester.

below: *"Men of Mark."* Composite photograph by Bradley & Rulofson, San Francisco, 1876.

The lecture circuit of Twain's time was a popular form of public entertainment that aimed to enlighten as well as amuse. Twain appears top row, fourth from left, among a gallery of his male peers.

"MEN OF MARK."
BRADLEY & RULOFSON, PHOTO., S. F.

Mark Twain in sealskin coat. Photograph, 1880s.

Mark Twain's sealskin coat startled proper Bostonians and staid New Englanders accustomed to more formal wear. Worse still was his behavior during a 70th birthday tribute to beloved poet William Greenleaf Whittier on December 17, 1877. That night, he spoke with casual irreverence of the city's literary legends: Henry Wadsworth Longfellow, Ralph Waldo Emerson, and Oliver Wendell Holmes.

The biggest boost came out of straitlaced Boston, where no one less than William Dean Howells, soon to become the influential editor of the venerable *Atlantic Monthly,* and Oliver Wendell Holmes, the magisterial Autocrat of the Breakfast Table, gave Twain high marks, although Holmes withheld permission to use his remarks for publicity, perhaps fearing the backlash to his own lofty position. Such praise from American men of letters and the immense popular success of *Innocents Abroad* helped Twain

overcome the reservations of Livy's family. After a rigorous vetting of Twain's past relationships and escapades by Jervis Langdon on behalf of his daughter, Twain was accepted by Livy and her family, and they were married in February 1870, moving into an elegant, fully furnished and staffed house, gifted by her father, in Elmira, New York, 144 miles from Buffalo.

In love and ecstatic over his new life and marriage, he wrote to his old Hannibal friend Will Bowen, "She is the most perfect gem of womankind that I ever saw in my life–& will stand by that remark till I die." Settling into his surroundings, Twain found that old memories of Hannibal came streaming back. To Bowen he wrote, "The fountains of my great deep are broken up & I have rained reminiscences for four & twenty hours. The old life has swept before me like a panorama." Thinking back on his childhood, the outlines of his youth took shape once more in his mind, offering a glimpse of incidents and themes he would employ in his greatest works.

While Americans continued to argue over political, economic, ethnic, and racial divisions, Twain tried to settle down. The success of *Innocents Abroad* made him much sought after on the lecture circuit. He joined James Redpath's prestigious lecture bureau, sharing the stage with notable novelists and commentators. Jervis Langdon, seeking to corral his son-in-law into more steady employment, offered him a position in his coal company, but Twain declined, determined to write and lecture. Hoping to support the couple and compel Twain to put down roots, Langdon loaned him the money to purchase a part interest in the local Buffalo newspaper the *Express,* and for a few months Twain hunkered down in domestic bliss, working daily to revamp the newspaper and contribute editorials.

His and Livy's unalloyed joy was ephemeral. That August, Jervis Langdon succumbed to cancer; Twain's mother, Jane Clemens, came to visit, exhibiting worrisome "wooly-headed" symptoms;

above: Samuel and Livy Clemens with daughters sitting in a gazebo, Hartford. Photograph, cabinet card by H. L. Bundy, 1884.

Livy Clemens helped design the dream house they built in Hartford, Connecticut, home to the American Publishing Company and a literary community which included Harriet Beecher Stowe and Twain collaborator Charles Dudley Warner.

right: The Mark Twain House & Museum, where Samuel Clemens and his family lived from 1874 to 1891, Hartford, Connecticut. Photograph by Carol Highsmith.

Renowned photographer Carol Highsmith gifted to the Library of Congress without rights restrictions her entire archives of photographs documenting American landmarks, from the Twain House in Hartford to Manhattan's World Trade Center.

and Livy's close friend Emma Nye, while on a visit, died in their home from typhoid fever. Livy's first pregnancy proved difficult; Langdon Clemens, born in November 1870, was sickly and premature, and Livy's frail health further compromised. She would soon survive a bout of the same disease that killed her friend.

Taking on Livy's suffering along with his own anxieties, Twain kept working, reluctantly completing an exhausting fall tour. He gathered his western letters with the help of his brother Orion. Joe Goodman, his editor in Nevada, came east to visit and stayed to help Twain edit his growing manuscript for *Roughing It*, slated to be his next book. But the Elmira home became

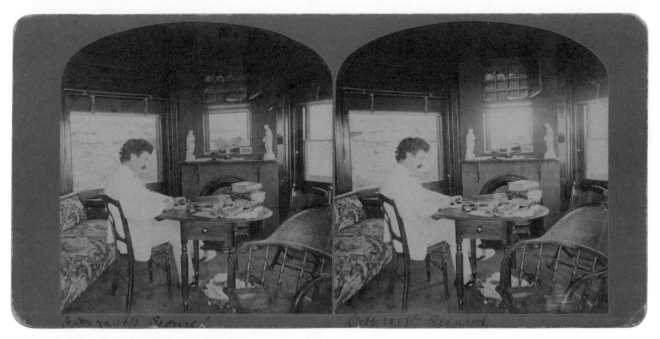

Twain working at desk, Quarry Farm, Stereograph, 1874.

Quarry Farm outside Elmira, New York, owned by Livy's sister, became a favorite summer retreat for Sam Clemens and his family. In an octagonal study built for him by Livy on a picturesque hill overlooking the Chemung Creek, Twain produced pages for his most revered books, including *The Adventures of Tom Sawyer, A Tramp Abroad, The Prince and the Pauper, Life on the Mississippi, Adventures of Huckleberry Finn,* and *A Connecticut Yankee in King Arthur's Court.*

a haunted residence to Twain, and he spent his days working at Quarry Farm, a Langdon country home outside the city, where he found peace from young Langdon's wailing and Livy's debilitating prostration.

In the fall of 1871, the couple sold the Elmira home at a loss and relocated to Nook Farm, outside Hartford, a writers' compound where they rented the home of Isabella Beecher Hooker, who developed the community and had been his shipmate and friend on the *Quaker City.* There they lived in close contact with celebrated neighbors, among them Isabella's half-sister Harriet Beecher Stowe and novelist Charles Dudley Warner. From Hartford Twain was easily able to visit both New York and Boston on business and for pleasure; he caused a sensation in Boston by wearing a western sealskin coat in a town more suited to tails and topcoats.

At Nook Farm, Twain and Livy started fresh. His manuscript for *Roughing It* was in the works,

and his busy lecture schedule had amplified his fame, catapulting him into the rarefied circles of fine American literature. He joined forces with his old California colleague Bret Harte, whose extended poem featuring Ah Sin, the Heathen Chinee, and publication of his seminal book of sketches, *The Luck of Roaring Camp,* had given him a national profile. The two collaborated on a stage version of *Ah Sin,* though it never caught on with audiences. Over time, their separate and collected

opposite, top: *Mark Twain House, Hartford, Conn.* Photograph, Detroit Publishing Company, ca. 1905.

opposite, bottom: **Twain House, Hartford.** Photograph from the Historic American Building Survey/Historic American Engineering Record (HABS HAER) collection in the Library of Congress.

Among the Library's numerous depictions of Twain residences are photographs and architecturally rendered plans produced in the 1930s by the Historic American Building Survey, a public program documenting the country's most revered sites.

work would inspire a new strand of realism in American fiction.

Life with Livy, her family, and her friends altered Twain's outlook, while his views toward the world underwent slow but measurable evolution. His circle now included many of the best and brightest in the country, and he was moved to reconsider his views on race and women. Livy, though physically slight and vulnerable, was strong-minded, answering Twain's sometimes chauvinistic acts with the retort, "I am women's rights." Having met Frederick Douglass and Harriet Beecher Stowe, he became more sensitive to the plight of blacks, responding to accounts of a black man cleared of rape charges only after he had been lynched. With caustic derision, he wrote in a short essay, "Only 'a Nigger,'" "Ah well! Too bad to be sure! A little blunder in the administration of justice by Southern mob-law; but nothing to speak of. Only 'a nigger' killed by mistake–that is all."

Mark Twain's Curious Dream. London: George Routledge & Sons, 1871.

Mark Twain. Photograph by Rogers & Nelson, London, 1872.

London, home of the humor magazine *Punch,* was the epicenter of English comic art and literature as Mark Twain emerged on the world literary scene. The land of Swift, Dickens, and Gillray and the Cruikshanks had long enjoyed a good laugh at others' expense. England embraced Twain from the start of his career, and his fame spread quickly through the British Empire.

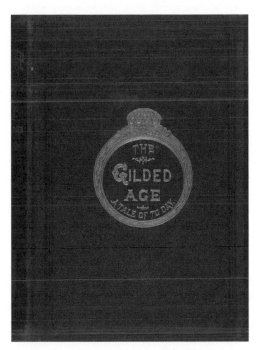

above: *The Gilded Age* book cover, 1873.

Mark Twain named the Gilded Age as it began, in this spirited collaboration with popular author Charles Dudley Warner, a Clemens family neighbor at Nook Farm, outside Hartford, Connecticut.

right: *Colonel Sellers Feeding His Family on Expectations.* Frontispiece, *The Gilded Age*

James Lampton, a favorite cousin of Twain's mother, could, like Colonel Mulberry Sellers, the main character in *The Gilded Age,* verbally turn turnips into T-bone steaks; he became the model for the ever-optimistic Colonel in *The Gilded Age.*

COLONEL SELLERS FEEDING HIS FAMILY ON EXPECTATIONS.

A daughter, Olivia Susan Clemens, was born in March 1872, followed soon by the death of their firstborn, Langdon, in June at Nook Farm. Death had become Twain's companion, as it was for so many before the advent of modern medicine and antibiotics. He kept working on new material for books and lectures while contributing stories and essays to a variety of journals. The popular success of *Roughing It* encouraged Twain, but he was very concerned about his lack of control over pirated versions of his books and letters. In the fall he spent several months in London meeting his authorized English publishers and making the social rounds of banquets and receptions.

As the effects of the war diminished and the economy improved, the middle class was rising fast, with a boost from public education, public works and American industry, new towns and new markets. Speculation and graft, too, became part of the social fabric. Industrial moguls, called robber barons for their unapologetic fleecing of the public, helped move the country forward, while helping themselves to the lion's share of the profits. Twain's short stints in Washington, DC, had given him a glimpse of governmental affairs, and he was soon contracted to produce a modern book of manners with his neighbor Charles Dudley Warner. *The Gilded Age*

COL. SELLERS BLOWING BUBBLES FOR WASHINGTON.

Col. Sellers Blowing Bubbles for Washington. Illustration in *The Gilded Age*.

The Gilded Age was a satire of modern morals; here the effervescent Colonel Sellers beguiles gullible young innocent Washington Hawkins with airy dreams of get-rich-quick schemes. Twain modeled Washington after his older brother Orion.

featured characters drawn from Twain's past and contemporary types pulled from the latest headlines.

Written alternately (in clumps of chapters) by Twain and Warner in the spring of 1873, apparently conceived as a result of a challenge issued by their wives, who tired one evening of hearing their husbands complain about the state of current American fiction, this satirical novel interweaves the lives of characters caught up in the modern quest for riches and romance. Twain's chapters recount in fictional form his father, Marshall's, tale of speculation and despair; the Clemens family serves as the model for the Hawkins family, with

Squire Hawkins a fair representation of Marshall Clemens. Female lobbyists, greedy speculators, corrupt politicians, and misguided entrepreneurs fill out a cast of characters notable for their venality and vanity. Endearing scoundrels populate the pages with earnest men and driven women. The central figure, Col. Beriah Sellers, was based on a Clemens cousin, James Lampton, a generous, warmhearted man plagued, like Twain's father, with an unquenchable thirst for speculation and get-rich-quick schemes:

He'll make anybody believe in that notion that'll listen to him ten minutes—why I do believe he

would make a deaf and dumb man believe in it and get beside himself, if you only set him where he could see his eyes tally and watch his hands explain. What a head he has got! When he got up that idea there in Virginia of buying up whole loads of negroes in Delaware and Virginia and Tennessee, very quiet, having papers drawn to have them delivered at a place in Alabama and take them and pay for them, away yonder at a certain time, and then in the meantime get a law made stopping everybody from selling negroes to the south after a certain day—it was somehow that way—mercy how the man would have made money! Negroes would have gone up to four prices.

In another scene, Col. Sellers fills the head of young Washington, Squire Hawkins's eldest son, with visionary schemes:

Washington was so dazed, so bewildered—his heart and his eyes had gone so far away among the strange lands beyond the seas, and such avalanches of coin and currency had fluttered and jingled confusedly down before him, that he was now as one who has been whirling round and round for a time, and, stopping all at once, finds his surroundings still whirling and all objects a dancing chaos. However, little by little the Sellers family cooled down and crystalized into shape, and the poor room lost its glitter and resumed its poverty.

For Twain, this dramatic, measured collaboration with Warner, an established Eastern author, supplied the gravitas some critics found wanting in Twain's earlier efforts. Underlying the book's comic passages were the pathos of failure and the sense of futility that those who pursue chimerical riches face; yet there was also an irrepressible belief in the unprecedented opportunities available to those who seize their chance:

Laura Receives Dillworthy's Blessing. Illustration in *The Gilded Age.*

In *The Gilded Age,* formidable Laura Hawkins makes her way to Washington as a professional lobbyist for pet projects. Male lobbyists peddle their influence for $3,000, while charismatic female lobbyists like Hawkins command as much as $10,000 from special interests—the same price it would take to buy a senator. Twain's disdain for politicians was legendary: "Reader. Suppose you were an idiot. And suppose you were a member of Congress. But I repeat myself."

To the young American, here or elsewhere, the paths to fortune are innumerable and all open; there is invitation in the air and success in all his wide horizon. He is embarrassed which to choose, and is not unlikely to waste years in dallying with his chances, before giving himself to the serious tug and strain of a single object. He has no traditions to bind him or guide him, and his impulse is to break away from the occupation his father has followed, and make a new way for himself.

Several of the characters in *The Gilded Age* are like the tailors in the fable who create a new suit of clothes for the emperor; reality in appearance is often quite different from their descriptions. With a few well-chosen words, the smallest stream becomes a mighty waterway teeming with commerce:

"This, gentlemen," said Jeff, "is Columbus River, alias Goose Run. If it was widened, and deepened, and straightened, and made long enough, it would be one of the finest rivers in the western country."

As the sun rose and sent his level beams along the stream, the thin stratum of mist, or malaria, rose also and dispersed, but the light was not able to enliven the dull water nor give any hint of its apparently fathomless depth. Venerable mud-turtles crawled up and roosted upon the old logs in the stream, their backs glistening in the sun, the first inhabitants of the metropolis to begin the active business of the day.

The story opens in Tennessee and Missouri (chapters written by Twain) and then moves to Washington, DC, exposing the vanity and cupidity of public officials, the hidden mechanics behind the burgeoning federal juggernaut. The anti-corruption campaign by cartoonist Thomas Nast and New York newspapers against Boss William Magear Tweed and the Democratic Tammany Hall political machine was fresh in people's minds. "Honest graft" was the phrase of the day, and the authors of *The Gilded Age* chronicled the steps needed to advance a bill through Congress:

Why the — matter is simple enough. A Congressional appropriation costs money. Just reflect, for instance–a majority of the House Committee, say $10,000 apiece–$40,000; a majority of the Senate Committee, the same each– say $40,000; a little extra to one or two chairman of one or two such committees, say $10,000 each–$20,000; and there's $100,000 of the money gone, to begin with. Then, seven male lobbyists, at $3,000 each–$21,000; one female lobbyist, $10,000; a high moral Congressman or Senator here and there–the high moral ones cost more,

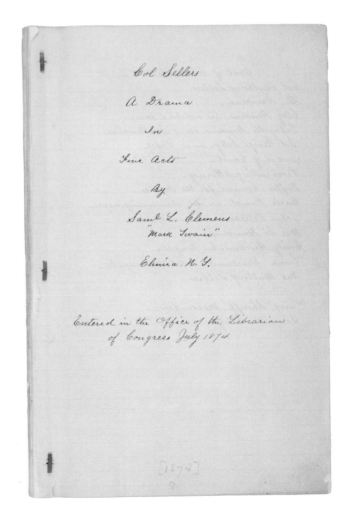

Col. Sellers. *The Gilded Age* stage play manuscript, 1874

The Library of Congress collections include a draft manuscript for a theatrical version of *The Gilded Age,* entitled "Col. Sellers, A Drama in Five Acts" by Sam[ue]l. L. Clemens, "Mark Twain," submitted for copyright registration in 1874 from Elmira, New York.

because they give tone to a measure—say ten of these at $3,000 each, is $30,000; then a lot of small-fry country members who won't vote for anything whatever without pay—say twenty at $500 apiece, is $10,000; a lot of dinners to members—say $10,000 altogether; lot of jimcracks for Congressmen's wives and children—those go a long way—you can't spend too much money in that line.

The Gilded Age itself proved as ruinous as it was rewarding, even to those with pluck and enterprise. In the fall of 1873, less than six months after Twain and Warner finished writing their novel, panic enveloped Wall Street, and the stock market closed for ten days to stem the tide of investors trying to sell off increasingly worthless shares of stock. More than five thousand businesses failed, and thousands of people were left destitute, depending on soup kitchens for their meals. As for Twain, even as his literary career flourished, he ignored the lessons of his father and cousin, pouring more and more money and mental effort into his own surefire inventions: a harness to hold up men's pants, a patented girdle for women, an adhesive scrapbook—the last actually did make money—and educational games for children. Still quivering over his own rough school days, he sought to make learning more fun and engaging for young Americans.

In Hartford, surrounded by admiring friends and a doting family, Twain found his rhythm, producing the essays, sketches, and stories that would make him the country's most widely read author. He was already known by name, and True Williams's illustrations for *Innocents Abroad* and *Roughing It*, along with promotional advertisements and lecture broadsides, made his distinct features familiar to all. When not distracted by Livy's illnesses or his own financial missteps, Twain was pouring out thousands of words each day.

Inspired by his love of the stage, Twain wrote a theatrical version of *The Gilded Age* entitled

Edwin Booth as Hamlet Photograph, cabinet card, ca. 1870.

Twain loved the theater, wrote several stage plays, and admired Edwin Booth above all other actors. In the 1880s, Booth founded the Players Club in New York City for fellow aficionados, actors, and producers; Twain was a prominent member.

Col. Sellers, A Play in Five Acts, just as he would later authorize stage versions of *Huckleberry Finn, The Prince and the Pauper,* and *A Connecticut Yankee in King Arthur's Court.* He followed the career of celebrated American actor Edwin Booth, brother of Lincoln assassin John Wilkes Booth, and enjoyed his renowned turn as Shakespeare's Hamlet. With Booth and others he founded the Players Club, a social group of prominent men in the world of theater—actors, writers, and producers.

KIRALFY BROS. "BLACK CROOK."

Kiralfy Bros. "Black Crook" poster. Color lithograph, Boston: Forbes Co., ca. 1882. Copyright by Imre and Bolossy Kiralfy.

The perennially popular drama *The Black Crook* debuted in New York City in September 1866, prefiguring future Broadway and Hollywood blockbusters. Crowds flocked to experience the lavish sets, brilliant costumes, song and dance, and huge cast of skilled performers. Patrons watched attentively as a hundred lovelies in skimpy costumes strutted to "March of the Amazons."

He enjoyed lavish theatricals like the Kiralfy Brothers' *The Black Crook,* a prototype for Cecil B. DeMille's epic Hollywood productions, with a huge cast and extensive stage sets. He found Robert Louis Stevenson's horror classic *Dr. Jekyll and Mr. Hyde* fascinating, shedding light on his own dual identity. The Siamese twins Eng and Chang Bunker, famous on the lecture circuit, were another favorite; Twain wrote a humorous sketch about them in 1875, in the last sentence giving their ages as fifty-three and fifty-

one years old. He used twins repeatedly as a dramatic device in his own works; for example, the plots for *The Prince and the Pauper* and *Pudd'nhead Wilson* revolved around switched identities.

By 1880 he and Livy had three daughters, Susy, Clara, and Jean. On the strength of his earnings and Livy's inheritance, the Clemenses built a picturesque and eccentric Victorian residence in Hartford, with plentiful nooks and crannies and an unusual picture window over the hearth. Now

DR. JEKYLL and MR. HYDE

THE TRANSFORMATION
"GREAT GOD! CAN IT BE !!"

Dr. Jekyll and Mr. Hyde: The Transformation, "Great God! Can It Be!!" Poster, Chicago: National Printing & Engraving Co., ca. 1886.

Robert Louis Stevenson's 1886 suspense novel, *Dr. Jekyll and Mr. Hyde*, became a best seller and rekindled Mark Twain's interest in duality and the possibility of multiple personalities existing within a single soul.

Eng Chang. Print by J. T. Bowen, July 1, 1837.

The conjoined brothers whose fame gave rise to the term "Siamese twins" lived much of their lives in America. For a time, they appeared on stages around the country, where Twain would have seen them. He wrote a humorous sketch about them in 1875, later turning the idea of twins into something much darker in *Pudd'nhead Wilson* (1894).

Yr Truly
Mark Twain

restored as the Mark Twain House and Museum, this residence, designed by architect Edward T. Potter and completed in 1874, became a center for entertaining Twain's and the couple's growing circle of friends and admirers. Twain played billiards, smoked cigars, and produced his most important works, *Tom Sawyer, Huck Finn,* and *A Connecticut Yankee in King Arthur's Court,* while living there.

More secure in his personal life and professional circle, he went back to his youth, to the river, mining his past for present truths. *Tom Sawyer* overturned the conventions of children's literature. It was an antidote to the strained morality of Horatio Alger's popular Ragged Dick character, the pious urchin rewarded for his good behavior. Good behavior found little purchase in Tom Sawyer, whose antics frazzled his good-hearted Aunt Polly. *Huck Finn* took another step beyond the pale, entering moral territory never before encountered in prose geared toward families.

Even after the publication of *Tom Sawyer,* when Twain had reached new heights of fame, he craved further recognition from America's literati. Most of them gathered in Boston at the Hotel Brunswick on December 17, 1877, to celebrate the seventieth birthday of the august abolitionist essayist John Greenleaf Whittier, who for decades remained at the center of the country's intellectual and political life. Twain was asked to speak at the event. The evening was meant to be a tribute, but his eagerly anticipated remarks treated it as a roast, tweaking Whittier and his Boston Brahmin colleagues as "imposters." His performance set him up for a vicious backlash for his bad taste and public miscue. William Dean Howells, who had introduced Twain, was mortified, and the rest of the crowd seemed stunned by Twain's hubris. Who was he to call out the gods of American literature, even in jest?

Twain fled to Europe with his family to escape the fallout from his faux pas. He produced a book from the trip, *A Tramp Abroad,* published in 1880. Following up on his previous experiences on the Continent during the *Quaker City* excursion, Twain evoked the Old World customs that differed so much from contemporary life in America. He included an extended section on dueling among German students, proudly displaying their wounds in the street. He attended a German-language performance in Mannheim of *King Lear* that left him unmoved: "It was a mistake. We sat in our seats three whole hours and never understood anything but the thunder and lightning; and even that was reversed to suit German ideas, for the thunder came first and the lightning followed after."

In *Innocents Abroad,* he had roundly dismissed the work of the Old Masters, explaining that all the martyrs they depicted looked alike to him. In Germany, Twain took instruction in art; he had always been a sketcher and doodler. Facetiously, he painted his own "great picture" portraying Heidelberg Castle.

Still, he remained fascinated by certain aspects of life in Europe, the monarchies and quaint habits of centuries providing food for thought. *The Prince and the Pauper,* published in 1881, attacked feudal laws and medieval ways but did it so politely that Twain himself later questioned its effect, asking an interviewer:

> *Perhaps you have read my book* The Prince and the Pauper? *You have? Well, that is a story that is not in my usual vein. At first I intended to publish it anonymously but I was persuaded not to do so by my family, because they liked it. But afterwards I was sorry I did not. Mind you, I like the book myself, but what I felt about it was that the signature Mark Twain is a kind of trademark. The public buying a book by Mark Twain expects to get a book of a certain type. And I felt it was not quite fair to my readers to publish a book of quite*

above: Cover for *A Tramp Abroad.*

right: *The Author's Memories.* Illustration in *A Tramp Abroad.*

Twain himself was a frequent character in his own books, encouraging familiarity, recognition, intimacy, and celebrity among his readers.

THE AUTHOR'S MEMORIES.

another type under that signature. I may be wrong but that is how I look at it. If a man puts a certain trademark upon a certain brand of cloth he has no rights to sell the public another sort of cloth under that same trademark.

But authors as a rule do not look upon a nom de plume as a trademark, do they?

Perhaps not, but I do. Mark Twain is my trademark.

Inspired further by Thomas Malory's romance *Le Morte d'Arthur*, Twain produced *A Connecticut Yankee in King Arthur's Court* in 1889. In his version of Camelot, an old-school monarchy confronts Hank Morgan, a modern-day Connecticut man employed

at an arms factory resembling Colt's Patent Firearms Manufacturing in Hartford. Chivalry, feudalism, and ignorance, foundations of British rule and the Church of England, wilt before the ingenuity of Hank, the Yankee whose progressive ideas are a mouthpiece for the author's thoughts on law, government, and religion.

In one scene, Hank accompanies Sandy, a young woman whose mistress and household are beset by ogres, on a mission to solve a problem. A chance encounter is a vehicle for poking fun at the class system in medieval England.

We were off before sunrise, Sandy riding and I limping along behind. In half an hour we came

Leaving Heilbronn

upon a group of ragged poor creatures who had assembled to mend the thing which was regarded as a road. They were as humble as animals to me; and when I proposed to breakfast with them, they were so flattered, so overwhelmed by this extraordinary condescension of mine that at first they were not able to believe that I was in earnest. My lady put up her scornful lip and withdrew to one side; she said in their hearing that she would as soon think of eating with the other cattle—a remark which embarrassed these poor devils merely because it referred to them, and not because it insulted or offended them, for it didn't. And yet they were not slaves, not chattels. By a sarcasm of law and phrase they were freemen. Seven-tenths of the free population of the country were of just their class and degree: small "independent" farmers, artisans, etc.; which is to say, they were the nation, the actual Nation; they were about all of it that was useful, or worth saving, or really respect-worthy, and to subtract them would have been to subtract the Nation and

above: *Leaving Heilbronn.* Illustration in *A Tramp Abroad.*

right: *Painting My Great Picture.* Illustration in *A Tramp Abroad.*

One of the running jokes in *A Tramp Abroad* was Twain attempting to illustrate his own adventures with crude drawings such as "Leaving Heilbronn," which in turn allowed him to comment on the art of the Old Masters he saw while touring the Continent. Illustrator William Francis Brown then turned the tables on Twain, depicting him in Moorish garb in an artist's studio whose walls are filled with his "great pictures."

PAINTING MY GREAT PICTURE.

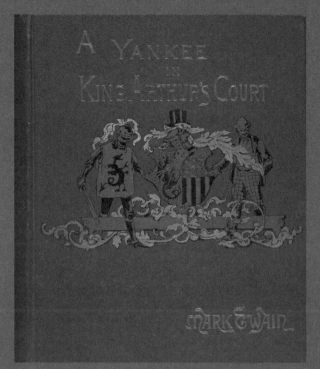

A [Connecticut] Yankee in King Arthur's Court cover.

"QUEEN GUENEVER WAS AS NAÏVELY INTERESTED AS THE REST."

"Queen Guenever Was as Naïvely Interested as the Rest." Illustration by Daniel Carter Beard in *A Connecticut Yankee in King Arthur's Court,* New York: Charles L. Webster & Co., 1889.

"I saw he meant business." A medieval knight tilts against a visitor from the nineteenth century. Pen and ink over graphite underdrawing, frontispiece in *A Connecticut Yankee in King Arthur's Court* by Daniel Carter Beard. "New York: Charles L. Webster & Co., 1889.

Daniel Beard produced the original illustrations for *A Connecticut Yankee in King Arthur's Court, The American Claimant,* and *Following the Equator.* Beard founded a youth organization, The Sons of Daniel Boone, which eventually became part of the original Boy Scouts of America. His papers, including numerous items related to his personal and professional relationship with Twain, reside in the Library of Congress's Manuscript Division.

Advice to Little Girls. By Mark Twain. Wood engraving by Thomas Nast, *Nast's Illustrated Almanac,* 1872.

Readers looking for a moral in Twain's comic work were often shocked; domestic mayhem directed by mischievous children was the norm.

leave behind some dregs, some refuse, in the shape of a king, nobility and gentry, idle, unproductive, acquainted mainly with the arts of wasting and destroying, and of no sort of use or value in any rationally constructed world.

Above all, in nearly everything he wrote during these years, Twain remained wickedly funny. In Thomas Nast's comic almanac for 1872, he parodied Benjamin Franklin's obsolete aphorisms–for example, "Never Put Off Till To-Morrow What You Can Do the Day After To-Morrow Just as Well." By 1888 he

was producing his own comic almanac, *Mark Twain's Library of Humor,* an anthology filled with essays by contributors including Bret Harte and Harriet Beecher Stowe, along with amusing illustrations by Edward Kemble, who had created the art for *Huckleberry Finn.*

To his everlasting regret, in the manner of his father, he also made terrible business decisions. *Tom Sawyer* and *Huck Finn* made Twain a rich man, but he poured much of his income, and Livy's inheritance, into ill-considered investments. Most notorious among them was a new invention, the

THE LATE BENJAMIN FRANKLIN.

BY MARK TWAIN.

[NEVER PUT OFF TILL TO-MORROW WHAT YOU CAN DO THE DAY AFTER TO-MORROW JUST AS WELL.—B. F.]

The Late Benjamin Franklin. By Mark Twain. Wood engraving by Thomas Nast, *Nast's Illustrated Almanac,* 1872.

"Never Put Off Till To Morrow What You Can Do the Day After To-Morrow Just as Well—B. F."
Benjamin Franklin's *Poor Richard's Almanac,* full of useful information and pious aphorisms, had no chance against the irreverent combination of Thomas Nast and Mark Twain.

Paige Compositor, an allegedly innovative but ultimately unworkable typesetting device. In 1884, he started his own publishing house, with his nephew Charles T. Webster at the helm, in an attempt to control his profits and gain independence. Twain was following in Franklin's footsteps here, attempting to control the means of production and distribution for his artistic output. Few writers between these two giants of American letters had thought to do the same, but Twain was naturally inclined to maximize his income—and he was living in an age that prized wealth above all else.

Though the Webster Publishing Company's first book, *Huckleberry Finn,* was a success, with one exception, subsequent books did not sell well, and the venture lost money in the wake of high expenses and tepid sales for, among others, biographies of Pope Leo XIII (which Twain mistakenly assumed would be required reading for every Catholic in America) and controversial Union general George B. McClellan, who frustrated the Lincoln administration with his inactivity toward the Confederate army in the early days of the war and then ran unsuccessfully for president on the opposition Democratic ticket in 1864.

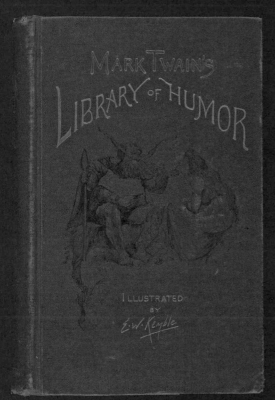

A NOVEL RATTLE.

A Novel Rattle, illustration of baby with rattlesnake in *Mark Twain's Library of Humor.*

Mark Twain's Library of Humor. Cover illustrated by E. W. Kemble.

The *Library of Humor,* a huge compilation of comic material published by Twain's own firm, did not sell well but remains an important source for some of Twain's funniest writing.

right: "Ah Sin," illustration and text in *Mark Twain's Library of Humor.*

Bret Harte, who preceded Sam Clemens as a chronicler of the frontier West, shaped Twain's style and career. Harte edited Twain's writing in California and helped him get published. In 1876, they collaborated on *Ah Sin,* a theatrical version of Harte's celebrated 1870 sketch "The Heathen Chinee." When Harte's career dwindled, Twain loaned him money and published his work, but ultimately he derided his former friend. Responding in an 1885 interview to George Washington Cable's defense of Crane during Cable and Twain's shared lecture tour, Twain remarked, "I tell you, when Harte tried to write frontier dialect it was idiocy. Do you mean to tell me there was any literary merit in an effort that contained five or six dialects? Why, he could have taken it to any miner and had it remedied; but he did not."

"HE WENT FOR THE HEATHEN CHINEE."

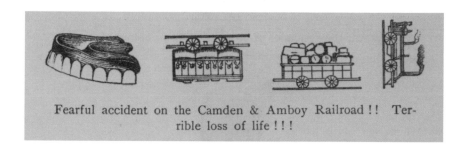

Fearful Accident on the Camden & Amboy Railroad!! Comic illustrations in *Mark Twain's Library of Humor.*

Twain parodies the generic images that early illustrated journals used to portray sensational contemporary events.

Fearful accident on the Camden & Amboy Railroad ! ! Terrible loss of life ! ! !

Between November 1884 and February 1885 Twain embarked with Southern writer George Washington Cable, famous for his genteel Creole tales, on what proved to be a wildly successful tour, Twins of Genius, embracing 103 stops in eighty cities over the course of three months. Reading from their most popular works, Twain and Cable took turns addressing the audience, as Twain explained in an interview at the time: "Our entertainment lasts one hour and three quarters. The fact that Mr. Cable and I alternate makes us able to extend it to that length. Were I lecturing alone, one hour and five minutes is as much as I would dare impose on the audience. The strain on them in the humorous direction would be too much. But now Mr. Cable soothes them, then I excite them to laughter, or

try to, at least." Twain took in $16,000 for the tour as *Huckleberry Finn* rolled off the press.

Aside from *Huck Finn,* Twain did enjoy one major coup as a publisher, as well as securing the thanks of the nation, by putting out another Union general's memoirs to great acclaim. Ulysses S. Grant, following his success in the war and two terms as president, was by 1885 gravely ill with throat cancer and destitute. Twain was the first to suggest to the general that he pen his memoirs, yet publishing houses rejected his manuscript for its straight-shooting, unrepentant description of the war.

At heart, in spite of his ambitions for wealth, fame, social status, and recognition, Twain was a populist, devoted to the idea of the American Republic for which Grant was a symbol of victory and strength. A dying Grant hurriedly dictated his memories and, after his voice gave out, wrote them out longhand in shaky script on lined paper, finishing the work just days before his death in July. Twain had offered him an advance of $200,000 for the book, a payment more than doubled with royalties from sales, which sustained Grant's widow for

Paige typesetter. Photograph, 1890.

Twain's desperate devotion to the Paige Compositor, an unworkable machine in which he invested and lost a fortune, became a counterpart to his father's debilitating speculation in Tennessee land that hamstrung the Clemens family for years.

Mark Twain and George Washington Cable. Photograph, ca. 1884.

The Twins of Genius tour of 1884—1885 was a great success for Twain and George Washington Cable, celebrated author of *Creole Tales*. Asked how the tour came about, Twain responded, "Each of us needed company, also somebody to do half the work."

GENERAL GRANT AT MT. McGREGOR.
(FROM A PHOTOGRAPH OF GENERAL GRANT AND FAMILY, JUNE 19, 1885, BY RECORD & EPLER, SARATOGA SPRINGS, N. Y.)

the rest of her life—also resulting in arguably the best military memoir in American history.

But by 1891 Twain was tapped out. Maintaining a lifestyle of ease, comfort, and hospitality in his Hartford mansion was costing him dearly. Between his lost money in the Paige typesetter and ill-considered and badly managed book contracts, he was close to bankruptcy. He remained one of the world's best-known and most productive writers and a star of American popular culture, yet his profligate spending and incompetent investing brought him near financial ruin. In a desperate attempt to cut expenses and shed his creditors, Twain took his family back to Europe, where the cost of living was relatively low and they could live in peace. He remained prolific and creative, sending articles home for publication and

left: **General Grant memoir.** Handwritten opening page.

right: *General Grant at Mt. McGregor.* From a photograph June 19, 1885, by Record & Epler, Saratoga Springs, N.Y.

Twain's devotion to former Union general and U.S. President Ulysses S. Grant resulted in one of the surprise bestsellers of its day. As the terminally ill Grant raced to complete his memoirs, Twain offered immense advances from his own publishing company, convinced that the book would reap a fortune for the Grant estate and for him as publisher. For once, Twain's investment instincts were right on the money.

preparing new works. His financial problems did not vanish with the journey; they were simply postponed. It would only be with his return to the United States in 1893, and the intercession of a robber baron, that his career as one of the world's great populist writers could continue.

CHAPTER 4

American Oracle

As the nineteenth century came to a close, Americans self-consciously distanced themselves from their recent tumultuous past, approaching the future with energy and idealism. In 1893, Chicago hosted the World's Columbian Exposition, an international fair commemorating Christopher Columbus's discovery of America and flaunting the nation's latest technological advances and cultural aspirations. Seventeen years before, the 1876 Centennial Exposition held in Philadelphia had rung the revolutionary bell, recalling the fight for independence and proudly clothing its buildings in traditional brick, echoing the city's patriotic past. This event was more forward-looking.

For the 1893 exposition, the first generation of professionally trained American architects, led by Daniel Burnham (and including Sophia Hayden Bennett, the first woman to graduate from the Massachusetts Institute of Technology with an undergraduate degree in architecture), created a "White City" of huge pavilions, which in their pristine rationalism and austere, classical simplicity evoked Greek and Roman precedents for civilization and democracy. Their snowy exteriors hid a sensory riot of Turkish carpets and exotic Egyptian dancing girls; the rumble of crowds; the intoxicating scent of popcorn, hot dogs, cotton candy, and ice cream; the gleaming displays of new engines, machines, and implements designed to improve lives, speed production, and free housewives, farmers, and factory workers from onerous, routine labor.

The proud and patriotic presentation, in Chicago, of America as a shining, unified symbol of democratic ingenuity and independence

Mark Twain greeting unidentified man. Photograph, Bain News Service, ca. 1908.

White City, World's Columbian Exposition, Chicago, Illinois, 1893. Platinum photograph by Frances Benjamin Johnston, 1893.

Frances Benjamin Johnston, based in Washington, DC, built a highly successful business portraying signal events and influential leaders at the turn of the century. Impeccably educated, she studied art in Paris before becoming a professional photographer. She uniquely combined commercial and documentary interest with strong aesthetic concerns. Like Twain, she connected with a broad public, from presidents to pupils; her Hampton Institute portraits of African American children in school is a landmark in feature photojournalism.

obscured the nation's social lesions and class conflicts. For many, the 1890s were far from gay. African Americans continued to face Jim Crow laws in the South and hostile competition for jobs in the North. Native Americans, Jews, and Chinese, Polish, German, and Irish immigrants confronted prejudice and derision in the streets and in the press, as if such satire, stereotyping, abuse, and attacks might turn the demographic tide and keep diversity at bay.

Women fought for the vote and some measure of political influence. By contrast, in churches, schools, and settlement houses, a new generation of dedicated reformers addressed social ills, bent on reducing poverty and disease; expanding education; regulating child labor and sanitation; providing care for the elderly, unwed, orphaned, abandoned, indigent, blind, deaf, or disabled; and advocating for humane treatment of animals.

left: *Jim Crow [London].* Etching and ink. New York & Philadelphia: published by Hodgson, 111 Fleet Street, and Turner & Fisher, 1835—1845.

White performer Thomas "Daddy" Rice put on blackface and became the blissfully bumbling and ignorant Jim Crow for a traveling minstrel troupe that performed in Hannibal, Missouri, in 1845 before a rapt ten-year-old Sam Clemens. Later, laws named after this folk character mirrored the brutal but familiar stage stereotype. Mark Twain became an international ambassador for human rights, even as the boy in him never lost passion for "Daddy" Rice.

below: *Uncle Sam's Lodging-House.* Chromolithograph by Mayer Merkel & Ottmann, *Puck*, published by Keppler & Schwarzmann, centerfold, June 7, 1882.

Uncle Sam: "Look here, you, everybody else is quiet and peaceable, and you're all the time a-kicking up a row!" During the Gilded Age and beyond, waves of immigration transformed the nation. Chinese, Polish, Germans, and Italians were among the most numerous of newcomers. The Irish, derided in caricature as loud, drunken louts, were a generation ahead in creating communities and building strong and vocal political power bases in American cities and towns, most visibly in New York City, where Irish Democrats ran Tammany Hall for generations. Uncle Sam, whether he liked it or not, needed the Irish for their labor and votes, but here he's clearly exasperated with his tenant's behavior.

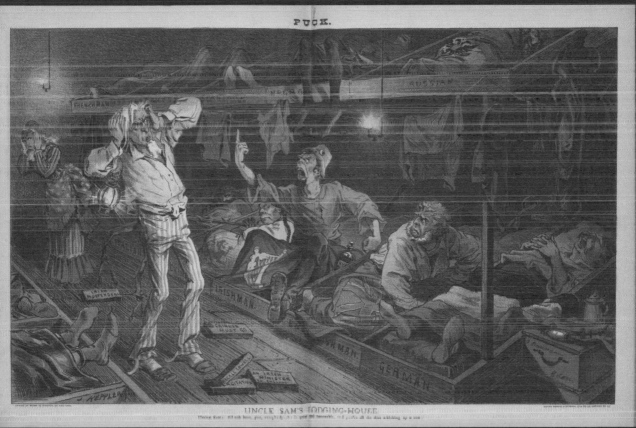

UNCLE SAM'S LODGING-HOUSE.

above: Cigar factory, Indianapolis Indiana. Photograph by Lewis Hine, August 1908.

left: Girls in packing room. Photograph by Lewis Hines S. W. Brown Mfg. Co., Evansville, Indiana, 1908.

American children spent their hard-earned pennies on dime novels featuring Mark Twain's tales. Documentarian Lewis Wickes Hine portrayed the ways they earned their wages, advancing workers' rights with his unprecedented portfolio of photographs for the National Child Labor Committee, founded in 1904.

Big business and bigger government were still in their infancy, with fewer rules and regulations to inhibit the national appetite for initiative, innovation, and investment. The country's borders were largely established, and the vast interior teemed with people inventing new products and new lives, building new towns and cities illuminated by electric lights, linked by rail, road, and river, connected to the larger world by post, telegraph, and, soon, telephone. The world was changing swiftly, with technology and opportunities there for the taking by bold politicians and businessmen, like Henry Huttleston Rogers of Standard Oil, who controlled their markets and protected their interests through financial and political maneuvering and manipulation. Pitfalls were many, however, and

Panic, as a Health Officer, Sweeping the Garbage out of Wall Street. Illustration by Frank Bellew, *The [New York] Daily Graphic,* Sept. 29, 1873.

The notion that financial panics might beneficially purge the economy is not new. Cartoonist Frank Bellew covered *The Daily Graphic's* front page with a gargantuan tramp bearing a huge broom, sweeping clean the city's financial sector during the 1873 financial crisis.

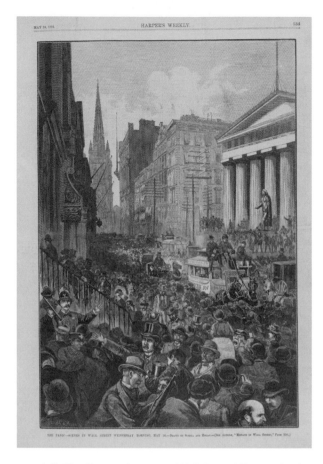

left: *The Panic—Scenes in Wall Street Wednesday Morning, May 14.* Engraving after Schell and Hogan, *Harper's Weekly,* May 24, 1884, p. 333.

right: *The Recent Panic—Scene in the New York Stock Exchange on the Morning of Friday, May 5th.* Engraving after Charles Broughton from sketches on the spot, published in *Frank Leslie's Illustrated Newspaper,* May 18, 1893, p. 322.

Americans rode an economic roller-coaster during the Gilded Age, as repeated downturns threatened the country's finances. From one crisis to the next, the scene remained much the same: citizens desperate for cash and answers converging on banks and brokerages.

periodic panics in 1873, 1884, and 1893 left even canny investors in ruin.

Despite financial catastrophes, labor strikes, and race riots, the economy grew, industry flourished, and the United States moved out from the diplomatic shadow of Great Britain and continental Europe, aggressively pursuing its own commercial, political, and military objectives around the globe. The government opened new markets to trade, wresting through war with Spain control of Cuba, Puerto

Rico, Guam, and the Philippines. Increasingly, U.S. warships and marines supported foreign policy where American interests were perceived to be at stake.

Into this volatile mix Mark Twain stirred his own combustible comments and opinions, such as: "The political and commercial morals of the United States are not merely food for laughter, they are an entire banquet. The human being is a curious and interesting invention." Eight years before the Columbian Exposition, *Adventures of*

BE SURE TO ASK FOR THE SUPPLEMENT.

ALFRED HENRY LEWIS, Editor.

THE VERDICT

VERDICT PUBLISHING COMPANY, BY O. H. P. BELMONT, President.

VOL. II. No. 4.   NEW YORK, (FOR WEEK ENDING) JULY 10, 1899.   PRICE, 10 CENTS—24 PAGES

TRUSTS—THE MAIN ISSUE.

Trusts—the Main Issue.
Photomechanical print after E. Noble, from statue by Frémiet. Published in *The Verdict,* July 10, 1899, cover.

Corporate trusts became the public face of robber barons following the Gilded Age, and the subject of intense public scrutiny and debate. Muckraking journalists and politicians sought to limit their monopolistic advantage, economic influence, and political power. Well before King Kong first appeared in movie theaters in 1933, the story of a great ape embracing a frightened young woman was familiar. French sculptor Emmanuel Frémiet used the motif in a study for a bronze, which the cartoonist for *The Verdict,* a short-lived comic journal, drew from to create this cartoon.

Huckleberry Finn had sparked controversy and was famously banned by the public library committee in Concord, Massachusetts, spiritual home of the Transcendentalists ("the veriest trash," the committee members said with a sniff). Twain would address the race question in *The Tragedy of Pudd'nhead Wilson* (1894); attack American imperialism in *Following the Equator* (1897), an account of his round-the-world lecture tour with Livy in 1895–96; and celebrate powerful women in *Joan of Arc* (1896). He challenged monarchies, autocracies, plutocracies, and leaders of the civilized world to free, educate, and employ their subjects. He railed against his Christian God (Twain was not, as some would have it, a nonbeliever) for fostering ignorance and suffering, creating havoc in the lives of humankind; he would take on religious zealots for their hypocrisy and intolerance. He wrote scenarios in which Satan lured good Christians into temptation and damnation, and where humans were made not of clay but mud, murky in their motives

According to Scripture:

"Blessed are the meek, for they shall inherit the earth."

As Practiced:

"I ought to have known that a meek little fellow like you could never make a successful salesman, anyway. We want a man who can go out and push and bluff his way to success, understand?"

According to Scripture:

"Agree with thine adversary quickly."

As Practiced:

R. R. ATTORNEY.—That old man who sued us ten years ago has appealed his case again, but I think we can tire him out.

According to Scripture:

"Blessed are the merciful, for they shall obtain mercy."

As Practiced:

"Aha, we've got Small, Green and Co. where we want 'em at last, and now, by thunder, we'll put the screws on 'em!"

According to Scripture:

"Take no thought of your life, what ye shall eat or what ye shall drink."

As Practiced.

THE SERMON ON THE MOUNT AS APPLI

According to Scripture:

"Lay not up for yourselves treasures upon earth."

As Practiced.

LAID UP FOR A RAINY DAY
BONDS
MORTGAGES
INTEREST
JEWELS
STOCKS
REAL ESTATE
AUTOMOBILES
HORSES
YACHTS
CLOTHES
HOUSES
LAND

Art Young

TO A COMMERCIAL AGE.

The Sermon on the Mount as Applied to a Commercial Age. Color lithograph by Art Young. New York: published by Keppler & Schwarzmann. *Puck,* centerfold, March 15, 1911.

Art Young led a generation of politically active cartoonists and illustrators. He famously drew himself snoring in the courtroom in 1918 while on trial for his life after the U.S. government indicted him for sedition, along with fellow contributors to the radical journal *The Masses.* In the event, Young and his colleagues were acquitted.

Montauk Point, Rough Riders, Col. Roosevelt. Cyanotype by Frances Benjamin Johnston, 1898.

Cyanide turns photographs blue, a beautiful if dangerous photographic process called "cyanotype." Frances Benjamin Johnston produced this dramatic 1898 equestrian portrait of Colonel Theodore Roosevelt training troops on Long Island in advance of the Spanish-American War.

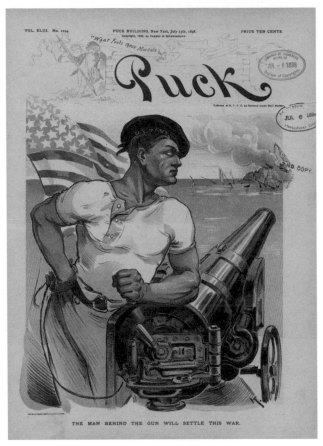

The Man Behind the Gun Will Settle This War. Chromolithograph by Udo Keppler, *Puck,* July 13, 1898.

The Spanish-American War began in April 1898 and was over by August. In its midst, *Puck* published this cartoon of a brawny American sailor, making it clear who the victor in the conflict would be.

and often befuddled by their fate. Twain became a cultural lightning rod; when he spoke, people listened.

The irony of Twain's rise to this lofty position is that for more than a decade, between 1891 and 1904, he and his family lived largely in Europe, moving from capital to capital: Vienna, Berlin, Paris, London. They visited healthful spas to lift Livy's spirits and soothe Sam's gout and rheumatism. Clemens returned regularly to New York, attending to business, pursuing contracts, and monitoring inventions and investments. He marketed a new Memory Builder game and worried over the fate of the Paige Compositor. He had never worked harder or been better known. He became an ambassador of American letters, an oracle of information, and an inspiration to his readers around the globe.

Facing bankruptcy, resulting largely from his money going down the black hole known as the Paige Compositor, however, presented a challenge. Although nearing sixty, and with Livy as frail as ever, Twain recognized that a world tour represented his best opportunity to recoup his losses and pay off his debts. He could make ready money on the road while continuing to publish.

He worked feverishly to overcome his own poor speculations. During a visit to New York in September 1893, he fortuitously befriended Henry Huttleston Rogers, an avid admirer and one of the country's richest and most powerful men of industry. (Ron Powers called him "Colonel Sellers without the buffoonery.") Rogers took Clemens under his financial wing, taking on power of attorney, working with creditors, and transferring the Twain intellectual copyrights to Livy to allow the family to benefit from his work as he paid down his debt. Like a Renaissance painter supported by the Medicis, Twain had found a benefactor and patron to help clear financial obstacles and smooth his creative path.

Having created his own financial disaster, Clemens suffered a fate with which his readers could empathize. They felt his pain and forgave his flaws, the least they could do for the creator of Tom Sawyer and Huck Finn. They knew of his tragic personal life as well, the sad losses of son Langdon and, later, daughters Susy and Jean, and Livy, in 1904. They were familiar with the terrors of his youth, as told in his own words: the early deaths of a brother and sister and the mayhem he had witnessed running through the streets of Hannibal. Mark Twain lived a public life, paying the price of privacy for the rewards of celebrity and public adulation; his reported money woes actually sparked offers of cash contributions from readers responding to his plight.

Henry Huttleston Rogers and Samuel L. Clemens. Photograph, Bain News Service, 1908.

Friend and patron Henry Huttleston Rogers took over Mark Twain's finances, loaned him money, and managed his personal and professional affairs. His advice and assistance sustained Twain and his family through hard financial times.

Beefsteak Dinner at Reisenweber's to Honor H. H. Rogers & Mark Twain. Photograph, Bain News Service, 1908.

By contrast with extravagant menus typical of nineteenth-century tribute dinners, this no-frills meal honoring Twain and his benefactor, Henry Rogers (in the rear, standing under the windows), offered just two courses: steak and beer.

Rogers's intercession bought Clemens time to pay his debts and restore his fortunes. To fund his comeback, he embarked in 1895 with Livy and Clara on a world lecture tour. As his opinions and reputation matured, Twain's self-described brand had gone global with sales of foreign and foreign-language editions. *Huckleberry Finn* and other books of his were published first in London before appearing in the United States, and were sent on to colonial booksellers in the Middle East, Hong Kong, and Australia. They reached readers in German and French colonies. In a fine irony, the imperialism he fought on principle in his writing made possible his international celebrity, spreading his fame from Europe to distant cities and far-flung outposts.

During the 1890s, Twain achieved statesmanlike status with a popular mandate and a tendency to speak his mind and tell the truth as he saw it. His books gave him uncommon credibility, his lectures visibility and press coverage. His comments on race, religion, and ethnicity in columns, sketches, and interviews stirred controversy and garnered publicity. Some considered him the nation's conscience, while others, like those members of the Concord, Massachusetts, public library committee, found his words distasteful.

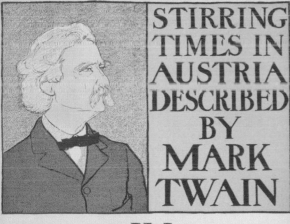

above: **Twain at police parade.** Bain News Service, 1908.

While Twain's writings attacked God and the church, clergymen were among his closest companions, and he mingled with prominent religious leaders. In New York City, he was the toast of the town, dubbed "the Belle of New York" for his celebrity, a welcome addition to high-profile parades and public events.

left: *Stirring Times in Austria Described by Mark Twain in* Harper's *March.* Color lithograph poster by Edward Penfield, designer. New York: Harper & Brothers, 1898.

While abroad in Europe during the 1890s, Twain continued to produce for the American market, writing new books and essays. He was a prolific contributor to popular magazines. Illustrator Edward Penfield, who drew this cover for *Harper's Monthly* magazine from March 1898, became celebrated for his bold new approach to fashion and design.

Twain as Huck Finn. Lithograph, unattributed, n.d.

Blending Twain with his characters is a long-running theme among cartoonists. This caricature was created for the Mark Twain Project at the University of California, Berkeley, where many of Twain's important papers, including his manuscripts for his autobiography, are housed.

Two reactions to the American publication of *Huckleberry Finn* in 1885 summed up the split. The *New York World,* in an unsigned review, described the book as the chronicles "of a wretchedly low, vulgar, and sneaking Southern country boy of forty years ago. He runs away from a drunken father in company with a runaway negro." The reviewer continued, "That such stuff could be considered humor is more than a pity"; the book was "a piece of careless hackwork in which a few good things are dropped amid a mass of rubbish." The critic acknowledged Twain's attempts to re-create regional dialects as a "pleasant literary exercise." The *San Francisco Chronicle,* in an unsigned review dated March 15,

1885, spoke for most of Twain's readers, however, crowing its acclaim:

> The Adventures of Huckleberry Finn *must be pronounced the most amusing book Mark Twain has written for years. It is a more minute and faithful picture of Southwestern manners and customs fifty years ago than was* Life on the Mississippi *while in regard to dialect it surpasses any of the author's previous stories in command of the half-dozen species of patois which passed for the English language in old Missouri. Mark Twain may be called the Edison of our literature. There is no limit to his inventive genius, and the best proof of its range and originality is found in this book, in which the reader's interest is so strongly enlisted in the fortunes of two boys and a runaway negro that he follows their adventures with keen curiosity, although his common sense tells him that the incidents are as absurd and fantastic as* The Arabian Nights. *Here is where the genius and the human nature of the author come in. Nothing else can explain such a tour de force as this, in which the most unlikely materials are transmuted into a work of literary art.*

Twain became an American Aesop, creating new fables with a modern twist. He cloaked his pronouncements in dialect and description, burying the bones of his opinions under fertile literary soil. In *Pudd'nhead Wilson,* he created another controversial novel filled with memorable characters, most prominently Roxana, a slave of mixed blood who switches babies to give her own child a life of freedom. There were few precedents in literature for Twain's portrait of his mulatto leading lady, light-skinned Roxy, damned by the fraction of black blood in her veins. While Huck and Jim paddle upriver toward dreams of Northern liberty, Roxy's haunting story of miscegenation and abduction takes readers southward, "down the river" toward a nightmare of captivity. Roxy's desperate act spawns a social monster: Her own child becomes a ruthless, spoiled tyrant while his white counterpart lives in submission as an obedient slave.

Twain embedded his tale of deception, betrayal, bloodlines, and racial relations within a larger context, hinging the plot on modern science and fingerprinting, a technique then being developed in criminal forensics. He opened each chapter with observations from "Pudd'nhead Wilson's Calendar," charming, funny, irreverent, and unforgettable aphorisms set amid relentless drama. Twain spent hours drafting potential entries for the calendar, saving the best for publication. Chapter 19 opens, "Few things are harder to put up with than the annoyance of a good example." To paraphrase Twain's famed preface to *Huckleberry Finn,* seeking a moral in "Pudd'nhead Wilson's Calendar" could be dangerous.

In Twain's own words, the book "changed itself from a farce to a tragedy" in adding a story of the extraordinarily close Italian twins, Luigi and Angelo Capello. Visiting the story's setting, Dawson's Landing, Missouri, they are subsumed by Roxana's tragic odyssey. In an early draft of the book, Twain portrayed them as conjoined twins. He was likely inspired by attending, while in Europe, an appearance by the Toccis, a famed set of conjoined Italian twins, and by his old obsession with the Chinese pair Eng and Chang, about whom he wrote a sketch in 1869. Mixing twins and switched identities had long been a popular motif in fairy tales and romances, as well as in Shakespeare, and Twain himself had already explored the subject in *The Prince and the Pauper* (1881). Here he found the device an effective vehicle for probing questions about character and identity, as well as revealing the virtues and flaws inherent in human nature. The book touched nerves with its twisted tale of misguided motherly devotion and the unredeemed cruelty of her only child, who is eventually sold down the river into the heart

Pudd'nhead Wilson. Photograph, cabinet card, 1896.

Actor Frank Mayo, who performed the title role in *Pudd'nhead Wilson* in 1896 (also writing the stage adaptation), first met Twain in Virginia City during the 1860s. Becoming the personification of Pudd'nhead, the fingerprint expert who solves a case of switched identities, he later wrote, "I seemed to become the hand and instrument of 'Mark Twain.'" Twain had finished the book in Florence, Italy, in 1893, but its roots lay in earlier drafts, the original titled *Those Extraordinary Twins.* Twain said he "had worked out Pudd'nhead a long time previous, and at Florence I had the opportunity to dress him up in language."

of slavery's darkness for his sins. The characters are bound and determined by their upbringing in a society of two worlds, one black and one white.

Pudd'nhead Wilson appeared thirty years after slavery was abolished, but African Americans still faced hostility and discrimination. In his *Devil's Dictionary,* published in 1906 under its original title,

above: *The Political Farce of 1876.*

right: *A Truce—Not a Compromise, but a Chance for High-Toned Gentlemen to Retire Gracefully from Their Very Civil Declarations of War.* Wood engraving by Thomas Nast, *Harper's Weekly,* February 17, 1877.

The 1876 presidential election pitted Democrat Samuel Tilden against Republican Rutherford B. Hayes in a referendum on the Civil War and Reconstruction. Tensions rose and violence flared, and the outcome proved too close to call; Tilden won the popular vote but lost out in the Electoral College following an apparent backdoor deal that included ending federal occupation of the South. "The Political Farce" poster names the men who crafted the compromise and, in the view of the artist, reversed the popular vote in four disputed states. Thomas Nast, famous for his incendiary Civil War cartoons detailing Southern atrocities, calls in his

The Cynic's Word Book, Ambrose Bierce included this entry:

> Negro, *n.* The *piece de resistance* in the American political problem. Representing him by the letter *n,* the Republicans begin to build their equation thus: "Let *n* = the white man." This, however, appears to give an unsatisfactory solution.

The Fifteenth Amendment faltered as Jim Crow laws and the Ku Klux Klan made life hard for blacks in the South, while Northern trade unions closed their doors to freed men of color. Race relations took a step back even as the country moved forward. In a cry of protest entitled "The United States of Lyncherdom" (written about 1901, published posthumously in 1923), Twain wrote, "Why does it [the heart] lift no hand or voice in protest? Only because it would be unpopular to do it, I think; each man is afraid of his neighbor's disapproval—a thing which, to the general run of the race, is more dreaded than wounds or death."

Twain showed little fear. He was a pioneer in race relations, bridging the social gap, welcome at both ends of the span. Growing up poor among slaves, he knew them as individuals and friends. Their stories and songs entertained and sustained him. He was comfortable and familiar in their midst, praying and singing. Longtime Clemens household maid Katy Leary recalled an account of Clemens joining in song with a black congregation:

Laying the Corner Stone at Vicksburg. Wood engraving by J. A. Wales, *Wild Oats,* Jan. 13, 1875, p. 1.

Vicksburg's rebirth from the ashes of the Civil War is celebrated sardonically by cartoonist James A. Wales. Virtually unremembered, Wales produced some of the era's most powerful graphic satire, first for *Wild Oats,* an early comic journal for men, and later for *The Judge,* an influential illustrated weekly guided by Republican Party politics.

A BOLD STROKE FOR FREEDOM.

A Bold Stroke for Freedom. Illustration, 1872.

An illustration from the 1872 history *The Underground Railroad*, by William Still, showing escaping slaves armed and ready to fight their white pursuers. Still, a black man who aided and abetted many fugitive slaves, wrote his book out of those experiences. It had an enormous impact on the consciousness of white Americans less than a decade after the end of the Civil War.

[Twain] just stood up with both his eyes shut and begun to sing soft like–just a faint sound–just as if there was a wind in the trees, she said, and he kept right on singing kind of low and sweet, and it was beautiful, and made your heart ache somehow. And he kept on singing and singing, and became kind of lost in it, and he was all lit up–his face was! 'Twas like something from another world, and she told me when he got through he just put his two hands up to his head, as though the sorrow of them Negroes was upon him, and begun to sing "Nobody Knows the Trouble I Sees. Nobody Knows But Jesus."

Booker T. Washington, a former slave and the leading civil rights advocate of his time, wrote of Huck's friend Jim, "One cannot fail to observe that in some way or other the author, without making any comment and without going out of his way, has somehow succeeded in making his readers feel a genuine respect for 'Jim,' in spite of the ignorance he displays. I cannot help feeling that in this character Mark Twain has, perhaps unconsciously, exhibited his sympathy and interest in the masses of the negro people."

Jews, too, felt the lash of bigotry in America from the Gilded Age into the next century. Twain defended the race, writing, in "Concerning the Jews" (1899), that "shabbiness and dishonesty are not the monopoly of any race or creed, but are merely human." He acknowledged that no race, no nationality, and no religion made people bad or stupid, or imposed moral will on individuals; rather, character was shaped by circumstance and surroundings, superstition and ignorance, as much as by education and enlightenment. For Twain, that is what defined expectations and formed personalities.

There was no question of his view toward women. He not only loved them but idealized them, surrounding himself with females young and old throughout his life. "Girls are charming creatures," he observed. "I shall have to be twice seventy years old before I change my mind as to that." He remained a devoted son, husband, and father, outgrowing his youthful chauvinism as Americans also began to embrace a larger political role for women. Suffragettes moved into the public arena after the Civil War expanded roles for women beyond

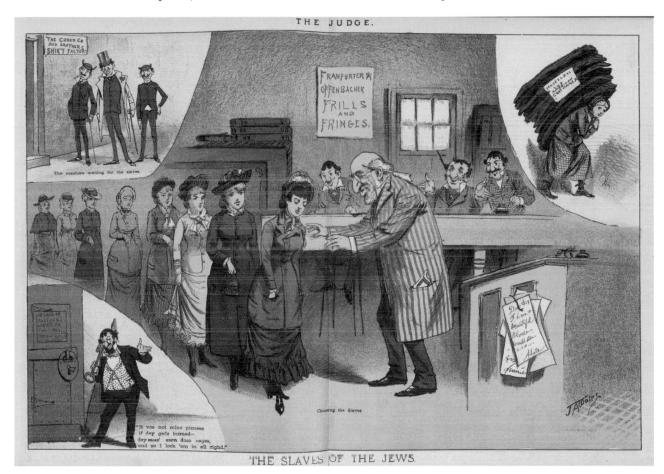

The Slaves of the Jews. Chromolithograph by J. A. Wales, *The Judge,* December 9, 1882.

James Wales and his publishers at *The Judge* pulled no punches with their social satire, depicting in this unfunny cartoon a lecherous, greedy Jewish sweatshop owner fondling and enslaving his female workers. With prejudice against the immigrant tidal wave came the inevitable anti-Semitism.

Mark Twain and Helen Keller. Photograph, 1909.

Mark Twain was captivated by blind and deaf Helen Keller (born 1880), helping her find support for her ongoing education. He sponsored other young students, black and white, providing a willing guide to young minds, mindful of his own incomplete, insufferable schooling.

textile mills, settlement houses, and city sweatshops. As a young man, shortly before he married Livy, Twain wrote,

> *I dearly want the women to be raised to the political altitude of the negro, the imported savage, and the pardoned thief, and allowed to vote. It is our last chance, I think.... I wish we might have a woman's party now, and see how that would work. I feel persuaded that in extending the suffrage to women this country could lose absolutely nothing and might gain a great deal.... We all know, even*

with our eyes shut upon Congress and our voters, that from the day that Adam ate of the apple and told on Eve down to the present day, man, in a moral fight, has pretty uniformly shown himself to be an arrant coward.

He met Helen Keller when she was just fourteen but nonetheless a prodigy. Mute, deaf, and blind, the young woman worked relentlessly with her teacher, Anne Sullivan, to overcome the obstacles her disabilities presented. He recalled their initial meeting, arranged by H. H. Rogers. She made a strong impression, Twain writing, "The wonderful child arrived now, with her about equally wonderful teacher, Miss Sullivan. The girl began to deliver happy ejaculations, in her broken speech. Without touching anything, and without seeing anything, of course, and without hearing anything, she seemed to quite well recognize the character of her surroundings. She said, "Oh, the books, the books, so many, many books. How lovely!"

Twain was completely smitten and the feeling became mutual. For a centennial tribute to Twain, published in 1935, she wrote of their first encounter through writer Laurence Hutton and subsequent visits to Twain's final home: "I met Mark Twain first at the home of Laurence Hutton when I was fourteen years old, and from that day until his death we were friends. I felt nearest to him during the few days I spent with him in the quiet of Stormfield. Whether we talked or sat by the fire or walked out under the snow-wreathed cedars surrounding the house, I caught unforgettable touch-pictures of his face that never laughed, but was full of tenderness whenever I read his lips."

Mark Twain's Joan of Arc. Color lithograph poster by Eugène Grassel. Harper & Brothers Publishers, 1894.

Joan of Arc was first serialized anonymously. "It is not in my usual vein," Twain said, teasing reporters, "I never deny authorship of anything good." He told one scribe, "Everything I have ever written...has had a serious philosophy or truth as its basis. I would not write a humorous work merely to be funny.... My *Joan of Arc,* published in 1892, was the first of the historical novels, and it was not a pretense of history; it was real history."

Twain passionately urged Rogers to find funding for her continuing education, which he did. "It won't *do* for America," he argued, "to allow this marvelous child to retire from her studies because of poverty–If she can go on with them she will make a fame that will endure in history for centuries." In 1906 she sent a letter to Twain, quoted in his *Autobiography,*

acknowledging his role as ambassador to the blind and explaining her own ambitions to educate and employ them: "You cannot bring the light to the vacant eyes; but you can give a helping hand to the sightless along their dark pilgrimage. You can teach them new skill. For work they once did with the aid of their eyes you can substitute work that they can do with their hands. They ask only opportunity, and opportunity is a torch in the darkness." Completely smitten by her "great heart" and "marvelous mind," he likened Keller to Joan of Arc, another transcendent teenager overcoming adversity.

In fall 1892, traveling through France with Livy and Susy, Twain passed the birthplace of fifteenth-century Christian martyr Joan of Arc, the young woman who achieved mythic status after she led French troops to victory over England, challenged king and church, and was burned at the stake during the Inquisition, in 1431. Her worst sin was communing directly with God, bypassing the priests. She claimed God and the saints spoke to her; she heard voices and had visions, and became a military and religious phenomenon. For Twain, she symbolized the best of Old World values–chastity, humility, godliness, confidence, courage, intelligence, and honesty–while opposing the worst elements of her time: an ungrateful king and a vengeful church. Garbed in white and fighting under Christ's banner for king and country, she was a shining vision of militant womanhood.

Twain was surrounded by bright, capable, and willful women, and Joan of Arc's story and its lessons were not lost on Livy and the girls. He wrote the book with Susy in mind; Ron Powers quotes her writing to her sister Clara, then in Berlin, that their father's latest book "promises to be his loveliest. The character of Joan is pure and perfect to a miraculous degree. Hearing the M.S. [manuscript] read aloud is an uplifting and revealing hour to us all. Many of Joan's words and sayings are historically correct and Papa cries when he reads them." When he read the passage describing Joan's death, Susy cried, too.

The work first appeared in serial form, under the title "Personal Recollections of Joan of Arc," in *Harper's* magazine, where it was presented as a translation of an account by a contemporary of the subject, the Sieur Louis de Conte. It was as if Twain wasn't quite sure how readers might respond. *Harper's* ran it anonymously, and Twain was not identified as the author when the book was first published, only adding his name to a later edition. He opened the book with wise words we might apply to Twain himself:

> To arrive at a just estimate of a renowned man's character one must judge it by the standards of his time, not ours. Judged by the standards of one century, the noblest characters of an earlier one lose much of their luster.... But the character of Joan of Arc is unique.... When we reflect that her century was the brutalest, the wickedest, the rottenest in history since the darkest ages, we are lost in wonder at the miracle of such a product from such a soil. The contrast between her and her century is the contrast between day and night. She was truthful when lying was the common speech of men; she was honest when honesty was become a lost virtue; she was a keeper of promises when the keeping of a promise was expected of no one; she gave her great mind to great thoughts and great purposes when other great minds wasted themselves upon pretty fancies or upon poor ambitions; she was modest, and fine, and delicate when to be loud and coarse might be said to be universal; she was full of pity when a merciless cruelty was the rule; she was steadfast when stability was unknown, and honorable in an age which had forgotten what honor was; she was a rock of convictions in a time when men believed in nothing and scoffed at all things; she was unfailingly true to an age that was false to the core.

The Maid of Orleans, woman, soldier, and, eventually, saint, was for Twain a medieval marvel and contemporary cautionary tale. Unlike with his famed preface to *Huckleberry Finn*, readers searching for a moral would not be banished, for there were lessons in her life and death. In Twain's rendering, Joan's heroism became universal. She brought light to darkness, assaulting the twin monoliths of entrenched royalty and established religion. He wrote,

> Joan of Arc, a mere child in years, ignorant, unlettered, a poor village girl unknown and without influence, found a great nation lying in chains, helpless and hopeless under an alien domination, its treasury bankrupt, its soldiers disheartened and dispersed, all spirit torpid, all courage dead in the hearts of the people through long years of foreign and domestic outrage and oppression, their King cowed, resigned to its fate, and preparing to fly the country; and she laid her hand upon this nation, this corpse, and it rose and followed her. She led it from victory to victory, she turned back the tide of the Hundred Years' War, she fatally crippled the English power, and died with the earned title of DELIVERER OF FRANCE, which she bears to this day.

Recounting the Loire campaign, Twain, in the guise of her aide, describes her uncanny ability to inspire fighting men with feminine grace:

> "She was clothed all in white armor save her head, and in her hand she carried a little battle-ax; and when she was ready to mount her great black horse he reared and plunged and would not let her. Then she said, 'Lead him to the cross.' This cross was in front of the church close by. So they led him there. Then she mounted, and he never budged, any more than if he had been tied.

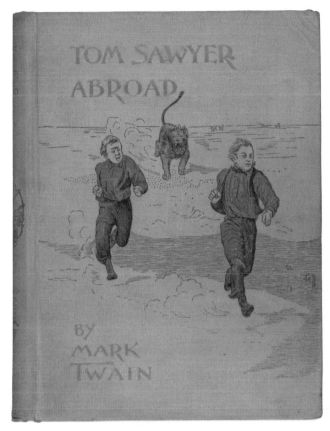

left: *Tom Sawyer Abroad.* Cover, 1894.

right: *Tom Sawyer Detective.* Cover illustration in *Harper's,* August, 1896.

It was one thing for Twain to spin off *Huckleberry Finn* from *The Adventures of Tom Sawyer.* But in the 1890s, two more Sawyer books (one first appearing in *Harper's*) were published. Although Twain professed to enjoy writing them, and as much as the public loved them, they have come to be regarded as lesser works, written more for Twain's bank account than out of any real artistic itch.

Then she turned toward the door of the church and said, in her soft womanly voice, 'You, priests and people of the Church, make processions and pray to God for us!' Then she spurred away, under her standard, with her little ax in her hand, crying 'Forward—march!'"

Joan's story encompassed the best and worst in human nature. It was that of a simple yet heroic woman of the people destroyed by larger forces arrayed against her, namely, church and state. Her life spoke to his own quest for moral and religious certainty, and to his admiration of spirited women.

In 1894, *Pudd'nhead Wilson* was published and distributed to booksellers by Harper & Brothers while the American Publishing Company, the Hartford firm that had produced Twain's early bestsellers, sold copies by subscription. Writing relentlessly to generate income, Clemens managed to complete two additional manuscripts promoting the Twain–Tom Sawyer brand. *Tom Sawyer Abroad* (1894) gave the plot reins to Tom Sawyer, while Huck narrated their Baron Munchausen/Jules Verne–type journey over oceans and continents to Africa and back in a hot-air balloon. *Tom Sawyer Detective* (1896) featured Tom and Huck in a high-octane response

Clemens with Kittens and the Little Girl's Family, Norwegian Shanty Town, Great Falls, Montana. Photograph by James Pond, July 31, 1895.

In the summer of 1895, Twain crossed the northern tier of states, speaking in towns great and small, here making an unscheduled appearance.

to the popular dime-novel genre of boy detectives, prototypes for the Hardy Boys. Although these titles never sold well, they pleased Twain, who was happy writing for young readers.

Unfortunately, Clemens still needed $100,000 to make up his deficits. Leaving his business affairs in the capable hands of Henry Rogers, he embarked with Livy and Clara on a one-year round-the-world tour. They left Elmira, where they summered at Quarry House, in mid-July 1895, and traveled across America and on to India, South Africa, and

Australia, among other destinations, Twain carrying his comic style and commentary across the globe.

The American tour was organized by Major James B. Pond, who had arranged Twain's triumphant Twins of Genius tour with George Washington Cable in 1884–85. An Australian agent booked the overseas events. They traveled first through the United States, beginning in Cleveland and heading west by boat and rail. In *Mark Twain: The Complete Interviews,* Major Pond declared Twain "[t]he most magnetic man I ever saw," on- or offstage. "I never

Twain and company, shipboard, Victoria, British Columbia. Photograph, 1895.

Twain's round the world tour in 1895–1896 used as its jumping-off point Victoria, British Columbia, where this shipboard photo was taken. James Pond, Twain's American tour manager; his wife, Martha; Olivia Twain; and their daughter Clara were all on deck.

saw anything like it. Everywhere we go crowds flock to hear him. Why, on the steamer coming up the lakes the passengers sat around him on the decks all day long in one grand laughing party. I don't believe that there is another man in America that attracts the people as he does."

In Minneapolis, a reviewer commented,

To the casual observer, as [Twain] lay there, running his fingers through his long, curly locks, now almost gray, he was anything but a humorist. On the contrary, he appeared to be a gentleman of great gravity, a statesman or a man of vast business interests. The dark blue eyes are as clear as crystal and the keenest of glances shoots from them whenever he speaks. Although his gravity might make one think him something else than a humorist, the kindly smile that lights up his face and the general appearance of happy abandon proclaim the author who is no bookworm. He talks easily and quietly yet with marked deliberation.

157

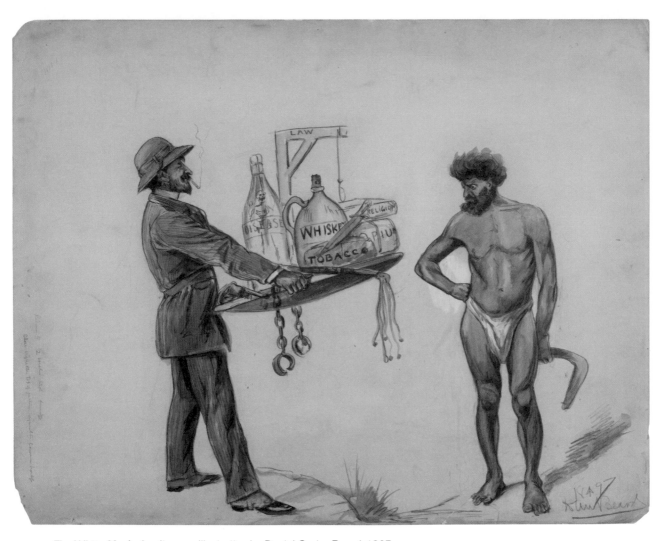

The White Man's Appliances. Illustration by Daniel Carter Beard, 1897.

Among Twain's concerns during his career was imperialism. Daniel Beard provided this pointed illustration for Twain's account of his round-the-world trip, *Following the Equator.*

Upon first setting eyes on him, an Australian critic voiced the same surprise at Twain's dour demeanor:

Mark Twain landed in Sydney today. He is spare and undersized, and there is nothing about him to fill the eye. Physically he is disappointing. Intellectually he is like many another humorist; he seems cast in a somewhat somber mould. "Life," he said looking from beneath his fair shaggy eyebrows, "is not at all a humorous thing. I have never found it a joke, and I am serious if nothing else. Man as a normal creature is serious now and then. One of us, say a scribbler like myself, pen in hand, may get a moment of enlightenment. A sudden thought may slip in, and then comes humor. That, however, is a contribution which the gods have sent his way, and which really is not of man. It comes from some place, the key of which he does not possess to open it at his will. Yes, life is serious, and man is the most serious part."

Twain's "kind eyes" and "humor" soon disarmed his interviewers and the public, his steamer cap a familiar accessory as he traveled from venue to venue. While still giving "the general appearance of happy abandon," Twain increasingly addressed serious subjects. In South Africa he encountered militant Boer farmers growing restive under a repressive British regime led by Cecil Rhodes. Native Africans were caught in the middle. Twain wrote caustically in *Following the Equator,*

> The great bulk of the savages must go. The white man wants their lands, and all must go excepting such percentage of them as he will need to do his work for him upon terms to be determined by himself. Since history has removed the element of guesswork from this matter and made it certainty, the humanest way of diminishing the black population should be adopted, not the old cruel ways of the past. Mr. Rhodes and his gang have been following the old ways. They are chartered to rob and slay, and they lawfully do it, but not in a compassionate and Christian spirit.

One Sunday afternoon in Africa a group of brightly costumed black women approached him across a square. The scene took him back to Hannibal and Quarles Farm: "I seemed among old, old friends; friends of fifty years, and I stopped and cordially greeted them. They broke into a good-fellowship laugh, flashing their white teeth upon me, and all answered at once. I did not understand a word they said. I was astonished; I was not dreaming that they would answer in anything but American." He had moved on in his attitude toward slavery, could not abide its legacy, yet thought with nostalgia of the servants of his youth, recalling their friendship, not their suffering.

India surpassed his preconceived notions, inspiring heartfelt passages admiring the country's vibrancy and its culture:

> This is indeed India! the land of dreams and romance, of fabulous wealth and fabulous poverty, of splendor and rags, of palaces and hovels, of famine and pestilence, of genii and giants and Aladdin lamps, of tigers and elephants, the cobra and the jungle, the country of a hundred nations and a hundred tongues, of a thousand religions and two million gods, cradle of the human race, birthplace of human speech, mother of history, grandmother of legend, great-grandmother of tradition, whose yesterdays bear date with the mouldering antiquities of the rest of the nations— the one sole country under the sun that is endowed with an imperishable interest for alien prince and alien peasant, for lettered and ignorant, wise and fool, rich and poor, bond and free, the one land that all men desire to see, and having seen once, by even a glimpse, would not give that glimpse for the shows of all the rest of the globe combined. Even now, after the lapse of a year, the delirium of those days in Bombay has not left me, and I hope never will.

Not every experience in India was endearing to him. He could barely stomach watching citizens washing themselves and their clothes in the filthy, sacred Ganges River, drinking mouthfuls of the muddy, murky water. It provoked revulsion and disgust in him.

On his travels, he noted harsh and cruel treatment of animals and spoke out on their behalf. He found the Australian dingo particularly admirable and condemned efforts to destroy the native creature, its very wildness and independence a boon to man and nature:

> In that garden I also saw the wild Australian dog—the dingo. He was a beautiful creature—shapely, graceful, a little wolfish in some of his aspects, but with a most friendly eye and sociable disposition. The dingo is not an importation; he was present

in great force when the whites first came to the continent. It may be that he is the oldest dog in the universe; his origin, his descent, the place where his ancestors first appeared, are as unknown and as untraceable as are the camel's. He is the most precious dog in the world, for he does not bark. But in an evil hour he got to raiding the sheep-runs to appease his hunger, and that sealed his doom. He is hunted, now, just as if he were a wolf. He has been sentenced to extermination, and the sentence will be carried out. This is all right, and not objectionable. The world was made for man—the white man.

Pudd'nhead Wilson addressed Twain's disdain for human behavior in his New Calendar: "Man Is the Only Animal That Blushes. Or Needs To." During the last two decades of his life, Twain transcended his humorist roots, speaking out forcefully and without equivocation on politics and social issues. In long-winded essays and short sound bites, he made his case for humane government and a humanist perspective. Pudd'nhead quipped, "It is by the goodness of God that in our country we have those three unspeakably precious things: freedom of speech, freedom of conscience, and the prudence never to practice either of them." Twain held on to his convictions in the face of mainstream movement away from his views. Pudd'nhead cautioned, "Don't part with your illusions. When they are gone you may still exist but you have ceased to live."

He maintained no illusions regarding America's growing jingoism. "Is it, perhaps, possible that there are two kinds of Civilization—one for home consumption and one for the heathen market?" Twain queried in his landmark 1901 anti-imperialism essay, "To the Person Sitting in Darkness." Should we not ask before we impose our own way of life on others? In his "salutation-speech from the Nineteenth Century to the Twentieth Century," which ran in the New York *Herald* on December 30,

1900, he angrily denounced military and religious aggression:

I bring you the stately matron named Christendom, returning bedraggled, besmirched, and dishonored, from pirate raids in Kiaochow, Manchuria, South Africa, and the Philippines, with her soul full of meanness, her pocket full of boodle, and her mouth full of pious hypocrisies. Give her soap and towel, but hide the looking glass.

He admonished Americans to look at themselves individually and judge their collective actions, asking,

Shall we? That is, shall we go on conferring our Civilization upon the peoples that sit in darkness, or shall we give those poor things a rest? Shall we bang right ahead in our old-time, loud, pious way, and commit the new century to the game; or shall we sober up and sit down and think it over first?...The Person Sitting in Darkness is almost sure to say: "There is something curious about this—curious and unaccountable. There must be two Americans; one that sets the captive free, and one that takes a once-captive's new freedom away from him, and picks a quarrel with him with nothing to found it on; then kills him to get his land."

Twain said and wrote all these things as Teddy Roosevelt was making his way up the political food chain, from New York police commissioner to colonel of the Rough Riders to vice president and finally president of the United States. Roosevelt carried a big diplomatic stick, intimidating nations with the threat of U.S. troops and warships. He also declared war on the country's huge new corporate trusts—sugar, oil, railroads, tobacco—following the lead of investigative muckrakers who were uncovering corruption and graft among businessmen and politicians. He instituted social reforms and protected the wilderness, all policies Twain could embrace.

Caricature of the church as death's head of "slavery," "superstition," and "ignorance" performing exorcism. Illustration by Daniel Carter Beard, 1891.

Beard's engraving for the first edition of *A Connecticut Yankee in King Arthur's Court* reveals how deeply Twain's skepticism about the church ran. Amazingly, as embittered as he became in his later years, the public continued to admire and love him and his work.

They did come to loggerheads over the issue of imperialism, however; to Twain, Teddy's bluster sounded like imperialist claptrap and bad policy. They saw America's place in the world differently–Roosevelt pushing American adventurism and Twain holding fast to a country that valued old traditions in company with new ventures. Twain gave a nod to technological advances while maintaining that the sovereignty of the human soul must be respected: "It is a fine thing to have them alongside each other–the sentiment that takes kindly to the swift lift and the electric wire, and the sentiment that preserves the old plough that turned your first sod, or where your explorers camped when they opened up your country...you generally find out that they are very precious when they are gone."

By August 1896, Twain, Livy, and Clara were in London. The tour had raked in about $25,000, which would go toward paying off his debt. It was an encouraging sum later augmented by sales of his account of the trip, *Following the Equator*. This happy development was offset by the saddest of news. While Sam, Livy, and Clara had toured the world, back in the States young Susy's health deteriorated. She made her way to Hartford and the old Twain house, now rented by family friends, and died there that month, with sister Jean at her side. In London, Mark Twain grieved apart, as Livy and Clara had sailed to America, too late to reach Susy's side. His family circle had suddenly become smaller.

CHAPTER 5

Twain's Circle

"I was seven years old when I came so near going to Heaven that time," recalled Mark Twain in his *Autobiography,* writing about one of his many childhood illnesses. "I do not know why I did not go; I was prepared." He claimed castor oil saved his life as his family gathered around to say good-bye: "I had begun to die, the family were grouped for the function; they were familiar with it, so was I. I had performed the star part so many times that I knew just what to do at each stage without rehearsal, although so young; and they–they had played the minor roles so often that they could do it asleep."

He later commented, "I have never enjoyed anything in my life anymore than I enjoyed dying that time." No doubt, he drew upon this memory for the sequence in *The Adventures of Tom Sawyer* in which Tom, thought to be drowned in the river, is given a funeral, which he sneaks into. Tom had previously imagined this scenario as a way of wallowing in childish self-pity: "Oh, they would miss me if I were gone, all right!"

Instead, he finds himself feeling pity for others, especially his strict Aunt Polly, who are genuinely grieving his death.

From his earliest years, which were marked by many ailments, Twain had a special relationship with death. It shaped his spiritual and religious life. His mother thought he'd never live through infancy and called him a miracle child. His early illnesses made him wonder at his

The offending illustration of Clemens in flames above his urn in *Life on the Mississippi.*

The first American edition of *Life on the Mississippi* (1883) included this provocative portrait of Twain in flames above an urn with his initials on it. In the text, he wrote, "As for me, I hope to be cremated. I made the remark to my pastor once, who said, with what he seemed to think was an impressive manner, 'I wouldn't worry about that, if I had your chances.'" Livy was not amused, finding the image distasteful; it was removed from future editions.

The Search for the Drowned: Tom and Huck Watching as Hannibal Sounds Mississippi for Their Bodies. Illustration in *The Adventures of Tom Sawyer.*

Twain was obsessed with his mortality much of his life, and even a relatively lighthearted work such as *Tom Sawyer* depicted a scene in which his young hero is thought to be swept under by the river, followed later by Tom's funeral, which he surreptitiously attends.

own existence, why he had been spared when others succumbed. "Nameless terrors" assailed him when the family embarked from his birthplace in Florida, Missouri, for their new home in Hannibal, somehow forgetting young Sammy for hours before sending an uncle back to retrieve him. "I was well frightened," he recalled in the *Autobiography,* "and I made all the noise I could, but no one was near and it did no good. I spent the afternoon in captivity and was not rescued till the gloaming had fallen and the place was live with ghosts." In 1845, aged ten, he tempted the devil to take him, purposefully visiting his stricken pal Will Bowen's bedside during a measles epidemic, contracting the disease and nearly killing himself.

He was marked by his family as a spiritual soul. Just before the death of their older sister Margaret, in 1839, his brother Orion watched in amazement as four-year-old sleepwalking Sammy appeared at her sickbed, a ghostly sign of her impending demise and his unearthly sensitivity. Young Sammy soaked in the beliefs of the slaves living with his family at the

Quarles farm. One of the slaves in particular, Uncle Dan'l, filled the impressionable youth with spiritual curiosity and supernatural dread. Aunt Hannah, an elderly slave living in a nearby cabin, inspired awe in the Clemens children, "for we believed she was upwards of a thousand years old and had talked with Moses.... She was superstitious like the other negroes; also, like them, she was deeply religious."

Twain wrote that in growing up, "All the negroes were friends of ours, and with those of our own age we were in effect comrades…and yet not comrades; color and condition interposed a subtle line which both parties were conscious of, and which rendered complete fusion impossible." Twain kept many black friends for life, professionally and personally. He responded to character, not color. In 1877, John T. Lewis, a neighboring tenant farmer, prevented a terrible carriage accident outside Quarry Farm, saving the lives of Livy's sister-in-law, her daughter, and a nursemaid. Twain and Lewis struck up a thirty-year friendship.

The superstitious fears of slaves and his mother's religious warnings attached to the real horrors Sam saw in his Hannibal youth: dead men lying in the street, corpses floating in the river, a man burned alive inside a fiery jail. When his younger brother Henry died in 1858 from burns suffered in a steamboat fire, Sam blamed himself; he had persuaded Henry to join him on the boat and then, before the accident, Sam got thrown off for arguing with the captain. He took responsibility as well for the death of his own son, Langdon, in 1872, from pneumonia brought on, Twain believed, by a wet, frigid carriage ride they shared one night. In time, death left only his daughter Clara, from whom he was at times estranged, to see him to his grave.

Death was a terrible equalizer in the nineteenth century, as cholera, dysentery, septicemia, other diseases, and infections ran unchecked, taking young and old, rich and poor. Swill milk, spoiled meat, and bad oysters poisoned consumers, and an untreated

Mark Twain and John T. Lewis. Photograph, ca. 1900.

In 1877, at Quarry Farm, the home of Livy's sister Susan Crane outside Elmira, New York, a runaway carriage threatened the lives of her brother's wife, their daughter, and nursemaid. John T. Lewis, an African American veteran of Gettysburg and tenant farmer on the Cranes' land, stopped the careening buggy and made a friend of Twain for life.

cold could wipe out a promising life. There were few effective treatments for Livy, who had a weak heart; Jean suffered epileptic fits, for which there was also no cure. Susy had no chance against the viral meningitis that claimed her life at twenty-four. Religion offered Twain scant comfort, and he became increasingly bitter as the family's losses mounted. No loving God would make humans suffer so; no reasonable deity desiring to create a being in His image could have produced such a flawed, fragile creature.

Family and friends were a buffer for Twain, keeping him engaged and distracting him from dark thoughts and a worried mind. He built concentric circles of support: family, friends, colleagues, and even rivals sustained his creative energy and fueled his art. At the core were his two families: his mother, Jane Clemens, his older brother Orion, and his older sister Pamela; and Livy and their three daughters. For Twain, family was both boon and bane, a source of love and exasperation.

Jane set high standards for young Sammy; she was his Aunt Polly. In the long run, her Christian piety and moral sense set a hook in Twain he would never manage to remove, despite his best efforts. Orion proved an itch Twain scratched to no effect. Sam inherited his mother's good humor and inventive mind; Orion took on their father's failed legacy of serious, fruitless activity, his life downwardly mobile after his brief whirl of influence in Nevada in the 1860s. Similarly, Livy's love and support could be tempered by her prim modesty, which served as both a brake on Twain's rambunctiousness and a source of frustration.

In the West, Twain added a circle of colleagues, taking on friendships with editors, writers, reporters, and humorists, including Joe Goodman, Dan De Quille, Bret Harte, Artemus Ward, and others. Back East, his growing literary reputation garnered the affection of William Dean Howells and exposed him to the country's literati, while friendships he made on the *Quaker City* excursion lifted him into a new social circle and the world of Olivia Langdon.

In Elmira, he became wealthy and, briefly, a part of that stratum of upstate New York society. At Nook Farm he joined an exclusive literary circle that included Harriet Beecher Stowe and Charles Dudley Warner. Joining James Redpath's Lyceum lecturing circuit brought him into contact with the region's leading intellectuals. He was a celebrity among celebrities: He knew and admired Thomas Nast, performed with humorists Josh Billings and Petroleum V. Nasby, and shared a stage for months with George Washington Cable.

Ironically, for a man of dubious faith, Twain embraced men of the cloth as the closest of friends. His marriage into the Langdon family introduced him into a circle of leading Congregationalist ministers, including Joseph Twichell, whom he met in Hartford, and the Reverends Thomas K. Beecher and his brother Henry Ward. These men were militant abolitionists; Twichell had served as a Union Army chaplain during the Civil War, while Henry Ward

Petroleum Vesuvius Nasby. Negative, glass, wet collodion, 1860–1875.

Petroleum Nasby (real name David Ross Locke) was a comic writer and lecturer who, like Sam Clemens, began working at an early age (ten) as a printer and drifted into journalism, in his native Ohio. He adopted his pseudonym on the eve of the Civil War as a means of writing in the voice of a racist, states' rights—loving, and supremely ignorant preacher. Twain admired his wit and in his *Autobiography* described their memorable first meeting at a Hartford lecture in 1868 or 1869.

Beecher supplied guns before the war to antislavery forces in Kansas. Twain and Twichell became lifelong great companions. During his years in Hartford they rambled frequently together for miles on foot, discussing the affairs of God and men.

Twichell and Twain were spectators at Henry Ward Beecher's sensational trial for adultery. The charges were filed by fellow preacher and apparent cuckold Theodore Tilton on behalf of his wife, Elizabeth. Despite the public scandal, a hung jury declined to convict Beecher. Clergymen like Joseph Twichell and the Reverend Henry Ward Beecher were close and frequent companions of Twain's; they countered his skepticism and debated his views. Their encounters were based in friendship, but Twain could also gleefully recount the time he handed out "Long Nines," his favorite foul, cheap cigar, effectively smoking and choking a room full of ministers right out of his house.

His happiest years were the first decade in Hartford, where life was good for the Clemens family. Beyond writing his best work during summers at Quarry Farm–including *Tom Sawyer*, *Huck Finn*, and *A Connecticut Yankee in King Arthur's Court*–he reveled in his home life, surrounded by people he

Testimony in the Great Beecher-Tilton Scandal Case Illustrated. Lithograph designed and drawn by James E. Cook, 1875.

In 1872, suffragette and presidential aspirant Victoria Woodhull accused Henry Ward Beecher, famed pastor of Brooklyn's Plymouth Church, of an illicit affair with a parishioner. The trial became a sensation, and Twain, a friend of the preacher, weighed in, musing, "[T]he general thought of the nation will gradually form itself into the verdict that there is some fire somewhere in all this smoke of scandal."

Twain and Susy in costume, Onteora Park, New York. Photograph, 1890.

Plays and charades occupied the Twain family and their friends during idyllic summers spent in New York State. Susy and Clara devised original dramas with parts for their father and guests. "Our children," Twain recalled in his *Autobiography,* "and the neighbors' children played well; easily, comfortably, naturally, and with high spirit. How was it that they were able to do this? It was because they had been in training all the time from their infancy."

cared for who cared for him. Livy and the girls sustained him, inspiring and informing his work. *The Prince and the Pauper* and *Joan of Arc,* in particular, show their influence. He was writing for them and about them; they were part of his creative process, even editing his new pages: "The children always helped their mother to edit my books in manuscript. She would sit on the porch at the [Quarry] farm and read aloud, with her pencil in her hand, and the children would keep an alert and suspicious eye upon her right along, for the belief was well grounded in them that whenever she came across a particularly satisfactory passage she would strike it out."

His last decade, 1900–1910, found him surrounded by well-wishers but suffering the ongoing pain

of watching his family circle dwindle. All of the Clemens women suffered physical or mental disabilities. Susy's death in 1896 formed dark clouds in her father's mind that only gathered with time. He lost Orion in 1897. In June 1904, after a prolonged illness, Livy succumbed to heart disease, in Florence, Italy. As Sam Clemens mourned his wife, daughter Clara visited sanitariums seeking relief from overwhelming grief. In late July, Jean, already afflicted by epileptic seizures, was severely injured in a horse-riding accident. Adding to Sam's woes, his older sister Pamela passed away at the end of August 1904.

He augmented his family circle as it tightened. Before Livy's death he hired Isabel Lyon as his confidential secretary in charge of his personal

Mark Twain and Dorothy Quick. Photograph, Bain News Service, 1907.

During Twain's shipboard return from England in 1907, eleven-year-old Dorothy Quick from New Jersey took the seventy-one-year-old author under her young wing. When questioned about their relationship by a reporter, Twain deferred to Dorothy, who "sat in his lap and leaned her head trustfully against his shoulder. 'You can tell them,' she consented, patting his cheek by way of encouragement."

Twain and Isabel Lyon. Photograph, 1908.

Isabel Lyon became Twain's close confidante and private secretary following Livy's death in 1904. Their relationship soured after Isabel, taking advantage of their relationship, insinuated herself in his financial affairs and ran afoul of Clara.

Twain playing billiards with Angelfish. Photograph, ca. 1907.

At Stormfield, inspired by the sea life he found during trips to Bermuda, Twain nurtured an "aquarium" of "Angelfish," young girls with whom he corresponded and invited to his home for billiards and tea parties. Clara finally found the presence of all of these surrogate grandchildren to be unseemly and dismissed them from the home.

affairs, a move he would later regret. For a few years after he turned seventy, in an apparent attempt to re-create the Hartford idyll he had enjoyed with his daughters, he stocked an "Aquarium" of young women he called "Angelfish" to brighten his afternoons of billiards, tea, and tobacco. Newspapers took note, illustrating their matter-of-fact coverage with photographs portraying the old author arm in arm with young girls. Clara eventually realized the

Mark Twain   Jan. 24/08

dangers and urged him to stop the get-togethers. The aging, increasingly vulnerable legend took a further hit before he died when he suspected that Isabel Lyon and a male accomplice had sought to gain control of the lucrative Twain estate. In the aftermath of Livy's death, he saw Lyon abusing his trust.

When he wasn't entertaining guests, out on the town socializing, or summering in Dublin, New Hampshire, or Bermuda, Mark Twain spent a great deal of his day in bed–a huge carved Italian affair he and Livy had purchased in Florence–puffing on his pipe or cigar, reading, writing essays and correspondence, greeting visitors, and dictating his life to his authorized biographer, Albert Bigelow Paine. William Dean Howells recalled: "Whenever he had been a few days with us, the whole house had to be aired, for he smoked all over it from breakfast to bedtime. He always went to bed with a cigar in his mouth, and sometimes, mindful of my fire insurance, I went up and took it away, still burning, after he had fallen asleep. I do not know how much a man might smoke and live, but apparently he smoked as much as a man could, for he smoked incessantly."

In his last decade, Twain entrusted Paine, also Thomas Nast's biographer, to write his authorized biography from Twain's dictation. This would be published only after Twain's death. Excerpts from Twain's *Autobiography*–strictly speaking, an aggregation of self-reflective writing and dictation produced over many years–began appearing serially in 1906. They appeared in newspapers all over the world, reviving international interest in Twain and his views. Americans, though growing in

Twain photo inscribed to Isabel Lyon. Photograph, 1908.

There has been much speculation about the nature of Twain's relationship with Lyon, but in the end, what mattered most was his distrust of her. Given how many times his instincts for finance had been off the mark and how vulnerable he felt in the wake of Livy's death, his suspicions may not have been rational, but they were understandable.

sophistication, still took Twain's homespun humor to heart. They bought his books and celebrated his legacy as a living legend, loved for his honesty and independence of mind. They forgave him his irritable, iconoclastic outbursts.

"If you pick up a starving dog and make him prosperous he will not bite you. This is the principal difference between a dog and man," wrote Twain in *Pudd'nhead Wilson*. Mark Twain sometimes bit the hand that fed him. He quarreled with colleagues and had rows with friends over slights perceived and real. He derided former drinking companion and collaborator Bret Harte as a "sham" after a falling-out: "Harte could not write dialect…when Harte tried to write frontier dialect it was idiocy. Do you mean to tell me there was any literary merit in an effort that contained five or six kinds of dialect? Why, he could have taken it to any miner and had it remedied; but he did not." Twain made nephew Charles Webster's life a living hell; after handing him the reins of their publishing company, he arguably hounded the younger man to an early grave over book contracts.

Even lifelong friends and family could feel his wrath, particularly Orion when he was asking for money or pursuing an ill-conceived speculation. His family found him moody and unpredictable. They expressed fear at his explosions, a reaction he revealed with surprise to William Dean Howells. He considered himself the most thoughtful of fathers, not recognizing the impact of his moods on family and friends. His friendship with Howells, the most staunch and influential of his supporters, also lapsed occasionally, as Clemens sulked or raged. "It was not ingratitude that he ever minded," recalled Howells, "it was treachery that really maddened him past forgiveness."

The last decade of Twain's life solidified his reputation and popularity, even as his writing grew more introverted, more concerned with mortality, the nature of evil, and the extreme folly of man, offering fewer amusing observations of human foibles. The books and stories he published were less accessible, less widely read, and yet no one begrudged him his standing even as he raged in his growing isolation.

With the loss of Susy and Livy, he gave vent to his suffering, lashing out against the God that betrayed him and civilization's appetite for war and social repression. His anti-imperialist tracts damned the American dream of conquest and its Christian underpinnings. Having mapped the civilized world for millions in his books, he turned inward, looking to penetrate and describe the human soul. He wrote about moral sense, conscience, and the role of circumstance and environment, asking existential questions and seeking insights into human nature. He had begun those explorations long before; they drove the plot in his short story "The Facts Concerning the Recent Carnival of Crime in Connecticut" (1876), in which our tormented and anonymous hero demolishes his nemesis–namely, his conscience–after it has been rendered submissive by his aunt Mary's incessant nagging:

With an exultant shout I sprang past my aunt, and in an instant I had my lifelong foe by the throat. After so many years of waiting and longing, he was mine at last. I tore him to shreds and fragments. I rent the fragments to bits. I cast the bleeding rubbish into the fire, and drew into my nostrils the grateful incense of my burnt-offering. At last, and forever, my Conscience was dead!

The devil and his minions made life miserable for well-meaning citizens in Twain's later work, as he punctured the bigotry, greed, ignorance, hypocrisy, pomposity, complacency, corruption, self-righteousness, and self-delusion that he felt characterized the era. His vitriol did have limits. Twain could and did censor himself, postponing publication of his more extreme efforts until after his death, while other strident essays went unsold. "The

Mysterious Stranger," an unfinished novella begun in Vienna in 1898 and completed and published in 1916 by his estate, introduced an underworldly angel in the guise of a youth:

"Why, naturally I look like a boy, for that is what I am. With us what you call time is a spacious thing; it takes a long stretch of it to grow an angel to full age." There was a question in my mind, and he turned to me and answered it, "I am sixteen thousand years old–counting as you count."

Lucifer's young disciple astonishes a trio of Austrian adolescents, including the Huck-like narrator, with his powers. They watch in horror as the stranger, called Satan, conjures a miniature castle built by Lilliputian laborers and then cruelly destroys the construction along with thousands of tiny lives, mocking God. When reproached for his cruelty, the stranger responds, "Oh, it is no matter; we can make plenty more."

Humans are flawed and damned, a dime a dozen and toys for the gods. Satan says, "Man is made of dirt. Man is a museum of diseases, a home of impurities; he comes to-day and is gone to-morrow; he begins as dirt and departs as stench."

Life is a parade of woe and warfare,

a mighty procession, an endless procession, raging, struggling, wallowing through seas of blood, smothered in battle-smoke through which the flags glinted and the red jets from the cannon darted; and always we heard the thunder of the guns and the cries of the dying. "And what does it amount to?" said Satan, with his evil chuckle. "Nothing at all. You gain nothing; you always come out where you went in."

No wonder "The Mysterious Stranger" came out only after Twain's death; it would have been considered too extreme for most fans of *Huckleberry*

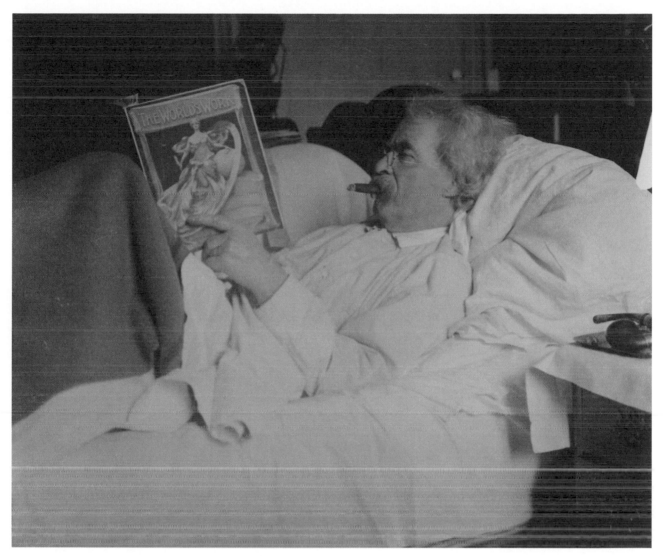

Twain in bed smoking. Photograph, 1906.

At his seventieth-birthday tribute dinner at Delmonico's in New York City in 1905, Twain remarked, "I smoke in bed until I have to go to sleep; I wake up in the night, sometimes once, sometimes twice, sometimes three times, and I never waste any of these opportunities to smoke."

Finn. In the story Twain returned to a familiar theme, humanity's duality:

> *Every man is a suffering-machine and a happiness-machine combined. The two functions work together harmoniously, with a fine and delicate precision, on the give-and-take principle. For every happiness turned out in the one department the other stands ready to modify it with a sorrow or a pain—maybe a dozen. . . . Sometimes for an hour's happiness a man's machinery makes him pay years of misery.*

A dozen miseries for every pleasure plagued Twain's later years; as he overcame one setback, another appeared. Finally, he tired of the contest. He described life as a game of dominoes. "You stand a row of bricks on end a few inches apart; you push a

"THE HOUSE WAS IN A ROARING HUMOR"

The House Was in a Roaring Humor. Illustration by Daniel Beard in "The Man That Corrupted Hadleyburg," 1900.

Twain's late satiric masterpiece, "The Man That Corrupted Hadleyburg," recounted a tale of greed and duplicity in a town renowned for the integrity of its citizens. Twain provided a pungent tagline: GO AND REFORM—OR, MARK MY WORDS—SOME DAY, FOR YOUR SINS YOU WILL DIE AND GO TO HELL OR HADLEYBURG—TRY AND MAKE IT THE FORMER.

brick, it knocks its neighbor over, the neighbor knocks over the next brick–and so on till all the row is prostrate. That is human life. A child's first act knocks over the initial brick, and the rest will follow inexorably." Our lives are ruled by circumstance and environment, while the twin engines of Christianity and civilization propel the ark, "leaving famine and death and desolation in their wake, and other signs of the progress of the human race."

His last works were not all grim. He found his funny bone again in "The Man That Corrupted Hadleyburg," a short story published in 1899. It was Twain's twist on Hebrews 13:2, which admonishes believers to welcome strangers, lest they be angels in disguise. Hadleyburg is an upright town brought low by greed and duplicity. A passing stranger seeking vengeance for ill-treatment concocts a scheme to corrupt the town with a bag of unclaimed gold. The citizens quickly drop their moral masks, embroiled in their own greed. Through a series of maneuvers choreographed by the vengeful outsider, the town's citizens reveal their individual avarice and collective greed, their righteous reputation rocked. "Going to Hell or Hadleyburg" became a familiar refrain.

Not everyone found Twain's relentless rants amusing; according to Howells, Livy preferred her sickbed to listening to her husband deride "the damned human race." Even as he raged, Twain was largely forgiven his excesses and trespasses; most of his readers remained mindful of his virtues and grateful for his contributions. At sixty-five, he was given a lavish party at New York's famed Lotos Club. His seventieth birthday in 1905 gave his close friends and legions of worldwide readers the opportunity to show their affection. His friends gathered at Delmonico's, the venerable New York City steakhouse, for a multicourse meal and multiple tributes. *Harper's Weekly* published a special pictorial supplement commemorating the event. Two years later, the popular magazine *Life* commented,

Age cannot wither, nor custom stale the heart and humor of Mark Twain; the cask grows old, but the wine grows riper in flavor and richer in bouquet with the years…by reaching the years of indiscretion—seventy—crowned with the success and still humorous…. He defies Time and mocks Convention. Cruelty and greed, wrong and oppression, humbug and pretension he has hated and harried, and he has laughed them out of court and lashed them into outer darkness…. Good-humor is rarer than good health, sanity than sense, serenity than sentiment; but this merry old philosopher who has punctuated life with laughter and sweetened it with honesty, goes down the shadowed road like a vagrant sunshine, blessed with health, sense and sentiment, and adorned with humor, sanity, and serenity.

Lotos Club dinner program, 1900.

In his old age, Twain seemed a constant center of celebration, as here at New York's famed Lotos Club, still very much in operation over 100 years later.

Following a darkened, diminishing path, Twain produced more late fireworks in *Eve's Diary*, an account of the Garden of Eden. The short story, published in book format in 1906 with provocative nude drawings of the first couple by illustrator Lester Ralph, Twain's first-person narrative of Eve's life sparked its share of outrage. In Puritan Massachusetts, where *The Adventures of Huckleberry Finn* had been banned twenty years earlier in

Mark Twain's 70TH Birthday
SOUVENIR OF ITS CELEBRATION

MARK TWAIN

SUPPLEMENT TO HARPER'S WEEKLY, December 23, 1905.

left: Seventieth-birthday bust of Twain.

below: Seventieth-birthday dinner photo with Twain and friends. Copyright by Harper & Brothers, 1905.

opposite: Seventieth-birthday program and menu. Designed by Daniel Carter Beard.

Twain was a legend in his own lifetime, immortalized in paintings, illustrations, and sculpture, as in honor of his seventieth birthday in 1905. A dinner at Delmonico's in New York was a grand and formal affair, as witnessed by this photograph of the guest of honor's table and the special program, designed by frequent Twain illustrator Daniel Beard. *Harper's* published a special issue devoted entirely to the evening.

Kate Douglas Riggs   Mark Twain   Rev. Joseph H. Twichell   Bliss Carman   Ruth McEnery Stuart   Henry Mills Alden   Henry H. Rogers
Mary E. Wilkins Freeman
Copyright, 1905, by HARPER & BROTHERS

Eve's Diary. Illustration by Lester Ralph, 1906.

Eve's Diary. Illustration by Lester Ralph, 1906.

Charlton, Massachusetts, banned Twain's fanciful *Eve's Diary* from its public library, offended by the nude drawings of Adam and Eve in the Garden of Eden. It echoed the banning of *Huckleberry Finn* from the Concord, Massachusetts, library twenty-one years earlier. Even in the last years of his life, Twain's work proved a lightning rod for controversy.

Concord, the literary witch hunt continued, this time in Charlton, whose public library board banned Twain's latest book.

Twain himself was unimpressed, and a bit disingenuous, claiming to prefer skin to clothes: "The whole episode has rather amused me. I have no feeling of vindictiveness over the stand of the librarians there–I am only amused. You see they did not object to my book; they objected to Lester Ralph's pictures. I wrote the book; I did not make the pictures. I admire the pictures, and I heartily approve

them, but I did not make them."

The book is itself lyrical and loving. Eve's bright intellect, strong curiosity, and self-awareness mark her as a modern, independent woman and role model. Livy lives in its pages as she becomes Eve to Twain's Adam:

It is not on account of his brightness that I love him–no, it is not that. He is not to blame for his brightness, such as it is, for he did not make it himself; he is as God made him, and that is sufficient. There was a wise purpose in it, THAT I know. In time it will develop, though I think it will not be sudden; and besides, there is no hurry; he is well enough just as he is.

It is not on account of his gracious and considerate ways and his delicacy that I love him. No, he has lacks in this regard, but he is well enough just so, and is improving.

Twain projects his own heartrending pain in Eve's last prayer:

But if one of us must go first, it is my prayer that it shall be I; for he is strong, I am weak, I am not so necessary to him as he is to me—life without him would not be life; how could I endure it? This prayer is also immortal, and will not cease

from being offered up while my race continues. I am the first wife; and in the last wife I shall be repeated.

Eve's epitaph declaimed Twain's love: WHERESOEVER SHE WAS, THERE WAS EDEN.

In the end, his circles were irreparably broken. He outlived most of his immediate family, many of his literary peers, even his rivals and enemies. The man he once described as "the best friend I have ever had and the best man I have ever known," corporate titan and personal financial savior Henry Rogers, died in 1909, one year before Twain's passing. From 1907 to 1910, Twain lived in a grand, outsized Italianate villa called Stormfield, after a favorite character in "Captain Stormfield's Visit to Heaven," a sketch

"STORMFIELD" REDDING, CONNECTICUT — MARK TWAIN'S LAST HOME
HOWELLS AND STOKES, ARCHITECTS.

"Stormfield." Photograph, 1910.

Twain breathed his last on April 21, 1910, at Stormfield, the villa in Redding, Connecticut, he built late in life. He named the house after the short story that had helped fund its construction, "Captain Stormfield's Visit to Heaven."

Twain in his white suit at Stormfield. Photograph, 1910.

With his health failing, in the last year of his life Mark Twain remained a powerful presence and an enduring symbol of American creativity.

first published in 1909. Built on a hill in Redding, Connecticut, it was designed by William Dean Howells's son. He played billiards, smoked constantly, and surrounded himself with cats and confidants.

Twain largely retired to his bed, having closed most of his life's chapters. In the wake of the Isabel Lyon dismissal, he leaned even more heavily on Albert Paine, who became his authorized biographer. They spent months with a stenographer spinning out his life story.

In 1902 he had taken his last trip to Hannibal and said a final good-bye to a town "full of Huck Finns, Tom Sawyers and Beckys," all wishing him well. In 1907, he returned triumphantly to England, where he first came to fame, to receive an honorary degree from Oxford University. His graduation gown and cap became a conceit, like the white serge suit he wore to such spectacular effect. He wore the academic outfit to Clara's wedding and other special occasions, at once representing his pleasure in the award and setting himself apart. Throughout his life, bold clothing choices defined him: the sealskin overcoat in Boston, the top hat and tails he affected on Broadway, the splendid white serge suit, and the Oxford cap and gown all made strong statements. Twain wore his heart on his sleeve and revealed his character in his clothes. "Honest," he said, "I can't get over the abomination of the American clothes. The garments the average man wears are a fright; but I have reached that age of discretion which gives to years the right of individuality in dress. I wear my white serge not as clothes. No, it's my uniform." He employed his image to great effect, as if on stage at all times. Appearing before a congressional committee on copyright protection, he made an impression on an observer: "Nothing could have been more dramatic than the gesture with which he flung off his long loose overcoat, and stood forth in white from his feet to the crown of his silvery head."

By his nature theatrical, Twain, clad in white, was an avenging angel, a force of nature, a strong, independent spirit guiding mankind by trial and error. His stories of love, loss, identity, and humanity remain among the most moral and moralizing in American literature. Featuring flawed characters and dubious scenarios, they teach unlikely lessons of honesty, resilience, courage and compassion, tolerance

Twain with Howells and others. Photograph, 1907.

At a luncheon for old friend William Dean Howells at Lakewood, New Jersey, in 1907, Twain posed with (from left) Howells; George Harvey, president of Harper & Brothers; H. M. Alden, editor of *Harper's* magazine for fifty years; and David A. Munro and M. W. Hazeltine, both of the *North American Review*, America's oldest literary magazine, published since 1815. The ginger-haired wild boy of Hannibal, the cocky riverboat pilot, the failed prospector and spinner of western folk tales, and the satirist of the high and the mighty was now a member in good standing of the establishment.

and understanding. He had lived his life publicly, becoming one of the world's most revered writers. Clemens's death at home in April 1910 released his haunted soul and an international outpouring of appreciation for the man Howells called our "Lincoln of Literature." The nation lost a brave heart and a strong voice. Mark Twain celebrated the best in American character and acknowledged the worst, using fiction to remind his readers that, being human, they are capable of both.

✤ 1835 ✤

Halley's Comet passes through the sky; its closest pass to Earth is on November 16.

Born this year: Andrew Carnegie and Belgian King Leopold II, subject of Twain's *King Leopold's Soliloquy.*

President Andrew Jackson pays off the national debt, continues to move Native Americans off their lands, and survives the first presidential assassination attempt.

A new Seminole war against whites in Florida Territory sees blacks fight alongside Native Americans in opposition to U.S. forces.

Anti-abolition riots break out in major cities across the Northeast.

The army of the Republic of Texas captures San Antonio, and the Texas Declaration of Independence is written in Goliad, Texas.

Alexis de Tocqueville publishes *Democracy in America.* Hans Christian Andersen publishes *Fairy Tales.*

P. T. Barnum begins a career in show business by exhibiting an infirm slave woman whom he claims to have been George Washington's nurse and over 160 years old.

Camp-meeting. Lithograph by Alexander Rider, ca. 1829.

✤ 1836 ✤

Born this year: Bret Harte, collaborator with Twain on *Ah Sin,* and Thomas B. Aldrich, author of *The Story of a Bad Boy* (1870), said to have laid the groundwork for *Tom Sawyer.*

Martin Van Buren, first president born as a U.S. citizen, is elected to the presidency. A crash in the economy immediately following his election earns him the nickname "Martin Van Ruin."

The Republic of Texas wins independence from Mexico and legalizes slavery. Free blacks and mulattoes are forbidden from entering the state.

U.S. missionary Marcus Whitman takes his wife, Narcissa, and Eliza Spalding to the Pacific Northwest. They are the first white women to cross the continent.

Arkansas, a slave state, is admitted to the Union as the twenty-fifth state.

Faced with a deluge of abolitionist petitions, the U.S. House of Representatives adopts a "gag rule" under which abolitionist materials are automatically tabled.

The Erie Canal, completed in 1825, is widened and deepened for barge traffic.

The Colt six-shooter revolver is patented by inventor Samuel Colt.

Ralph Waldo Emerson publishes "Nature." Charles Dickens publishes *Sketches by Boz* and *Pickwick Papers.*

✤ 1837 ✤

Born this year: Grover Cleveland, J. Pierpont Morgan, Sitting Bull, and evangelist Dwight L. Moody.

President Jackson recognizes the Republic of Texas on his last day in office, March 3, after approval by Congress.

Congress increases Supreme Court membership from seven justices to nine.

Michigan, a free state, is admitted to the Union as the twenty-sixth state.

Mississippi River Steamboat. Chromolithograph, Heliotype Printing Co., ca. 1895.

Blacks in Pennsylvania and Mississippi lose the right to vote. In New York, they petition for continued voting rights.

E. P. Lovejoy, editor of an abolitionist paper, is murdered by a mob in Alton, Illinois.

Gag rule becomes law to suppress debate on the slavery issue.

Seminole leader Osceola is tricked into coming out of the Florida Everglades under a flag of truce and is arrested.

His braves are defeated, and most of his tribe will be exterminated over the next few years.

Queen Victoria begins an almost sixty-four-year reign over the British Empire.

Horace Mann begins universal public education reforms in Massachusetts.

Charles Dickens publishes *Oliver Twist* and *The Posthumous Papers of the Pickwick Club.*

Nathaniel Hawthorne publishes *Twice-Told Tales*.

The New York and Harlem Railroad reaches Harlem with its horse cars and develops the world's first steam tram.

Economic depression begins in the United States and then in Britain. The sudden reduction of land speculators makes more U.S. farmland available for real farmers.

Samuel F. B. Morse gives a public demonstration of his magnetic telegraph and files for a U.S. patent.

✢ 1838 ✢

Born this year: John Muir and Victoria Woodhull, American feminist and leader in the women's suffrage movement.

The Underground Railroad, organized by U.S. abolitionists, transports southern slaves to freedom in Canada.

A Philadelphia proslavery mob burns down Pennsylvania Hall in an effort to thwart antislavery meetings May 17.

Hooping Crane. Color engraving by R. Havell after drawing by John J. Audubon.

The first transatlantic crossing by steamships is completed as two British steamers, the S.S. *Sirius* and the S.S. *Great Western,* arrive at New York.

Charles Dickens publishes *Nicholas Nickleby.* He also serializes *Oliver Twist, or the Parish Boy's Progress.*

Edgar Allan Poe publishes his only novel, *The Narrative of Arthur Gordon Pym.*

✢ 1839 ✢

Born this year: John D. Rockefeller and Henry George, American economist in whose newspaper, *The Standard,* Twain published "Archimedes" in 1889 under the name "Twark Main."

Hannibal, Missouri, is incorporated as a town.

Some 10,000 Mormons, driven from Missouri, settle in the Illinois town on the Mississippi called Commerce and rename it Nauvoo; it is the largest city in the state.

OSCEOLA of Florida. Lithograph by George Catlin, ca. 1838.

Steamboat Wharf, Washington, D.C. Illustration by Augustus Köllner, 1839.

Abolitionists form a national party called the Liberty Party, in Albany, New York.

Africans aboard the Spanish slave ship *Amistad* lead a mutiny; when the ship lands off the coast of Long Island, the slaves plea for freedom in court.

Theodore D. Weld publishes antislavery pamphlet "American Slavery, as It Is: Testimony of a Thousand Witnesses," an influence on Harriet Beecher Stowe's *Uncle Tom's Cabin.*

Charles Goodyear discovers the process of "vulcanization," making possible the commercial use of rubber.

Lowell Institute is founded by John Lowell Jr. in Boston to provide free lectures by eminent scholars.

⁜ 1840 ⁜

William Henry Harrison, the Whig Party candidate, wins presidential election.

The World's Anti-Slavery Convention opens in London, but Boston abolitionist William Lloyd Garrison refuses to attend, protesting its exclusion of women.

In Texas, slaves are barred from carrying weapons without written permission.

South Carolina enacts a "Black Code," under which slaves are denied basic rights, including the right to produce food, earn money, and learn to read.

James Fenimore Cooper publishes *The Pathfinder.*

Richard Henry Dana Jr. publishes *Two Years Before the Mast.*

Improvements to Cyrus McCormick's reaper will begin to reduce the number of hours that farmers spend in their fields.

Charles Darwin begins to develop his theory of evolution.

More than two hundred steamboats work the Mississippi, double the number in the mid-1820s. New Orleans is the fourth largest city in America and will soon overtake New York in volume of shipping, as more than half the nation's exports move out of New Orleans.

U.S. canals cover 3,300 miles, and the nation has 2,816 miles of railroad in operation.

During this decade Connecticut, Massachusetts, and Pennsylvania pass laws limiting the hours of employment of minors in textile factories.

⁜ 1841 ⁜

Born this year: Oliver Wendell Holmes Jr. and Sir Henry Morton Stanley, Welsh journalist and explorer of Africa.

President William Henry Harrison is inaugurated March 4 and dies April 4. John Tyler assumes full presidential duties, earning the nickname "His Accidency."

The Whigs expel Tyler from their party, and his cabinet resigns, except Secretary of State Daniel Webster. The Whigs and Tyler do agree to the "Log Cabin" bill, which enables a settler to claim 160 acres of land before it is offered publicly for sale and later pay $1.25 an acre for it, provided that a house has been built on the land and it is under cultivation. Before this bill, U.S. lands west

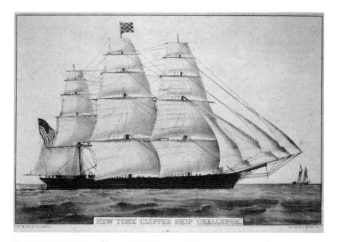

New York Clipper Ship Challenge. Lithograph by N. Currier (firm), 1835–1856.

of Wisconsin not offered for sale had 30,000 to 50,000 settlers on them.

The U.S. Supreme Court declares freedom for the Africans from the slave ship *Amistad*.

Texas citizens are allowed to apprehend runaway slaves and turn them in for return to their owners or to be sold at auction.

The first university degrees are granted to women in America.

Ralph Waldo Emerson publishes *Essays*.

James Fenimore Cooper publishes *The Deerslayer*, the principal subject of Twain's "Fenimore Cooper's Literary Offenses."

Charles Dickens publishes *Barnaby Rudge: A Tale of the Riots of 'Eighty* and *The Old Curiosity Shop*.

Edgar Allan Poe publishes "The Murders in the Rue Morgue," the world's first detective story.

Punch magazine begins publication in London.

Horace Greeley, 30, launches the *New York Tribune*.

Volney B. Palmer starts the first advertising agency in Philadelphia.

The first emigrant train bound for the Pacific is guided through northwestern Montana Territory by Irish American trapper and Indian trader Thomas Fitzpatrick.

John Augustus Sutter purchases California's Fort Ross from the Russian colonists who established it in 1811.

James Braid, a Scottish surgeon, discovers hypnosis, a practice that will figure into Twain's "The Arrival of the Mesmerist" and "How to Tell a Story."

P. T. Barnum opens the American Museum, an exhibition of freaks and oddities in New York City.

✢ 1842 ✢

Born this year: William James and Ambrose Bierce.

The Oregon Trail mapped by U.S. Army lieutenant John Charles Frémont, 29, will take thousands of emigrants westward. Frémont then begins four-year exploration of the Rocky Mountains.

The Quaker Giant and Giantess as Exhibited at Barnum's American Museum, New York. Print, 1849.

The U.S. Supreme Court, in *Prigg v. Pennsylvania,* upholds the constitutionality of most of the Fugitive Slave Act (1793), and the Court also rules that state personal liberty laws make unconstitutional demands on slave owners. Further, the federal government is held responsible for enforcement of the Fugitive Slave Act; previously, the responsibility had been that of the states.

The Georgia legislature declares that its free blacks will never be recognized as citizens.

Congressman Joshua R. Giddings from Ohio resigns his seat after being censured by the House for introducing antislavery resolutions, but Giddings is reelected and is back in his seat eight weeks later.

Henry Wadsworth Longfellow publishes *Poems on Slavery*.

Charles Dickens publishes *American Notes for General Circulation* after a reading tour in New York during which he finds Broadway swarming with untended pigs.

Edgar Allan Poe publishes "The Masque of the Red Death."

The first U.S. wire suspension bridge opens to span the Schuylkill River near Philadelphia.

Air-conditioning and mechanical refrigeration are pioneered by Florida physician John Gorrie.

✢ 1843 ✢

Born this year: Henry James.

John James Audubon travels up the Missouri River to Fort Union at the mouth of the Yellowstone River to sketch wild animals for his projected *Quadrupeds of North America.*

Hawaiian independence gains recognition November 28 from Britain and France in the Anglo-Franco Proclamation.

Ulysses S. Grant graduates from West Point.

Dorothea Lynde Dix reveals to the Massachusetts legislature inhumane treatment of mental patients.

Charles Dickens publishes *A Christmas Carol.*

The Virginia Minstrels give the first full-scale minstrel show in New York City.

Congress appropriates $30,000 to enable Samuel F. B. Morse to build an experimental telegraph line between Washington, DC, and Baltimore.

Charles Thurber pioneers the typewriter and patents a hand-printing "chirographer" with a cylinder that moves horizontally and contains a device for letter spacing.

✢ 1844 ✢

Born this year: Sarah Bernhardt, George W. Cable, and Friedrich Nietzsche.

Joseph Smith, Mormon leader and prophet, is murdered in Illinois.

U.S. Democrats nominate the first "dark horse" presidential candidate, James Knox Polk, with the slogan "Reoccupation of Oregon, reannexation of Texas." Polk wins election with 170 electoral votes to Henry Clay's 105.

Connecticut passes a personal liberty law. North Carolina denies citizenship to free blacks. Oregon prohibits slavery.

Karl Marx writes: "Religion is the sigh of the oppressed creature, the heart of a heartless world, and the soul of soulless conditions. It is the opium of the people," in his *Contribution to the Critique of Hegel's Philosophy of Right.*

Charles Dickens publishes *The Life and Adventures of Martin Chuzzlewit.*

Alexandre Dumas publishes *The Count of Monte Cristo.*

Samuel F. B. Morse transmits the first telegraph message, "What hath God wrought" (the words, from Numbers 23:23, were selected by Annie Ellsworth, the daughter of Morse's friend the governor of Connecticut) from the U.S. Capitol to Alfred L. Vail, of the B&O Railroad, in Baltimore.

The Methodist Episcopal Church splits into northern and southern conferences after Georgia bishop James O. Andrews refuses to give up his slaves on pain of losing his bishopric.

E. Z. C. Judson begins publishing *Ned Buntline's Own* magazine in Cincinnati.

P. T. Barnum presents a morality play about the evils of drink, William H. Smith's *The Drunkard; or, The Fallen Saved,* in Philadelphia, New York, and other cities.

✢ 1845 ✢

J. J. Hooper, a humorist who influenced Twain, publishes *Some Adventures of Captain Simon Suggs.*

British engineer William M'Naught develops compound steam engine.

A hydroelectric machine perfected by English inventor William Armstrong, 35, produces frictional electricity by means of escaping steam. Armstrong patents the "hydraulic crane."

New Bedford, Massachusetts, reaches the height of its whaling trade.

Florida joins the Union as the twenty-seventh state.

Texas is annexed to the United States over Mexican objections. It joins the Union as a slave state.

The United States claims the Oregon Territory "by the right of our manifest destiny to overspread and possess the whole of the continent." U.S. and British diplomats renew

Birds-eye view of the Camp of the Army of Occupation, Commanded by Genl. Taylor, near Corpus Christi, Texas, (from the North) Oct. 1845. Tinted lithograph after Charles Parsons, 1847.

the 49th parallel as the boundary line between Oregon and British territory.

Woman in the Nineteenth Century by feminist Margaret Fuller is published.

The Condition of the Working Class in England by Friedrich Engels reveals the exploitation of labor by capital.

"Report of the Exploring Expedition to the Rocky Mountains in the Year 1842, and To Oregon and North California in the Years 1843–44," by John C. Frémont, who proceeds to California on a third congressionally funded expedition with Kit Carson serving as guide.

Alexandre Dumas publishes *The Count of Monte Cristo.*

Edgar Allan Poe publishes *The Raven and Other Poems.*

Potato famines that kill 2.5 million from Ireland to Moscow accelerate emigration to America.

✣ 1846 ✣

Born this year: William F. "Buffalo Bill" Cody.

The Donner party is stranded crossing the Sierra Nevada.

Missouri removes restraints on interstate slave trade.

The Mexican War, precipitated by President Polk, begins.

Negotiations with Mexico for New Mexico fail.

Samuel Colt receives an order for revolvers as the Mexican War produces a shortage of firearms.

California's Bear Flag Revolt begins June 14 as settlers of Sacramento Valley proclaim a republic independent of Mexico and raise a flag bearing a black bear and a star at Sonoma.

An Oregon Treaty signed with Britain gives territory south of the 49th parallel to the United States, overriding cries of "54° 40' or Fight." Britain receives land north of the parallel on the mainland and Vancouver Island.

Iowa becomes the twenty-ninth state.

In response to the widespread potato famine, Americans raise $1 million and send relief ships, but the aid programs are mismanaged and at least half a million die of starvation and hunger-related typhus.

Britain and America will both benefit in the next fifteen years from the lowering and suspension of tariffs.

Brigham Young leads the Mormons from Nauvoo, Illinois, westward.

John Greenleaf Whittier's *Voices of Freedom* is published.

California's first newspaper begins publication in Monterey.

The Smithsonian Institution in Washington, DC, is founded.

The rotary "lightning press," patented by New York printing press manufacturer Richard Hoe, can run 10,000 sheets per hour, a rate far faster than that of traditional flatbed presses.

Born this year: Thomas A. Edison, Jesse James, Bram Stoker, and Alexander Graham Bell.

Missouri charters the Hannibal-to-St. Joseph railroad.

Escaped slave Frederick Douglass begins publication, in Rochester, New York, of an abolitionist newspaper, *The North Star.*

Liberia is proclaimed an independent republic, the first African colony to gain independence.

Nearly 15,000 Mormons led across the mountains by Brigham Young enter Salt Lake Valley in Mexican Territory. Young founds Salt Lake City.

A wagon route from Santa Fe to San Diego is opened by some 400 men of the Mormon Battalion under Lieutenant Colonel Philip St. George Cooke.

U.S. forces capture Mexico City.

Attack on Chapultepec, Sept. 13th 1847—Mexicans Routed with Great Loss, Colored lithograph by E. B. & E. C. Kellogg 1847 or 1848.

Karl Marx publishes *The Communist Manifesto.*

H. W. Longfellow publishes *Evangeline.*

Charlotte Brontë publishes *Jane Eyre.*

Emily Brontë publishes *Wuthering Heights.*

Oliver Wendell Holmes becomes dean of the Harvard Medical School.

The New York State Commissioners of Emigration begin to keep accurate records for the first time. Between now and 1860 some 2.5 million immigrants will enter the United States through the Port of New York and more than a million of these will be Irish.

The seagoing junk *Kee Ying* brings the first Chinese immigrants to New York.

✤ 1848 ✤

Born this year: Joel Chandler Harris and Belle Starr.

With the January 24 discovery of gold in northern California, the gold rush begins.

San Francisco loses three-fourths of its population in four months as men hurry to strike it rich in the goldfields.

The Pacific Mail Steamship Company is incorporated to employ a route across the Isthmus of Panama for California-bound gold seekers.

The Treaty of Guadalupe Hidalgo ends the Mexican War.

Zachary Taylor, Whig and Mexican War hero, is elected president.

Antislavery groups organize the Free Soil Party, a group opposed to the westward expansion of slavery and a forerunner of the Republican Party.

Connecticut law prohibits slavery by law.

South Carolina removes restrictions on interstate slave trade.

A child labor law to restrict the age of workers is enacted March 28 by the Pennsylvania legislature.

The first Woman's Rights Convention is held at Seneca Falls, New York, under the leadership of Elizabeth Cady Stanton and Lucretia Coffin Mott.

Wisconsin is admitted to the Union as the thirtieth state.

Zachary Taylor campaign poster. Colored woodcut by Thomas W. Strong, 1848.

Hawaii annexed by the United States as a territory.

Irrigation in U.S. agriculture is introduced by the Mormons, who begin plowing the shores of the Great Salt Lake.

G. N. Christy, of the Christy Minstrels, sings Stephen Collins Foster's "Oh! Susanna!" The song will remain in the repertoire of every minstrel show and will be sung by gold seekers en route to California.

The *Pioneer,* the Chicago and Galena Railroad's first locomotive to reach Chicago, inaugurates the city's career as transportation hub of the country.

✤ 1849 ✤

Born this year: Sarah Orne Jewett.

Edgar Allan Poe dies.

The Pacific Railroad is chartered in Missouri.

The Know-Nothings, a nativist political party, is formed.

Lucretia (Coffin) Mott, 1793–1880. Engraving by J. C. Buttre after Broadbenz & Philips, n.d.

The first ship of gold seekers lands in San Francisco. A rush of forty-niners causes California's population to jump in the next seven years from 15,000 to nearly 300,000 as the goldfields yield $450 million in precious metal.

Basque shepherds from Argentina and Uruguay flock by the hundreds to California in quest of gold. Many will later become sheepherders on the western range.

A cholera epidemic spread by gold rush emigrants crossing the Texas Panhandle wipes out the leadership of the Comanche tribe.

Railroad construction begins across the Isthmus of Panama to facilitate passage to California.

The Wheeling Suspension Railroad bridge is completed across the Ohio River at Wheeling and is the world's largest bridge, spanning more than 1,000 feet.

President Zachary Taylor creates the U.S. Department of the Interior.

Maryland slave Harriet Tubman escapes to the North and begins a career as "conductor" on the Underground Railroad. Tubman will make nineteen trips back to the South to free more than three hundred slaves, including her aging parents.

Virginia passes a law permitting the emancipation of any slave by will or deed.

Kentucky removes restraints on interstate slave trade.

The first licensed American female medical doctor, Elizabeth Blackwell, graduates at the head of her class at Geneva Medical College in Syracuse, NY.

Temperance reformer Amelia Bloomer begins American women's dress reform by promoting "bloomers" in her magazine *The Lily*.

Henry David Thoreau publishes "Civil Disobedience" and *A Week on the Concord and Merrimack Rivers*.

Harriet Tubman. Photograph by H. B. Lindsley, 1860–1875.

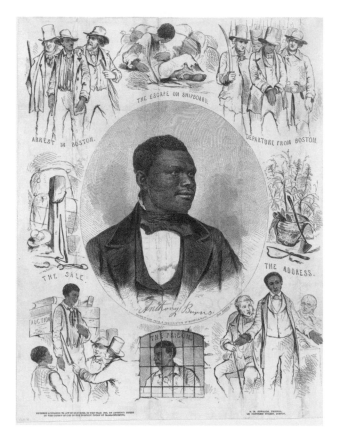

Anthony Burns, Fugitive Slave. Engraving by John Andrews, 1855.

Francis Parkman publishes *The California and Oregon Trail.*

Charles Ellet Jr. publishes *Physical Geography of the Mississippi Valley.*

Charles Dickens publishes *David Copperfield.*

✢ 1850 ✢

Born this year: Robert Louis Stevenson, Edward Bellamy, and Samuel Gompers.

President Zachary Taylor dies of typhus after sixteen months in office. He is succeeded by his vice president, Millard Fillmore.

The Compromise of 1850, introduced by U.S. senator Henry Clay, contains resolutions designed to reduce the growing polarity between North and South. California is admitted to the Union as a free state. Territorial governments are set up in the rest of the territory acquired from Mexico, with no congressional stipulation as to slavery in the territory, Texas is to give up her claim to part of the New Mexico Territory in return for federal assumption of the Texas state debt, slavery is to be abolished in the District of Columbia, and a stronger fugitive slave law is to be enacted.

Maryland removes restraints on interstate slave trade.

Virginia demands that emancipated slaves leave the state within a year and prohibits the legislature from freeing any slave.

The first National Women's Rights Convention is held in Worcester, Massachusetts.

Nathaniel Hawthorne publishes *The Scarlet Letter.*

Stephen Foster writes "Camptown Races."

Harper's New Monthly magazine begins publication.

U.S. railroad trackage reaches 9,000 miles, up from a little more than 3,000 in 1840. Canal mileage reaches 3,600, up from 3,000 in 1840.

The U.S. South has 1.8 million black slaves, 2.1 million whites.

✢ 1851 ✢

Born this year: Kate Chopin.

Solar eclipse over United States July 8.

Cholera epidemic strikes Hannibal in June.

Ballarat strike induces the Australian gold rush.

The U.S. Treasury turns out nearly four million $1 gold pieces. Congress votes to establish a mint in San Francisco. Minting of 3-cent silver coins is authorized to reduce the demand for large copper pennies.

The Fugitive Slave Act is defied by a mob of Boston blacks who rescue a fugitive from jail. President Fillmore calls upon Massachusetts citizens and officials to execute the law, but another fugitive slave is rescued by abolitionists at Syracuse, New York.

Sojourner Truth gives her "Ain't I a Woman?" speech at the Women's Convention in Akron, Ohio.

In the Oneida Community, men and women are treated equally and all classes of work are viewed as equally

Effects of the Fugitive-Slave-Law. Lithograph by Theodor Kaufmann, 1850.

honorable. Three hundred converts live in communal buildings made of timber from the community's farms.

The Erie Railroad becomes the first line linking New York City with the Great Lakes, providing competition for the Erie Canal.

Some 4,400 miles of railway track will be laid this year and next between the Atlantic seaboard and the Mississippi.

Herman Melville publishes *Moby-Dick*.

Nathaniel Hawthorne publishes *The House of Seven Gables*.

The first edition of the *New York Times* is published.

Fire destroys much of the Library of Congress on Christmas Eve. Two-thirds of the collection acquired from Thomas Jefferson in 1814 is destroyed along with thousands of other volumes. Congress appropriates $100,000 to buy new books and create a more fireproof room for the library.

Prohibition of "intoxicating liquors" begins in Maine.

The Young Men's Christian Association (YMCA) opens its first American offices at Boston and Montreal.

I. M. Singer patents his sewing machine.

A wet collodion process for developing photographic images is published by English architect Scott Archer, whose process will be used in photomechanical houses for nearly a century.

The United States will receive 2.5 million immigrants in this decade, up from 1.7 million in the 1840s.

✤ 1852 ✤

Franklin Pierce of New Hampshire is elected the 14th president of the U.S.

The governor of California calls for land grants to encourage the continued immigration of Chinese from "one of the most worthy of our newly adopted citizens." Close to 50,000 Chinese have defied China's death-penalty law against emigration to make their way to California's goldfields.

Massachusetts becomes first state to pass compulsory school attendance.

Brigham Young publicly endorses the doctrine of polygamy.

The Whig Party begins to dissolve over the slavery issue.

Harriet Beecher Stowe publishes *Uncle Tom's Cabin; or, Life Among the Lowly*. A dramatic adaptation of the book by George L. Aiken will have enormous success in the North.

Uncle Tom's Cabin: Little Eva Converting Topsy (detail). Lithograph, 1880.

193

Steamboat, possibly U.S.S. *Susquehanna,* Shown During Commodore Perry's Landing at Kurihama, Japan, July 8, 1853. Drawing, watercolor, 1855.

The first U.S. World's Fair opens in New York City's Crystal Palace Exhibition, modeled after London's (1851).

The Crimean War begins. Twain would later visit the main cities in which the war was waged and write about it in "The War Prayer" and "Luck."

Charles Dickens publishes *Bleak House.*

The Mount Vernon Hotel opens at Cape May, New Jersey, the world's first hotel with private baths.

A yellow fever epidemic at New Orleans kills 7,848.

Less than half of Americans are engaged in agriculture, down from 83 percent in 1820.

Boston, Massachusetts, public library founded.

Prohibition laws are adopted by Massachusetts, Vermont, and Louisiana.

David Livingstone explores the Zambezi River.

Herbert Spencer publishes "The Development Hypothesis," popularizing the use of the term "evolution"; ten years later, after reading Darwin's *On the Origin of Species,* he would first use the expression "survival of the fittest."

✤ 1853 ✤

Commodore Matthew C. Perry of the U.S. Navy arrives at Edo in July with the first formal bid for U.S. relations with Japan.

The Gadsden Purchase treaty signed with Mexico permits the United States to annex a tract of land south of the Gila River. Mexico receives $10 million under terms of the treaty.

The Molly Maguires, a secret society of miners, is formed in Pennsylvania.

Nook Farm, on whose land Mark Twain will build his family home, is founded in Hartford, Connecticut.

New York City is authorized by the state legislature to purchase land for a public park, which will become Central Park.

✤ 1854 ✤

Born this year: George Eastman and Oscar Wilde.

The Kansas-Nebraska Act creates the territories of Kansas and Nebraska and allows popular sovereignty to decide the slave status of each. It also repeals the antislavery clause of the Missouri Compromise.

In Kansas, a series of violent conflicts occurs in the new territory between supporters and opponents of slavery.

Scots-American journalist James Redpath of Horace Greeley's *New York Tribune* travels through the slave states urging slaves to run away.

The Republican Party is organized at Ripon, Wisconsin, by former Whigs and disaffected Democrats opposed to the extension of slavery.

The Treaty of Kanagawa, signed by Commodore Matthew C. Perry, opens the Japanese ports of Hakodate and Shimoda to U.S. trade, the first time in centuries Japan is opened to foreign relations.

Alfred, Lloyd Tennyson publishes "The Charge of the Light Brigade."

Henry David Thoreau publishes *Walden; or, Life in the Woods.*

Charles Dickens publishes *Hard Times.*

A paper mill at Roger's Ford in Chester County, Pennsylvania, procures paper from wood pulp at low cost.

The first railroad bridge across the Mississippi River connects Rock Island, Illinois, and Davenport, Iowa.

✤ 1855 ✤

Interstate slave trade restrictions are eased in Georgia and Tennessee.

The Elmira Female College is founded in Elmira, New York. It is the first U.S. institution to grant baccalaureate academic degrees to women.

The Young Women's Christian Association (YWCA) is founded in London to improve the condition of young

Walt Whitman, half-length portrait. Photographic print on card mount (albumen), 1873.

working women by providing good food and a decent place to live for those living away from home.

The Sault Ste. Marie ("Soo") River Ship Canal opens to link Lake Huron and Lake Superior and to make the Great Lakes a huge inland waterway navigable by large ships.

A telegraph line to link the Mississippi River with the Pacific Coast is authorized by Congress.

Prohibition laws are adopted by Delaware, Indiana, Iowa, Michigan, New Hampshire, New York, and the Nebraska Territory.

Frederick Douglass publishes *My Bondage and My Freedom.*

Thomas Bulfinch publishes *Age of Fable.*

Henry Wadsworth Longfellow publishes *The Song of Hiawatha.*

Walt Whitman publishes *Leaves of Grass.*

Frederick Douglass. Photograph, ca. 1850–1860.

✤ 1856 ✤

Born this year: George Bernard Shaw.

Pennsylvania Democrat James Buchanan is elected president.

Lawrence, Kansas, is sacked by proslavery "border ruffians" who have poured into the territory to pack the territorial legislature of "bleeding Kansas" with men who will vote to make Kansas a slave state.

The Wabash and Erie Canal opens after twenty-four years of construction that has been marked by loss of life to cholera and loss of money to embezzlers.

At the encouragement of his new employer, Adams Express Company, Andrew Carnegie makes his first investment and buys 10 shares of company stock at $50 per share.

The whaling ship *E. L. B. Jennings* returns to New Bedford, Massachusetts, with 2,500 barrels of sperm oil after a four-and-a-half-year voyage.

✤ 1857 ✤

Born this year: Joseph Conrad and William Howard Taft.

A nationwide celebration marks the linking by rail of New York and St. Louis.

The Dred Scott decision, announced by Supreme Court Chief Justice Roger B. Taney, denies citizenship to all slaves, ex-slaves, and descendants of slaves and denies Congress the right to prohibit slavery in the territories.

New Hampshire declares that African descent is no reason to deny citizenship. Richmond, Virginia, passes a restrictive slave code that bars self-hiring by slaves and bars blacks from areas of the city, specifying street etiquette.

The Mountain Meadows Massacre, in which Mormons and their allies kill 135 California-bound emigrants, occurs in Utah Territory.

Financial panic strikes New York, and a severe depression ensues in which 4,932 business firms will fail after a period of speculation and overexpansion.

The *Atlantic Monthly* begins publication at Boston under the editorship of James Russell Lowell.

Thomas Hughes publishes *Tom Brown's School Days.*

Gustave Flaubert publishes *Madame Bovary.*

The first Currier & Ives prints are issued as New York lithographer Nathaniel Currier takes into partnership his bookkeeper James Merritt Ives.

U.S. landscape architect Frederick Law Olmsted is appointed superintendent of New York's Central Park.

Harper's Weekly begins publication.

✤ 1858 ✤

Born this year: Theodore Roosevelt.

Minnesota enters the Union as the thirty-second state.

"A house divided against itself cannot stand," says former Illinois congressman Abraham Lincoln, in accepting nomination as the Republican candidate for U.S. senator. "I believe this government cannot endure permanently half slave and half free." Lincoln is defeated by Democrat Stephen A. Douglas.

Vermont's personal liberty law forbids denying citizenship to those of African descent.

U.S. senator from South Carolina James Henry Hammond says, in a speech taunting critics of the South: "You dare not make war upon cotton! No power on earth dares to make war upon it. Cotton is king."

New York's Central Park opens to the public.

Josiah Henson, a Maryland-born slave, publishes *Truth Stranger Than Fiction.*

Henry Wadsworth Longfellow publishes *The Courtship of Miles Standish.*

Charles Darwin publishes *On the Origin of Species.*

The pen name Artemus Ward appears in the Cleveland *Plain Dealer.* Charles Farrar Browne uses the name to sign a letter to the editor allegedly written by a shrewd showman with Yankee dialect and unconventional spelling.

The Overland Mail stage reaches St. Louis after 23 days and 4 hours on its first trip from San Francisco. A westbound stage that has left at the same time reaches San Francisco after 24 days, 20 hours, 35 minutes.

The first practical sleeping car is perfected by George Mortimer Pullman.

✛ 1859 ✛

Born this year: Arthur Conan Doyle.

A railroad links Hannibal to St. Joseph, Missouri.

Oregon enters the Union as the thirty-third state.

Work begins on the Suez Canal.

The gold strike of 1858 in the Colorado Rockies of Kansas Territory brings 100,000 prospectors determined to reach "Pike's Peak or bust."

Harriet E. Wilson, author of *Our Nig*, becomes the first female African American novelist published in the United States.

The Fugitive Slave Act of 1850 is upheld by the Supreme Court March 7 in *Ableman v. Booth*.

The last slave ship to bring slaves into the United States lands in Mobile Bay, Alabama.

A group of whites and blacks, led by John Brown, conducts an unsuccessful raid on Harper's Ferry, Virginia, in an attempt to undermine slavery in the South October 16.

Charles Dickens publishes *A Tale of Two Cities*.

Nevada's Comstock Lode, which Twain would write about in the West, is discovered.

Jim Bridger makes his first visit to the Yellowstone area.

Daniel Emmett writes the song "Dixie" as the finale to a minstrel show.

Charles Blondin walks a 1,100-foot-long tightrope across Niagara Falls on June 30.

✛ 1860 ✛

Born this year: Anton Chekhov and James Barrie.

Abraham Lincoln is elected the sixteenth president. On December 20, South Carolina issues an Ordinance of Secession in protest of the election.

The slave population reaches nearly four million; the ratio of free to enslaved Americans is approximately 7:1.

Elizabeth Cady Stanton urges women's suffrage in an address to a joint session of the New York State Legislature.

Portrait of John Brown. Photograph by Martin M. Lawrence, May 1859.

More than 1,000 steamboats ply the Mississippi, up from 400-odd in 1840.

John D. Rockefeller enters the oil business at age twenty. He persuades richer men to build more refineries for petroleum, which he foresees as a major energy source.

An internal combustion engine is patented in Paris by Belgian inventor Jean Étienne Lenoir.

Ann S. W. Stephens publishes the first dime novel, *Malaeska: The Indian Wife of the White Hunter*.

George Eliot publishes *The Mill on the Floss*.

William Wilkie Collins publishes *The Woman in White* (serialized beginning in 1859), a pioneer detective novel.

Popular songs include "Old Black Joe" by Stephen Collins Foster.

The first Pony Express riders leave St. Joseph, Missouri, April 3 and deliver mail to Sacramento, California, ten days later.

The first Flag of Independence raised in the South, by the Citizens of Savannah, Ga. November 8th 1860.
Lithograph by H. R. Howell, 1860.

The newspaper where Twain will work in the West, the *Territorial Enterprise,* moves to Virginia City, Nevada, in November.

✛ 1861 ✛

Born this year: E. W. Kemble, illustrator of several Twain books.

Kansas becomes the thirty-fourth state January 29.

The U.S. Congress refuses to hear proposals from Virginia's peace conference as it tries to preserve the Union.

Five Southern states, Mississippi, Florida, Alabama, Georgia, and Louisiana, following South Carolina's example, secede from the Union in January, followed by Texas. Virginia, Arkansas, Tennessee, and North Carolina secede later in the year.

The Union of Confederate States is formed February 18, with Jefferson Davis as president. It will call for more than 100,000 military volunteers March 6.

Nevada and Dakota become territories March 2. James W. Nye begins organizing the Nevada Territory July 8.

The Civil War begins when Confederate forces open fire on Fort Sumter, on an island in the Charleston, South

Carolina, harbor. In the first major battle of the conflict, the first Battle of Bull Run, Virginia, 847 are killed and 2,706 wounded.

The Union warship *Pawnee* sinks after striking a floating mine on the Potomac River on July 10.

President Abraham Lincoln proclaims martial law in Missouri on August 30.

Incidents in the Life of a Slave Girl, by Harriet Jacobs, is one of the first published autobiographies of an African American woman.

Seventy-five thousand blacks volunteering for the U.S. Army are rejected.

When slaves take refuge with Northern forces, they are treated as "contraband of war." The First Confiscation Act declares all property in support of rebellion, including slaves, subject to capture.

Charles Dickens publishes *Great Expectations.*

George Eliot publishes *Silas Marner.*

Antislavery satirist David Ross Locke publishes the Petroleum V. Nasby letters.

The *Territorial Enterprise* begins daily publication September 24.

✢ 1862 ✢

Born this year: Edith Wharton and O. Henry (William S. Porter).

Jefferson Davis is inaugurated as president of the Confederacy.

First federal income tax introduced to finance the Civil War.

Union forces capture Fort Henry, Roanoke Island, Fort Donelson, Jacksonville, and New Orleans; they are defeated at the Second Battle of Bull Run and Fredericksburg.

The Battle of Antietam in Maryland ends in a standoff but will become known as the bloodiest day of the Civil War.

Slavery is abolished in the District of Columbia by act of Congress and is abolished in the U.S. territories.

Lincoln writes in a letter to Horace Greeley, of the *New York Tribune,* "My paramount object in this struggle *is*

The Siege of Yorktown, Va. Stereograph by James F. Gibson, May 1862.

President Lincoln, Writing the Proclamation of Freedom, January 1st, 1863. Chromolithograph after David Gilmour Blythe, 1863.

to save the Union, and is *not* either to save or to destroy slavery. If I could save the Union without freeing *any* slave I would do it; and if I could save it by freeing *all* the slaves I would do it; and if I could save it by freeing some and leaving others alone I would also do that."

The president is authorized, through the Militia Act, to use all citizens, black included, in the military and the navy; enemy-owned slaves are awarded freedom in return for service to the Union.

The Emancipation Proclamation, issued September 22, declares that "persons held as slaves" within areas "in rebellion against the United States" on and after January 1, 1863, are free. Lincoln makes it clear that emancipation is a war aim.

Virginia, followed by other Southern states, authorizes the use of slaves to perform military labor.

South Carolina slaves take over a Confederate ship, the USS *Planter,* and deliver it to the Union army at Fort Sumter.

Admitted to the Union on condition that it is a free state, West Virginia drafts a constitution that calls for gradual emancipation.

Utah bans slavery.

Oberlin College in Ohio awards a degree to Mary Jane Patterson, the first black woman to graduate from an American college.

Congressional resolutions offer monetary incentives to states for emancipating slaves.

The Homestead Act declares that any U.S. citizen, or any alien intending to become a citizen, may have 160 acres of western lands free provided that certain improvements are made to the land and that the owner live on the tract for five years. There is a surge in U.S. immigration as a result.

Congress promises up to 100 million acres of federal lands to the Union Pacific, the Central Pacific, and other railroads that will connect the Mississippi with the Gulf and Pacific coasts.

The Morrill Land-Grant Act provides funds to start U.S. land-grant colleges for the scientific education of farmers and mechanics.

Artemus Ward (C. F. Browne) publishes *Artemus Ward: His Book.*

Victor Hugo publishes *Les Misérables.*

✣ 1863 ✣

Born this year: William Randolph Hearst.

Kit Carson and federal troops that have been joined by a band of Ute reach Fort Defiance in Arizona Territory and begin to resettle Navajo and Apache on a reservation at Fort Sumner in New Mexico.

West Virginia becomes a state.

The Shoshone, Washoe, and others in the Nevada Territory are awarded more than twenty-three million acres of land in the Nevada Territory through the Ruby Valley Treaty, but most of it is desert. The treaty gives whites the right to build railroads across the Indian lands.

The Emancipation Proclamation takes effect January 1. It frees nearly four million U.S. slaves.

Conscription for the Union army begins under the Conscription Act, which exempts any man who pays $300. Draft riots soon break out in Northern cities; the most violent riot, in New York, leaves 1,200 dead and thousands injured, including black victims of mob lynching.

Maryland state law abolishes slavery.

The Battle of Gettysburg in Pennsylvania marks the turning point of the war.

President Lincoln dedicates a national cemetery at Gettysburg and delivers the Gettysburg Address.

Lawrence, Kansas, is sacked by William Quantrill, whose forces kill every man in town.

Disruption of sugar plantations in the South sends U.S. sugar prices soaring and leads to a sharp increase in sugar planting in the Hawaiian Islands.

Confederate dead gathered for burial, Gettysburg, Pa. Stereograph, July 5, 1863.

President Lincoln signs a bill, passed in 1862, that guarantees builders of the Central Pacific and Union Pacific railroads extensive land grants.

The Territory of Idaho is formed from parts of Dakota, Nebraska, Utah, and Washington. Arizona is created as a separate territory cut from the New Mexico Territory.

President Lincoln names the last Thursday of November Thanksgiving Day, a commemoration of the feast offered by the Pilgrims in 1621 to the Wampanoag.

The Capitol dome in Washington is capped, completing construction of the building.

Lincoln asks Congress to establish a system for encouraging immigration.

Congress establishes free city mail delivery.

Charles Kingsley publishes *The Water Babies.*

Edward Everett Hale publishes "The Man Without a Country" in the *Atlantic Monthly.*

Jules Verne publishes *Cinq Semaines en ballon (Five Weeks in a Balloon).*

✢ 1864 ✢

Nevada enters the Union as the thirty-sixth state.

President Lincoln calls for 500,000 men to serve three years or for the duration of the war.

Ulysses S. Grant is commissioned lieutenant general and is given command of all Union armies.

President Lincoln gains reelection, running as a Union party candidate with support from the "War Democrats" and helped by General William Sherman's victory at Atlanta.

The Destruction of the City of Lawrence, Kansas, and the Massacre of Its Inhabitants by the Rebel Guerrillas, August 21, 1863. Wood engraving, 1863.

Ordnance Depot at Broadway Landing. Stereograph by William Frank Browne, 1864.

Congress passes a new Reconstruction plan, the Wade-Davis Bill, stipulating that only those who swear never to have fought against the Union can participate in the reconstruction of state governments. Lincoln refuses to sign the bill.

Black soldiers of the 54th Massachusetts (as well as those from other regiments) protest unequal compensation. A few months later, Congress passes the Equalization Bill, promising black Union soldiers equal pay.

The governments of Louisiana, Arkansas, and Tennessee are reconstructed under Lincoln's 1863 plan; Congress does not recognize them.

Louisiana, Arkansas, and Missouri abolish slavery.

"In God We Trust" is printed on every piece of U.S. currency for the first time by order of Treasury Secretary Salmon P. Chase.

Erie Railroad president Daniel Drew and New York State legislators sell New York Central and Hudson River Railroad stock short on the New York Stock Exchange. Cornelius Vanderbilt buys up all existing stock, plus another 27,000 shares delivered by speculators.

Montana Territory is formed out of Idaho Territory as prospectors flock to the goldfields of Virginia City

Navajos terrorized by Kit Carson and his men are marched three hundred miles to Fort Sumner in New Mexico Territory on the "Long Walk" to the Bosque Redondo resettlement camp.

California's Yosemite Valley is protected by Congress, which passes a bill at the urging of Frederick Law Olmsted to preserve the area as the first U.S. national scenic reserve.

Houghton Mifflin Co. publishers has its beginnings in the partnership Hurd & Houghton.

C. H. Webb founds the *Californian* in San Francisco.

Charles Dickens publishes *Our Mutual Friend*.

Jules Verne publishes *Journey to the Center of the Earth*.

The Brotherhood of Locomotive Engineers, the Iron Moulders' International, and the Cigar Makers' National Union are organized by U.S. workingmen.

✣ 1865 ✣

Born this year: Rudyard Kipling.

The Thirteenth Amendment to the U.S. Constitution abolishes slavery throughout the country.

At the recommendation of Robert E. Lee, the Confederate Congress signs and passes the Negro Soldier Bill, allowing slave enlistment.

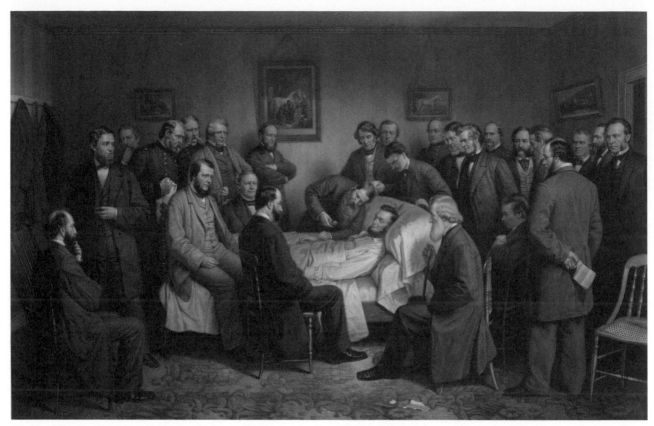

Death of Lincoln. Mezzotint. Painted and engraved by Alexander Hay Ritchie, ca. 1875.

General Lee surrenders to Union general Grant at Appomattox Court House in Virginia.

President Lincoln is assassinated. Andrew Johnson, a Southern Democrat, becomes president. Johnson's Reconstruction plan, which lasts twelve years, offers amnesty to those promising future loyalty and requires that leading Confederate officials submit for individual presidential pardons. States must also ratify the Thirteenth Amendment.

Congress refuses to acknowledge state governments formed under Johnson's Reconstruction plan.

Congress establishes the U.S. Bureau of Refugees, Freedmen and Abandoned Lands (the Freedmen's Bureau) to assist former slaves in the transition to freedom.

The Ku Klux Klan is founded in Pulaski, Tennessee, by six Confederate veterans; Confederate general Nathan Bedford Forrest is named its first Grand Wizard two years later, in 1867.

The Union As It Was. The Lost Cause. Worse Than Slavery.
Wood engraving by Thomas Nast, 1874.

Jefferson Davis is captured and imprisoned.

The Colorado River Indian Reservation is established by an act of Congress signed by President Lincoln a month before his death.

Rockefeller & Andrews is organized by Cleveland oil refiner John D. Rockefeller.

Andrew Carnegie enters the steel business with former blacksmith Andrew Klopman.

Leopold II becomes king of Belgium.

Jules Verne publishes *A Trip to the Moon.*

Josh Billings publishes *His Sayings.*

Lewis Carroll (Charles Lutwidge Dodgson) publishes *Alice's Adventures in Wonderland.*

Walt Whitman publishes *Drum Taps.* He is fired by the Department of the Interior's Bureau of Indian Affairs–charged by Interior Secretary James Harlan with immorality when proofs of a joint edition of *Leaves of Grass* (originally published in 1855, and now deemed sexually explicit by Harlan) and new war poems were discovered on Whitman's desk.

✢ 1866 ✢

Born this year: H. G. Wells.

The clipper ship the *Hornet* sinks in the Pacific. Mark Twain's account of the survivors' miraculous journey appears on the front page of the July 19 issue of the *Sacramento Union.*

Limits to the authority of martial law and to suspension of habeas corpus in time of war are set by the Supreme Court in the case of *Ex parte Milligan.*

The first U.S. train robbery is committed.

The Civil Rights Act is passed by Congress on April 9 over President Johnson's veto to secure former slaves all the rights of citizenship intended by the Thirteenth Amendment.

Efforts to introduce black suffrage into the Louisiana Constitution produce a July 30 race riot at New Orleans, with some 200 casualties.

Postwar economic depression begins in the United States as prices begin a rapid decline following Civil War inflation.

Two African Americans sit in the Massachusetts legislature. It is the first time black representatives have participated in this branch of American government.

Congress passes an act to expand the Freedmen's Bureau. Johnson vetoes the act, but again Congress overrides his veto.

Nearly 15,000 people gather in the nation's capital to celebrate Emancipation.

The former Confederate states enact "Black Code" laws to counteract the Thirteenth Amendment.

The American Equal Rights Association is founded on May 10 in New York at the Woman's Rights Convention.

The Black Crook opens on Broadway, with a Faustian plot, elaborate sets and costumes, and music adapted from various sources, including Giuseppe Verdi.

William Dean Howells publishes *Venetian Life.*

Fyodor Dostoyevsky publishes *Crime and Punishment.*

Leo Tolstoy publishes *War and Peace.*

Jack Daniel's sour mash whiskey is produced in Lynchburg, Tennessee.

✢ 1867 ✢

Nebraska becomes the thirty-seventh state.

Alaska is ceded by treaty to the United States by Russian czar Alexander II.

The first attempt to impeach U.S. president Andrew Johnson fails.

Congress overrides presidential vetoes to pass the first, second, and third Reconstruction acts, ushering in the period known as Radical Reconstruction.

Congress gives blacks the right to vote in Washington, DC.

Howard University, named after the head of the Freedmen's Bureau, is founded in Washington, DC, by white Congregationalists.

The Knights of White Camelia, a white supremacist organization, is organized in Louisiana.

A commission to conclude peace treaties with the Indians is appointed by Congress.

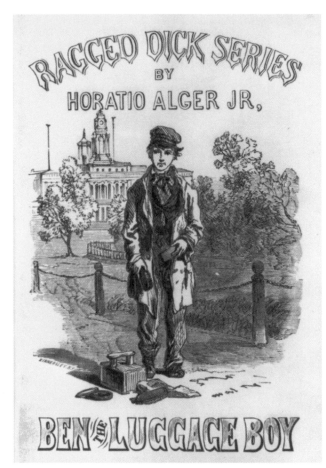

Ragged Dick series by Horatio Alger Jr., *Ben the Luggage Boy.* Book cover, 1867.

Construction begins at St. Louis on the Eads Bridge, which will span the Mississippi.

The Pullman Palace Car Company is founded by George M. Pullman.

Cornelius Vanderbilt gains control of the New York Central Railroad.

Oliver Wendell Holmes publishes *The Guardian Angel.*

Bret Harte publishes *Condensed Novels.*

Horatio Alger Jr. publishes *Ragged Dick.*

Ouida (Marie Louise de la Ramée) publishes *Under Two Flags.*

Karl Marx publishes *Das Kapital,* urging an end to private ownership of public utilities.

Charles Dickens begins final American tour.

More than half of all U.S. working people are employed on farms.

✣ 1868 ✣

Born this year: W. E. B. Du Bois and Maxim Gorky.

Americans observe Memorial Day (Decoration Day) for the first time. The holiday commemorates the Union dead of the Civil War.

The Fourteenth Amendment grants citizenship to former slaves.

The House of Representative votes to impeach Johnson. The United States Senate acquits him by one vote.

Civil War hero Ulysses S. Grant is elected president.

South Carolina, North Carolina, and Georgia, followed by Alabama, Arkansas, Florida, and Louisiana, are readmitted to the Union and allowed representation in Congress on the "fundamental condition" that black suffrage be retained in those states forever.

In South Carolina the first and only American legislature made up of a black majority is elected. African American representatives are expelled from the Georgia legislature. It takes them a year to gain readmittance.

Congress passes a fourth Reconstruction Act. Military rule continues in the South.

Navajo chiefs are forced by U.S. military authorities to sign a treaty agreeing to live on reservations and cease opposition to whites.

Congress enacts the Eight-Hour Law for U.S. government workers, but in private industry most laborers work ten to twelve hours per day.

Louisa May Alcott publishes *Little Women.*

Bret Harte publishes *The Luck of Roaring Camp.*

Overland Monthly begins publication in San Francisco with editor Bret Harte.

Rockefeller, Andrews & Flagler, predecessor of Standard Oil, tries to eliminate competition in the U.S. petroleum industry; Rockefeller creates a commanding market in kerosene by making it cheaper than coal and whale oil.

⊹ 1869 ⊹

Tennessee is the first of many Southern states to establish an all-white, Democratic "Redeemer" government sympathetic to the cause of the former Confederacy and against racial equality.

In *Texas v. White,* the U.S. Supreme Court rules that secession is illegal. Following this decision, Congress restores republican government in Texas.

The first black American diplomat is elected, as minister to Haiti.

The National Woman Suffrage Association is started by Susan B. Anthony.

The new Wyoming Territory enacts a law giving women the right both to vote and to hold office.

San Francisco sees street riots against Chinese laborers.

Union organizers found the Noble and Holy Order of the Knights of Labor.

An expedition to find Scottish missionary David Livingstone in central Africa is organized by *New York Herald* publisher James Gordon Bennett Jr. and correspondent Henry Morton Stanley.

Union and Pacific railways meet at Promontory Point, Utah.

The Suez Canal opens, linking the Mediterranean with the Gulf of Suez at the head of the Red Sea.

The "Cardiff Giant," a ten foot stone figure of a man, is unearthed in Cardiff, New York. The statue was the brainchild of an atheist, George Hull, who arranged for it to be carved and then buried as an elaborate hoax following a disagreement with a minister about whether Genesis 6:4 should be taken literally.

The canonization of Joan of Arc begins.

Harper's Weekly cartoonist Thomas Nast draws the first of many caricatures attacking New York's corrupt "Tweed Ring."

A National Prohibition party is founded in September in Chicago.

Bret Harte publishes *The Outcasts of Poker Flat.*

Wall Street has its first "Black Friday" September 24, and small speculators are ruined.

⊹ 1870 ⊹

Born this year: H. H. Munro (Saki).

Died this year: Charles Dickens and Robert E. Lee.

The first black U.S. legislators take their seats in Washington, DC: Hiram R. Revels of Mississippi in the Senate and J. H. Rainey of South Carolina in the House of Representatives.

Ratification of the Fifteenth Amendment to the Constitution is proclaimed by Secretary of State Hamilton Fish. The amendment forbids denial of the right to vote "on account of race, color, or previous condition of servitude."

Full suffrage to women is granted by the Territory of Utah.

Women enter the University of Michigan for the first time since its founding at Ann Arbor in 1817. By the end of the 1870s there will be 154 U.S. coeducational colleges, up from 24 at the close of the Civil War.

Standard Oil Company of Ohio is incorporated January 10 with John D. Rockefeller as president.

"Go west, young man," says *New York Tribune* publisher Horace Greeley who picks up the phrase first published in 1851 by John L. Soule in the *Terre Haute Express.*

Ralph Waldo Emerson publishes his essay "Civilization," writing, "Hitch your wagon to a star."

Jules Verne publishes *Twenty Thousand Leagues Under the Sea.*

Thomas B. Aldrich publishes *The Story of a Bad Boy.*

New York City gets its first apartment house.

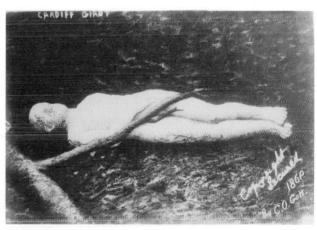

Cardiff Giant. Photograph, Bain News Service, 1910.

✢ 1871 ✢

Born this year: Stephen Crane.

The Ku Klux Klan Act (Enforcement Act of 1871, or Third Force Act) gives the federal government the power to use martial law against organizations that infringe upon civil rights.

The Second Enforcement Act is passed to secure rights granted to African Americans by the amended Constitution.

In South Carolina, Grant imposes martial law and suspends the writ of habeas corpus.

Whites in Georgia vote in a "Redeemer" government.

The African American Fisk Jubilee Singers go on national tour. The proceeds from the tour go toward the founding of Fisk University.

More than a dozen Chinese are killed in a race riot in Los Angeles.

The Indian Appropriation Act makes Indians wards of the federal government and discontinues the practice of according full treaty status to agreements made with tribal leaders.

Mormon leader Brigham Young is arrested in Salt Lake City in Utah Territory on charges of polygamy.

Horace Morton Stanley meets David Livingstone in Ujiji, now western Tanzania.

The 1836 Colt revolver is redesigned to extend its effective range.

Boss Tweed is arrested for fraud in part due to the attention drawn by Thomas Nast's cartoons.

William Dean Howells becomes editor of the *Atlantic Monthly*.

Joaquin Miller publishes *Songs of the Sierras* as John Muir explores them.

Lewis Carroll publishes *Through the Looking-Glass*.

George Eliot publishes *Middlemarch*.

Walt Whitman publishes *Democratic Vistas*.

The Great Chicago Fire starts in a barn owned by Patrick and Catherine O'Leary.

✢ 1872 ✢

Born this year: Calvin Coolidge and Zane Grey.

The federal income tax imposed during the Civil War is abolished by Congress.

The Freedmen's Bureau is abolished.

The Amnesty Act removes most remaining restrictions on Confederate officeholding.

Ulysses Grant is reelected president by 56 percent of the popular vote in spite of public scandals involving the "Erie Ring" of Wall Street speculators James Fisk and Jay Gould.

Equal pay for equal work in U.S. federal employment is ensured by a new law passed by Congress after lobbying by feminist Belva Ann Lockwood.

Susan B. Anthony and other women's rights advocates are arrested in Rochester, New York, for attempting to vote in the presidential election.

The anti-obscenity "Comstock Law" makes it a criminal offense to mail contraceptives and birth control literature through the mail.

The first U.S. consumer protection law is enacted by Congress; using the mail for fraudulent purposes is a federal offense.

Samuel Butler publishes *Erewhon,* a utopian novel about a country devoid of machinery.

Jules Verne publishes *Around the World in Eighty Days.*

Thomas Hardy publishes *Under the Greenwood Tree.*

Yellowstone National Park is created by an act of Congress.

The New York State Forest Commission halts sales of forest lands to commercial interests.

✢ 1873 ✢

U.S. vice president Schuyler Colfax is implicated in the Crédit Mobilier scandal, revealing further evidence of corruption in the Grant administration.

Financial panic closes the New York Stock Exchange for ten days.

The U.S. Congress doubles the president's salary, to $50,000 annually.

The James-Younger Gang robs its first passenger train, the Chicago, Rock Island and Pacific Rail Road Company's eastbound from Council Bluffs, Iowa, taking $2,000 in currency from a safe; an anticipated $75,000 in gold was in fact diverted to another train on the line.

The *Congressional Record,* a record of the U.S. Congress, begins publication.

The *New York Tribune* prints articles charging black representatives in South Carolina with corruption.

Colfax, Louisiana, is the scene of a clash between mostly black state militia and the White League, a group devoted to all-white government. Over 100 African Americans are killed.

Arkansas and Alabama vote in "Redeemer" governments.

A farmer's convention in Springfield, Illinois, attacks monopolies, calling them "detrimental to the public prosperity, corrupt in their management, and dangerous to republican institutions."

Demonitization of silver comes in the midst of new silver discoveries in Nevada.

John Stuart Mill publishes his *Autobiography.*

Anna Karenina, by Leo Tolstoy, is published in serial form over the next four years.

The world's first streetcar goes into service on Clay Street Hill in San Francisco.

"Home on the Range" and "Silver Threads Among the Gold" become popular songs.

American football clubs adopt uniform rules.

✢ 1874 ✢

Born this year: Gertrude Stein, Robert Frost, Winston Churchill, and Herbert Hoover.

U.S. senator from Minnesota William Windom heads a committee that proposes a government-built, government-operated double-track freight line between the Mississippi Valley and the eastern seaboard to prevent monopolies.

The first bridge to span the Mississippi at St. Louis is tested.

Federal troops at New Orleans put down a revolt by the

The Great Fire at Chicago. Print : wood engraving, 1871.

White League against black state government.

Some seventy-five blacks are killed in race riots at Vicksburg, Mississippi.

The Society for the Prevention of Cruelty to Children (ASPCC) is organized.

Thomas Hardy publishes *Far from the Madding Crowd.*

Josh Billings publishes *Encyclopedia of Wit and Wisdom,* which says, "It is better to know nothing than to know what ain't so."

The Remington typewriter introduced by F. Remington & Sons Fire Arms Company begins a revolution in written communication.

New York's Madison Square Garden opens in April under the name Barnum's Hippodrome.

Ku Klux Klan, Watertown [New York] Division 289.
Photographic print, ca. 1870.

Mary Baker Eddy publishes *Science and Health,* which explains the system of faith healing.

Richard Douglas publishes *The Jukes: A Study in Crime, Pauperism, Disease and Heredity.*

John Wesley Powell publishes *Explorations of the Colorado River of the West.*

William Tecumseh Sherman publishes his *Memoirs.*

The United States Hotel opens in Saratoga Springs, New York, with nearly 1,000 rooms for the summer season. The new hotel calls itself the world's largest.

✣ 1876 ✣

Born this year: Jack London.

The presidential election ends in a dispute when neither Democrat Samuel J. Tilden of New York nor Republican Rutherford B. Hayes of Ohio wins the necessary 185 electoral votes.

The International Association for the Exploration and Civilization of Africa is founded under the auspices of the Belgian king Leopold II. Twain and others will criticize Leopold greatly for his acts of colonization.

Black militiamen are massacred at Hamburg, South Carolina, the most dramatic of many racial clashes in that state over the gubernatorial election.

The Battle of the Little Big Horn, also called Custer's Last Stand, occurs in Montana.

Alexander Graham Bell invents the first practical telephone.

Thomas Edison builds his first laboratory in Menlo Park, New Jersey.

The United States Centennial Celebration opens in Philadelphia, Pennsylvania.

Colorado becomes the thirty-eighth state.

Wild Bill (James Butler) Hickok is murdered while playing poker.

Pyotr Ilyich Tchaikovsky composes *Swan Lake.*

Henry Robert publishes the ever popular *Robert's Rules of Order.*

✣ 1875 ✣

Henry Ward Beecher is tried for adultery in Brooklyn, NY.

Boss Tweed is released from prison and immediately arrested on other charges.

New York's "Tweed" Courthouse is completed north of City Hall at a cost of $13 million.

Congress passes a Civil Rights Act granting African Americans equal access to public accommodations, including transportation, and bans their exclusion from jury duty.

Whites in Mississippi vote in a "Redeemer" government.

The first Jim Crow law is enacted by the Tennessee legislature.

Oregon Territory, occupied under an 1855 treaty by the Nez Perce, is opened to white settlement by President Grant.

The Molly Maguires begin coordinated strikes of coal mines.

The electric telephone is pioneered by Alexander Graham Bell.

The first football game between Harvard and Yale is played.

The Whiskey Ring is broken by the arrest of 240 distillers and Internal Revenue officials.

The Suez Canal comes under British control.

Stenotype begins to facilitate courtroom reporting and to make records of legal proceedings more accurate.

The first carload of California fruit reaches the Mississippi Valley, but the freight rate is too steep for most growers.

⊹ 1877 ⊹

Cornelius Vanderbilt dies at age eighty-two, leaving a fortune of more than $100 million to his widow and ten children.

Under the "Compromise of 1877," Rutherford B. Hayes is inaugurated president by an electoral commission. Hayes is declared the winner on the condition that federal troops be removed from several Southern states.

The Socialist Labor Party is formed in the United States.

Portrait of George A. Custer. Brady National Photographic Art Gallery, digital file from original negative, 1865.

GENERAL CUSTER'S DEATH STRUGGLE.
The Battle of the Little Big Horn.

General Custer's Death Struggle. The Battle of the Little Big Horn. Lithograph by H. Steinegger, 1878.

San Francisco from California Street Hill. Panoramic photograph by Eadweard Muybridge, 1877.

Standard Oil Company of Ohio president John D. Rockefeller signs a contract with the Pennsylvania Railroad that strengthens his oil-rail monopoly.

Boston entrepreneur Augustus Pope converts his Hartford, Connecticut, air-pistol factory into the first U.S. bicycle factory.

Coal miners and railroad workers go on strike July through August.

A San Francisco mob burns down twenty-five Chinatown wash houses, setting off anti-Chinese riots that will last for months.

The phonograph is invented by Thomas Edison.

The Bell Telephone Company is founded. The first Bell telephones are sold. Mark Twain is one of the 778 buyers.

Henry James publishes *The American.*

John Wesley Powell publishes *An Introduction to the Study of Indian Languages.*

✢ 1878 ✢

Born this year: Carl Sandburg and Upton Sinclair.

President Hayes invites the children of Washington to an Easter egg roll on the White House lawn and begins an annual event.

The Greenback Labor Party is formed. Circulation of greenbacks is reduced by Congress.

The Bland-Allison Act makes the silver dollar legal tender and requires that the U.S. Treasury buy $2 million to $4 million worth of silver each month.

Thomas Edison founds the Edison Electric Light Co.

The relocation of former slaves to Kansas, called the Exoduster Movement, begins. Within the year, 30,000 blacks migrate to Kansas.

Popular songs this year include "Carry Me Back to Old Virginny," about an ex-slave in the North.

The U.S. Supreme Court rules against polygamy as a religious right.

The steamboat *J. M. White* launched on the Mississippi is the grandest ship ever seen on the river. Her smokestacks are 80 feet high, and her roof bell weighs 2,880 pounds.

In England, the Christian Mission is reformed and renamed the Salvation Army.

Henry James publishes *The Europeans*.

Thomas Hardy publishes *The Return of the Native*.

Allan Pinkerton publishes *Strikers, Communists and Tramps*.

Report on the Lands of the Arid Regions of the United States by John Wesley Powell points out that land west of the 96th meridian is arid–that only a few areas of the Pacific Coast can be successfully farmed.

Robert Louis Stevenson publishes *An Inland Voyage*.

Remington typewriters are first capable of printing both upper- and lower-case letters.

The Tiffany Diamond is discovered in South Africa's Kimberly Mine.

Born this year: Albert Einstein.

Congress authorizes a commission to improve Mississippi River navigation.

President Rutherford B. Hayes issues proclamation forbidding settlement of Oklahoma Territory.

U.S. women are given the right by Congress to practice law before the Supreme Court.

A large exodus of Southern blacks to Kansas begins as restrictions against former slaves increase in states of the old Confederacy.

George Washington Cable, New Orleans writer and lecturer-companion of Twain's, publishes *Old Creole Days*, which angers Southerners due to its criticism of slavery, prison conditions, and the mistreatment of blacks.

"In the Evening by the Moonlight" by James Bland is popularized through the Callender's Original Georgia Minstrels. He also writes "Oh, Dem Gold Slippers."

A bill that would restrict Chinese immigration into the United States passes Congress but is vetoed by President Hayes, who calls it a violation of the Burlingame Treaty (1868).

Thomas Edison invents first practical incandescent lamp using a carbon filament.

Application for a patent on a road vehicle to be powered by an internal combustion engine is filed by George B. Selden, who will not obtain the patent until 1895.

Progress and Poverty by U.S. economist Henry George points out that while America has become richer and richer, most Americans have become poorer and poorer.

Leadville, Colorado, becomes the world's largest silver camp, with more than thirty producing mines, ten large smelters, and an output of nearly $15 million.

The multiple switchboard invented by U.S. engineer Leroy B. Firman will make the telephone a commercial success and will help increase the number of U.S. telephone subscribers from 50,000 in 1880 to 250,000 in 1890.

Henry James publishes *Daisy Miller*.

Church of Christ Scientist (Christian Science) founded by Mary Baker Eddy.

The Boston park system is completed by Frederick Law Olmsted–an "emerald necklace" for the city.

The last of the southern bison herd is killed by U.S. hunters at Buffalo Springs, Texas.

✣ 1880 ✣

Republican James A. Garfield wins the presidency.

"War is hell," says U.S. Civil War general William Tecumseh Sherman in an address to a Columbus, Ohio, reunion. "There is many a boy here who looks on war as all glory, but, boys, it is all hell. You can bear this warning voice to generations yet to come."

African American veteran. Photograph, Franklin, Mass., ca. 1880.

Tennessee's 1875 Jim Crow law is called unconstitutional by a federal circuit court.

The first wireless telephone message is transmitted June 3 by Bell on the photophone he has invented.

Frenchman Ferdinand Marie de Lesseps starts company to build a Panama Canal.

Halftone photographic illustrations appear in newspapers for the first time.

Infrared photography techniques and film developed.

Dostoyevsky publishes *The Brothers Karamazov.*

Joel Chandler Harris publishes *Uncle Remus: His Songs and Sayings.*

Lew Wallace, governor of New Mexico Territory, publishes *Ben Hur: A Tale of the Christ.*

John Philip Sousa is appointed bandmaster of the United States Marine Band in Washington, DC.

The number of players in American-style football is reduced from fifteen to eleven, where it has remained.

The United States has more than 100 millionaires, up from fewer than 20 in 1840.

Joel Chandler Harris publishes "The Tar Baby."

✣ 1881 ✣

William H. Bonney (Billy the Kid) is killed.

Czar Alexander II is assassinated. Czar Alexander III makes Jews the scapegoats for the assassination of his father.

James Garfield is shot by Charles J. Guiteau in Washington, DC, and dies of his wounds three months later. Chester A. Arthur becomes president.

Drought strikes the eastern United States. New York City runs out of water, and people in many cities die of heat exhaustion.

The second Jim Crow law is passed by the Tennessee legislature. It segregates black passengers on railroads and establishes a precedent that will be followed by similar laws throughout the South.

The Tuskegee Institute is founded in Alabama. Local blacks invite Booker T. Washington to start the pioneer school.

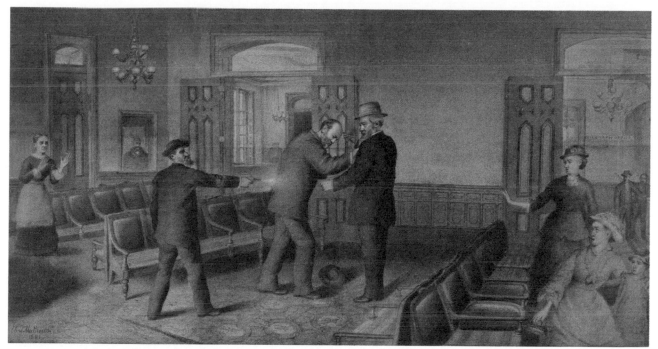

Scene of the Assassination of Gen. James A. Garfield, President of the United States (detail). Illustration, 1881.

The Supreme Court rules the U.S. federal income tax law of 1862 unconstitutional.

A decade of unprecedented railroad construction begins.

The American Association of the Red Cross is founded by Clara Barton.

Henry James publishes *Portrait of a Lady*.

Thomas B. Aldrich becomes editor of the *Atlantic Monthly*.

"The Story of a Great Monopoly," published in the *Atlantic Monthly*, is an attack on John D. Rockefeller's Standard Oil Company trust.

Andrew Carnegie donates funds for a Pittsburgh library, the start of a series of library gifts.

Some 669,431 immigrants enter the United States, up from 91,918 in 1861, as a decade begins that will see 5.25 million immigrants arrive.

✛ 1882 ✛

Born this year: Franklin Delano Roosevelt, Virginia Woolf, and James Joyce.

Jesse James is killed in St. Joseph, Missouri.

Ralph Waldo Emerson dies in Concord on April 27.

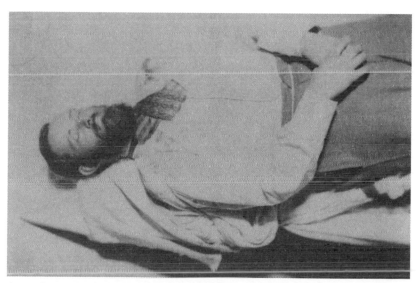

Jesse James dead. Photographic print, 1882.

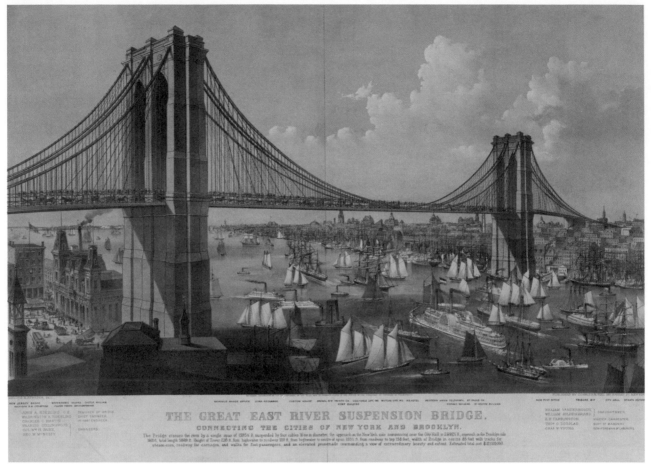

Brooklyn Bridge: The Great East River Suspension Bridge. Connecting the Cities of New York and Brooklyn. Colored lithograph by Currier & Ives, ca. 1874.

The first U.S. act restricting general immigration is passed by Congress. The new law excludes convicts, paupers, and defectives, and it imposes a head tax on immigrants.

The 1880 Chinese Exclusion Act takes effect and bars entry of Chinese laborers for a period of ten years. The loss of Chinese labor spurs development of machinery to clean and bone fish in California's salmon canneries.

An official record of the number of lynchings in the United States is started.

The U.S. Congress passes the Edwards Bill, disenfranchising polygamists.

Droughts spread throughout ranchlands, and only 2 percent of New York homes have water connections.

A three-mile limit for territorial waters is agreed upon by world powers at the Hague Convention.

Electricity illuminates parts of New York beginning September 4 as Thomas Edison throws a switch in the offices of financier J. P. Morgan to light the offices and inaugurate commercial transmission of electric power.

The Standard Oil Trust, incorporated by John D. Rockefeller and his associates to circumvent state corporation laws, brings 95 percent of the U.S. petroleum industry under the control of a nine-man directorate.

"The public be damned," says U.S. railroad magnate William H. Vanderbilt to a *Chicago Daily News* reporter when asked, "Don't you run it for the public benefit?"

John L. Sullivan wins bare-knuckle prizefight against Paddy Ryan, becoming World Heavyweight Champion.

Oscar Wilde arrives in New York in January and says, "I have nothing to declare except my genius."

Robert Louis Stevenson publishes *Treasure Island.*

✢ 1883 ✢

Born this year: Franz Kafka.

The Pendleton Civil Service Reform Act ends the abuses that culminated in the assassination of President Garfield.

Woman's Christian Temperance Union founded by Frances Elizabeth Willard.

The volcano Krakatoa erupts in Indonesia, an immense explosion that alters weather worldwide, an event alluded to in *The American Claimant.*

The Brooklyn Bridge (Great East River Bridge) opens.

Ferdinand de Lesseps begins work on the Panama Canal.

The Northern Pacific Railroad is completed with a last-spike ceremony at Gold Creek in Montana Territory.

Standard Time is established by international agreement. U.S. railroads adopt it, with four separate time zones: Eastern, Central, Rocky Mountain, and Pacific.

U.S. frontiersman W. F. Cody (Buffalo Bill) organizes his Wild West Show.

Keith & Batchelder's Dime Museum opens in Boston.

Joseph Pulitzer buys the *New York World.*

The humor magazine *Life,* not to be confused with the photojournalism magazine of the same name, begins publication in New York. Its first literary editor is Edward Sandford Martin, who, in 1876, had helped start the *Harvard Lampoon. Life* was to continue for more than half a century.

Robert Louis Stevenson publishes *Treasure Island.*

Hiram S. Maxim patents the first machine gun, capable of firing 600 rounds a minute.

More than 2,300 Remington typewriters were sold in the year 1882; by 1885, sales will reach 5,000 per year.

The United States has its peak year of immigration from Denmark, Norway, Sweden, Switzerland, the Netherlands, and China.

Reunion of Ex-Union POWs. Stereograph by Daniel W. Webb, ca. 1884.

✣ 1884 ✣

Born this year: Harry S. Truman.

New York governor Grover Cleveland is elected to the presidency.

United States recognizes King Leopold's International Association of Congo regime.

A Second Chinese Exclusion Act tightens the provisions of the 1882 act.

A Berlin conference on African affairs begins with delegates from fourteen nations, including the United States, who agree to work for the suppression of slavery and the slave trade.

The cornerstone for the Statue of Liberty is laid.

Sir Charles Parsons invents the first practical steam turbine engine.

More than 80 percent of the petroleum from U.S. oil wells is marketed by John D. Rockefeller's Standard Oil Trust.

George W. Cable publishes *Dr. Sevier* and *The Creoles of Louisiana*.

Helen Hunt Jackson publishes *Ramona*.

The *Oxford English Dictionary* begins publication.

George Bernard Shaw becomes a member of the Fabian Society, a British political organization promoting principles of democratic socialism.

Ottmar Mergenthaler patents the Linotype machine.

Chinese farm workers comprise half of California's agricultural labor force, up from 10 percent in 1870.

✣ 1885 ✣

Ulysses S. Grant dies. Twain publishes Grant's autobiography posthumously.

Belgium's king Leopold II creates the Congo Free State in central Africa, and his misrule of this colony will provoke much criticism from abroad, notably from Mark Twain.

Mormons split into polygamous and monogamous sects.

An identification system based on fingerprints is devised by English scientist Francis Galton.

Mark Twain. Lithograph, Advertising Card of Harris & Moxley, dealers in White & Fancy Goods, New London.

George Eastman markets the first "box camera."

William Dean Howells publishes *The Rise of Silas Lapham*.

George Washington Cable publishes *Silent South*.

Richard Burton publishes the English translation of *The Book of the Thousand Nights and a Night*.

The world's first successful gasoline-driven motor vehicle reaches a speed of 9 miles per hour in Mannheim, Germany.

Born this year: Van Wyck Brooks.

The Statue of Liberty is dedicated by President Grover Cleveland on Bedloe's Island in New York Harbor.

Chiricahua Indian chief Geronimo is captured by General George Crook, escapes, and is later captured by General Nelson Miles and agrees to end hostilities.

The National Cemetery of Custer's Battlefield Reservation is established in Montana.

Seattle has anti-Chinese riots, and 400 Chinese are driven from their homes. Some are sent to San Francisco before federal troops are called in.

Nine striking railroad workers are killed by St. Louis deputies.

A May 1 labor demonstration in Chicago's Haymarket Square sees police firing into the crowd, killing four. Four days later, a peaceful rally is disrupted by a bomb that kills seven policemen. Again, police fire into the crowd, this time killing over twenty.

Labor agitation for an eight-hour day and better working conditions makes this the peak year for strikes in nineteenth-century America.

The A.F. of L. (American Federation of Labor) forms with 150,000 members.

Robert Louis Stevenson publishes *The Strange Case of Dr. Jekyll and Mr. Hyde* and *Kidnapped*.

H. Rider Haggard publishes *King Solomon's Mines*.

William Dean Howells publishes *Indian Summer* and becomes editor of *Harper's*.

Karl Marx's *Das Kapital* is published in English three years after his death.

Henry James publishes *The Bostonians* and *The Princess Casamassima*.

A Mergenthal Linotype machine begins setting type at the *New York Tribune*, the first newspaper to use it.

✣ 1887 ✣

Henry Ward Beecher dies March 8.

The first Jim Crow law to segregate black passengers from whites on railway cars is passed by the Florida state legislature.

The Boone and Crockett Club to protect American wildlife from ruthless slaughter by commercial market hunters is organized by a group of "American hunting riflemen," one of whom is Theodore Roosevelt.

Thomas Hardy publishes *The Woodlanders*.

Sir Arthur Conan Doyle publishes "A Study in Scarlet," the first Sherlock Holmes story.

Britain celebrates Queen Victoria's Golden Jubilee.

U.S. telephone listings reach 200,000 by December 31, with 5,767 in Boston and neighboring towns, 1,176 in Hartford, and 1,393 in New Haven.

✣ 1888 ✣

Born this year: T. S. Eliot.

Republican Benjamin Harrison, fifty-five-year-old grandson of the ninth president, William Henry Harrison, is elected president, even though President Cleveland receives a 100,000-vote plurality. Harrison receives 233 electoral votes to Cleveland's 168.

A new Chinese Exclusion Act voted by Congress forbids Chinese workers who have left the United States to return.

A U.S. Department of Labor is created by Congress, which restructures the four-year-old Bureau of Labor, but the new department will not have cabinet status until 1903.

The Washington Monument, which will remain the world's tallest masonry structure, is completed after forty years of intermittent construction.

An immense and destructive blizzard strikes the U.S. Northeast in March.

A Suez Canal Convention signed at Constantinople declares the canal to be free and open to merchant ships and warships in both wartime and peacetime.

Andrew Carnegie gains majority ownership in the Homestead Steel Works outside Pittsburgh.

The National Geographic Society is established, and its magazine begins publication in October.

Standard Oil magnate H. M. Flagler's Ponce de Leon Hotel opens January 10 in St. Augustine, Florida.

George Eastman begins manufacturing the first Kodak camera.

The first escalator is installed at Coney Island's Iron Pier.

Nikola Tesla designs first practical generator for alternating electric currents.

Jack the Ripper terrorizes the East End of London.

✢ 1889 ✢

Born this year: Charlie Chaplin and Adolf Hitler.

Electric lights are installed at the White House, but neither President Harrison nor his wife will touch the switches. An employee turns on the lights each evening, and they remain burning until the employee returns in the morning to turn them off.

North Dakota, South Dakota, Montana, and Washington are admitted to the Union as the thirty-ninth, fortieth, forty-first, and forty-second states.

The Oklahoma Territory lands formerly reserved for Indians are opened to white homesteaders by President Harrison, and a race begins to stake land claims.

"The man who dies rich dies disgraced," writes steel magnate Andrew Carnegie in an article on "the gospel of wealth." He is praised for his philanthropies by John D. Rockefeller.

New York's first real skyscraper opens at 50 Broadway.

The Eiffel Tower is completed in Paris.

Thomas A. Edison invents the first alkaline battery.

Nellie Bly leaves Hoboken, New Jersey, in an attempt to outdo the hero of the 1873 Jules Verne novel *Around the World in 80 Days.*

Before the Storm (four Apaches on horseback under storm clouds). Photomechanical print: photogravure, by Edward S. Curtis, 1906.

The "safety" bicycle is introduced in the United States. Within four years, more than a million Americans will be riding new bikes.

I. M. Singer Company introduces the first electric sewing machines.

The first All-America football team has a backfield and linemen selected by Yale athletic director Walter Camp from among college varsity players across the country.

✢ 1890 ✢

The Sherman Antitrust Act curtails the powers of U.S. business monopolies, but the new law will have little initial effect.

The Tariff Act of 1890 (McKinley Tariff) increases the average U.S. import duty to its highest level yet.

The Supreme Court virtually overrules its 1877 decision upholding state regulation of business. The Court's decision in *Chicago, Milwaukee & St. Paul Railway Company v. Minnesota* denies Minnesota's right to control railroad rates and in effect reverses the Court's ruling in *Munn v. Illinois* (1877).

Kansas farmers are encouraged to "raise less corn and more hell" by Populist Party leader Mary Elizabeth Clyens Lease, who began speaking on behalf of Irish Home Rule in 1885 and who makes 161 speeches as she stumps the state.

A poll tax, literacy tests, and other measures designed to restrict voting by blacks are instituted by the Mississippi state legislature. Similar restrictions will be imposed by other southern states.

Sioux lands in South Dakota that were ceded in 1889 to the U.S. government are thrown open to settlement under terms of a presidential proclamation. Sioux chief Sitting Bull is arrested in a skirmish with U.S. troops and shot dead by Indian police at Grand River as Sioux warriors of the Ghost Dance uprising try to rescue him.

The Wounded Knee Massacre ends the last major Indian resistance to white settlement in America. Some 350 Sioux men, women, and children are killed in South Dakota by nearly 500 troops of the U.S. 7th Calvary.

Nellie Bly boards the SS *Oceanic* at Yokohama January 7 and sails for San Francisco after having crossed the Atlantic, Europe, and Asia in her well-publicized attempt to girdle the earth in less than eighty days.

The United Mine Workers of America is organized as an affiliate of the four-year-old American Federation of Labor.

The American Tobacco Company is founded by James Buchanan "Buck" Duke, who creates a colossal trust by merging his father's company with four other major plug tobacco firms.

Thomas Edison shows a short "motion picture" to a group in his workshop in New York.

Idaho and Wyoming enter the Union as the forty-third and forty-fourth states in July.

The Mormon Church bans polygamy.

Sequoia National Park and Yosemite National Park are established in California.

Poems by Emily Dickinson is published at the urging of Lavinia Dickinson, whose late sister, Emily, died in 1886 without ever having had her work appear under her own name.

The "Gibson Girl" created by New York illustrator Charles Dana Gibson makes her first appearance in the humor weekly *Life*.

The U.S. population reaches 62.9 million, two-thirds of it rural, down from 90 percent in 1840.

✢ 1891 ✢

Congress votes to establish a U.S. Office of the Superintendent of Immigration.

The Forest Reserve Act authorizes withdrawal of public lands for a national forest reserve as lumber king Frederick Weyerhaeuser expands his holdings.

Oklahoma Territory lands ceded to the United States by the Sauk, Fox, and Pottawattomie available to whites through a presidential proclamation that opens 900,000 acres.

U.S. Congress adopts the International Copyright Act.

A New Orleans lynch mob breaks into a city jail on March 14 and kills eleven Italian immigrants who have been acquitted of murder—the worst lynching in U.S. history.

Jim Crow laws are enacted in Alabama, Arkansas, Georgia, and Tennessee.

Carnegie Hall opens in New York with a concert conducted in part by Tchaikovsky.

Ambrose Bierce publishes *Tales of Soldiers and Civilians (In the Midst of Life)*.

Thomas Hardy publishes *Tess of the D'Urbervilles*.

Rudyard Kipling publishes *The Light That Failed*.

Oscar Wilde publishes *The Picture of Dorian Gray*.

The first football rule book is written by Walter Camp, who invents the scrimmage line, the eleven-man team, signals, and the quarterback position.

✢ 1892 ✢

Died this year: Walt Whitman and John Greenleaf Whittier.

Ellis Island, in New York, opens as immigration center February 14.

End of Mark Twain Log. Photograph by Charles C. Curtis, ca. 1892.

Grover Cleveland wins a second term as president. He wins 46 percent of the popular vote; Benjamin Harrison, 43 percent; the Populist candidate, 22 percent.

The Chinese Exclusion Act (Geary Act) extends for another ten years all existing Chinese exclusion laws and requires all Chinese residing in the United States to register within a year or face deportation.

Homestead, Pennsylvania, steel workers strike the Carnegie-Phipps mill and are refused a union contract by managing head Henry Clay Frick, who calls in Pinkerton guards to suppress the strike. Strike riots leave thirteen dead.

Lizzie Borden is arrested for the hatchet murder of her parents in Massachusetts.

The first title match in a prizefight to be fought in padded gloves, between James John "Gentleman Jim" Corbett and "Boston Strong Boy" John Lawrence Sullivan, results in a win for "Gentleman Jim."

The World's Columbian Exposition opens in Chicago.

Rockefeller's Standard Oil Trust is outlawed under the 1890 Sherman Act by the Ohio Supreme Court, but control of the trust properties are kept in Rockefeller hands by Standard Oil of New Jersey.

Economic depression begins in the United States, but the country has 4,000 millionaires.

Former clergyman Francis Bellamy composes the Pledge of Allegiance for U.S. schoolchildren to recite in commemoration of the discovery of America 400 years ago.

Sir Arthur Conan Doyle publishes *The Adventures of Sherlock Holmes.*

The Sierra Club is founded by John Muir and others to protect America's natural environment.

✧ 1893 ✧

A vast section of northern Oklahoma Territory opens to land-hungry settlers. Thousands of boomers jump at a signal from federal marshals and rush in to claim quarter-section farms.

The New York Stock Exchange crashes in June.

Kelly's Industrial Army marches on Washington, DC, to demand relief, which is not forthcoming from Congress. An army of unemployed workers from California arrives under the leadership of "General" Charles T. Kelly.

Chicago's Pullman Palace Car Company reduces wages by one-fourth and obliges workers to labor for almost nothing while charging them full rents and inflated prices at company food stores. The American Railway Union is founded.

Three of the men convicted of conspiracy in the 1886 Haymarket riot in Chicago are freed by the newly elected governor of Illinois, John Peter Altgeld.

Oscar Wilde publishes *A Woman of No Importance.*

Stephen Crane publishes *Maggie: A Girl of the Streets.*

Frederick Jackson Turner publishes "The Significance of the Frontier in American History." He observes that the American frontier has been the source of the individualism, self-reliance, inventiveness, and restless energy that have been so characteristic of Americans, but that the frontier is now closing.

Henry Ford builds his first car.

✦ 1894 ✦

The Wilson-Gorman Tariff Act reduces U.S. tariff duties by roughly 20 percent and includes an income tax on those who earn more than $4,000 per year. Lawyer Joseph H. Choate calls the 2 percent tax "communistic and socialistic."

Economic depression continues in the United States. Strikes cripple U.S. railroads. President Cleveland takes the position that the government has authority only to keep order, thus effectively supporting the railroad operators and their strikebreakers.

Coxey's Army arrives at Washington, DC, after a thirty-six-day march of unemployed workers from Massillon, Ohio, led by sandstone quarry operator Jacob Coxey. The 400 marchers demand that public works be started to provide employment and that $50 million in paper money be issued.

Pullman Palace Car Company workers strike in protest against wage cuts, and a general strike of western railroads begins as Eugene V. Debs orders his railway workers to boycott Pullman.

Labor Day is established as a legal holiday by Congress; the first Monday in September is set aside to honor the contribution of labor.

The United States and China sign a treaty on March 17 extending the exclusion of Chinese laborers from America for another ten years.

The Bureau of Immigration is created by Congress.

An Immigration Restriction League formed by a group of Bostonians campaigns for a literacy test that will screen out uneducated undesirables.

Washington rejects Britain's invitation to join a united move to intervene in the war between Korea, China, and Japan.

Planning for the first modern Olympic Games begins under Baron de Coubertin, the founder of the Olympic Committee.

Henry Demarest Lloyd publishes *Wealth Against Commonwealth,* a study of John D. Rockefeller's Standard Oil Company.

John Muir publishes *The Mountains of California.*

Rudyard Kipling publishes *The Jungle Book.*

George Bernard Shaw publishes *Arms and the Man.*

Popular songs include "I've Been Working on the Railroad," also known as the "Levee Song"; a University of Texas undergraduate, John Lang Sinclair, later adapted the tune for a student minstrel show, calling it yet another name, "The Eyes of Texas Are upon You," which eventually became both the school song and a state song.

✦ 1895 ✦

The Sherman Antitrust Act is emasculated by the Supreme Court on January 21 in *United States v. E. C. Knight Co.* H. O. Havemeyer's three-year-old Sugar Trust is upheld by the Court.

U.S. Treasury gold reserves fall to $41,393,000 as economic depression continues.

The income tax provision in the 1894 Wilson-Gorman Tariff Act is ruled unconstitutional by the Supreme Court.

The League of Struggle for the Emancipation of the Working Class is founded in St. Petersburg by Russian revolutionary Vladimir Ilyich Ulyanov, who will adopt the pseudonym Nikolai Lenin.

Booker T. Washington gives a speech agreeing to withdrawal of blacks from politics if education and technical training are guaranteed to blacks.

The Anti-Saloon League of America is organized in Washington, DC.

Cuban revolt against Spain begins.

Underwood Typewriter Company is founded by New York ribbon and carbon merchant John Thomas Underwood.

The New York Public Library is created by a merger of the forty-one-year-old Astor Library, the Lenox Library, and the Tilden Library.

Guglielmo Marconi invents wireless telegraphy, otherwise known as the radio.

Stephen Crane publishes *The Red Badge of Courage.*

Henry James publishes his autobiography, *The Middle Years.*

H. G. Wells publishes *The Time Machine*.

Oscar Wilde publishes *The Importance of Being Earnest*. Wilde is also convicted on moral charges and sentenced to two years of hard labor.

Thomas Hardy publishes *Jude the Obscure*.

"America the Beautiful," by Wellesley College English professor Katharine Lee Bates, will be set to the music of Samuel A. Ward's "Materna" and will become an unofficial national anthem.

John Philip Sousa composes "King Cotton" and "El Capitan."

The first U.S. automobile race is run Thanksgiving Day on a 53.5-mile course between Chicago and Milwaukee and is won by the only American-made gasoline-powered car in the race.

✤ 1896 ✤

Alfred Nobel's death creates from his estate the prizes that bear his name.

Nebraska fundamentalist William Jennings Bryan, in a speech at the Democratic National Convention, says, "You shall not press down upon the brow of labor this crown of thorns; you shall not crucify mankind upon a cross of gold."

Ohio governor William McKinley defeats Bryan for the presidency.

Utah becomes the forty-fifth state of the Union.

The Supreme Court upholds racial segregation by sustaining a Louisiana Jim Crow car law May 18 in the case of *Plessy v. Ferguson*.

Idaho women gain suffrage through an amendment to the state constitution.

First modern Olympic Games held in Athens, Greece, through the efforts of Greek nationalists and French educator-sportsman Pierre de Frédy.

First public viewing of a motion picture occurs at Koster and Bial's Music Hall, in New York; it is of a boxing match.

Joel Chandler Harris publishes *The Story of Aaron* and *Sister Jane: Her Friends and Acquaintances*.

Edmund Rostand publishes *Cyrano de Bergerac*.

The appearance of Richard Felton Outcault's comic strip character "The Yellow Kid" in Joseph Pulitzer's *New York World* will eventually suggest a name for sensationalist reporting, "yellow journalism."

✤ 1897 ✤

President Cleveland sets aside twenty million acres of additional western forest reserves.

The Dingley Tariff Act raises U.S. living costs by increasing duties to an average of 57 percent. A decade of prosperity begins in the United States.

U.S. railroads are subject to the Sherman Antitrust Act, says the Supreme Court.

The Hawaiian Islands are annexed to the United States.

Cubans reject an offer of self-government from Spain's Liberal Party premier Práxedes Mateo Sagasta, insisting on complete independence.

The first Zionist Congress opens in Basel.

News of the Klondike gold discoveries of 1896 sparks a new gold rush.

The drought that began on the U.S. western plains in 1886 finally comes to an end.

Joseph Conrad's *The Nigger of the "Narcissus"* is published.

Rudyard Kipling publishes *Captains Courageous*.

The Monotype typesetting machine introduced by U.S. inventor Tolbert Lanston is more practical for book publishers than the Merganthaler Linotype machine.

John Philip Sousa composes "The Stars and Stripes Forever."

A massive, ornate Library of Congress is completed in Washington, DC. The Renaissance-style structure has been built to house the books that have piled up in a room at the Capitol since 1851.

✤ 1898 ✤

The Spanish-American War, which lasts for 112 days, is precipitated by an explosion that destroys the U.S. battleship *Maine* in Havana Harbor.

A joint resolution of Congress recognizes Cuban independence, authorizes the president to demand Spanish

Explosion of the Maine. Chromolithograph, ca. June 21, 1898

withdrawal from the island, and disclaims any intention to annex Cuba.

Insurgents declare the Philippines independent.

Annexation of the Hawaiian Islands is proposed in a joint resolution of Congress three days after the American rout of the Spanish fleet at the Battle of Manila.

An Anti-Imperialist League to oppose annexation of the Philippines is founded at Boston's Faneuil Hall by leading intellectuals.

A peace protocol is signed with Spain, and the Spanish-American War is formally ended by the Treaty of Paris.

The U.S. Supreme Court declares that a child born of Chinese parents in the United States is a citizen and cannot be denied reentrance to the United States by the Chinese Exclusion Laws of 1880 and 1892.

Louisiana's new constitution contains a grandfather clause that restricts permanent voting registration to whites and to blacks whose fathers and grandfathers were qualified to vote as of January 1, 1867. The clause virtually disenfranchises blacks.

H. G. Wells publishes *The War of the Worlds.*

Henry James publishes *The Turn of the Screw.*

George Bernard Shaw publishes *Caesar and Cleopatra.*

✛ 1899 ✛

Born this year: Ernest Hemingway.

An open-door policy in China proposed by U.S. Secretary of State John Milton Hay receives support from the great powers, who agree that all the imperialist countries shall have equal commercial opportunity in spheres of special interest.

"The White Man's Burden," by Rudyard Kipling, appears in *McClure's* magazine. The *Times* of London calls it "an address to the United States."

Missouri congressman Willard D. Vandiver says, "I come from a state that raises corn and cotton and cockleburs and Democrats, and frothy eloquence neither convinces nor satisfies me. I am from Missouri. You have got to show me."

Thorstein Veblen publishes *The Theory of the Leisure Class.*

"Lift Every Voice and Sing," by composer and singer John Rosamond Johnson and his brother, the poet James Weldon Johnson, will be called the black national anthem.

Scott Joplin's "Original Rag" and "Maple Leaf Rag" are the first ragtime piano pieces to appear in sheet music form.

✛ 1900 ✛

President William McKinley successfully campaigns for reelection with "the full dinner pail" slogan symbolizing Republican prosperity. Thousands of workers cast their votes for the Socialist Party candidate Eugene V. Debs.

Hawaii becomes a U.S. territory June 14.

The Boxer Rebellion rocks China, as foreign legations at Peking are besieged by members of a militia force. "Boxers" was a name given by foreigners to the Yihequan or Yihetuan (translated variously as Righteous and Harmonious Fists, Righteous Harmony, etc.), a Chinese secret society.

The International Ladies' Garment Workers' Union is founded in New York.

Only 3.5 percent of the U.S. workforce is organized. Employers are free to hire and fire at will and at whim.

The Olympic Games held at Paris attract 1,505 athletes from 16 nations.

Kansas prohibitionist Carrie Nation declares that since the saloon is illegal in Kansas, any citizen has the right to destroy liquor, furniture, and fixtures in any public place selling intoxicants.

Sigmund Freud publishes *The Interpretation of Dreams.*

Joseph Conrad publishes *Lord Jim.*

The U.S. population reaches 76 million, with 10.3 million of the total foreign-born.

✛ 1901 ✛

Queen Victoria dies at age eighty-one after a reign of nearly sixty-four years.

Vice President Theodore Roosevelt lays down a rule for U.S. foreign policy that will influence the rest of the twentieth century: "There is a homely adage which runs, 'Speak softly and carry a big stick; you will go far.'"

President McKinley is shot at point-blank range by Polish American anarchist Leon Czolgosz in Buffalo, New York. The wounds are not properly dressed, and McKinley dies of gangrene. Theodore Roosevelt, 42, becomes the youngest chief executive in the nation's history.

The second Hay-Pauncefote Treaty gives the United States sole rights to construct, maintain, and control a trans-isthmian canal across Panama.

United States Steel Company is created by J. P. Morgan, who underwrites a successful public offering of stock in the world's first $1 billion corporation.

Wall Street panics as brokerage houses sell off stock so they can raise funds to cover their short positions in the Northern Pacific Railroad.

Booker T. Washington publishes *Up from Slavery.* That same year, Washington is entertained at a White House dinner by President Roosevelt.

Winston Churchill publishes *The Crisis.*

Rudyard Kipling publishes *Kim.*

John Muir publishes *Our National Parks.*

✛ 1902 ✛

President Roosevelt works through his attorney general Philander C. Knox to institute antitrust proceedings against various U.S. corporations.

Cuba is established as an independent republic. Washington withdraws the U.S. troops that helped the Cubans gain independence from Spain in 1898.

United States Steel Company has two-thirds of U.S. steelmaking capacity.

The History of the Standard Oil Company, by Ida M. Tarbell, published first in *McClure's* magazine and then in book form, reveals that John D. Rockefeller controls 90 percent of U.S. oil-refining capacity and has an annual income of $45 million.

Rudyard Kipling publishes *Just So Stories for Little Children*.

Owen Wister publishes *The Virginian*.

Helen Keller publishes *The Story of My Life*.

The Rose Bowl football game has its beginnings in a game played January 1 in Pasadena, California, as part of the Tournament of Roses.

The Teddy Bear is introduced in New York after a cartoon in the *Washington Evening Star* shows President "Teddy" Roosevelt refusing to shoot a mother bear while on a hunting trip.

Orville Wright aeroplane, in flight. Photograph, Bain News Service, 1908.

Immigration to the United States sets new records. Most of the arrivals are from Italy, Austro-Hungary, and Russia. Congress establishes a Bureau of the Census.

✣ 1903 ✣

The Hay-Herran Treaty signed by U.S. Secretary of State John Hay and the foreign minister of Colombia provides for a six-mile strip across the Isthmus of Panama to be leased to the United States for $10 million plus annual payments of $250,000.

U.S. anthracite coal miners win shorter hours and a 10 percent wage hike from President Roosevelt's Anthracite Coal Commission.

Congress votes to create a Department of Commerce and Labor, with its secretary to be a member of the president's cabinet.

The sonnet "The New Colossus," by Emma Lazarus, is engraved on the base of the Statue of Liberty.

Orville and Wilbur Wright achieve powered heavier-than-air flights at Kitty Hawk, North Carolina.

Jack London publishes *The Call of the Wild*.

George Bernard Shaw publishes *Man and Superman*.

New York has an outbreak of typhoid fever traced to Mary Mallon, a carrier of the disease who takes jobs that involve handling food.

The President in Panama, Teddy Roosevelt. Drawing by Clifford Kennedy Berryman, 1906.

Detail of Statuary, *Apotheosis of St. Louis,* St. Louis World's Fair. Stereograph by T. W. Ingersoll, ca. 1904.

✤ 1904 ✤

President Roosevelt wins reelection.

U.S. reformers organize the National Child Labor Committee to promote protective legislation.

The first New York City subway line of any importance opens to the public.

The third modern Olympic Games are held in St. Louis.

Joel Chandler Harris publishes *The Tar-Baby: And Other Rhymes of Uncle Remus.*

Albert Bigelow Paine publishes *Thomas Nast, His Period and His Pictures.*

Henry James publishes *The Golden Bowl.*

James Barrie publishes *Peter Pan.*

Joseph Conrad publishes *Nostromo.*

Jack London publishes *Sea Wolf* and *The War of the Classes.*

An International Exposition opens a year late in St. Louis to commemorate the centennial of the 1803 Louisiana Purchase. The Ferris wheel from the 1893 Chicago Midway is moved to St. Louis.

Montgomery Ward distributes its first free catalogs after having sold catalogs for years at 15 cents each. The company mails out more than three million of the four-pound books.

✤ 1905 ✤

The Treaty of Portsmouth, mediated by U.S. President Theodore Roosevelt, is signed between Russia and Japan at Portsmouth, New Hampshire.

President Roosevelt creates a Bureau of Forestry in the U.S. Department of Agriculture.

The Industrial Workers of the World (IWW) is formed as a new organization of U.S. workingmen who call themselves one big union for all the workers.

Edith Wharton publishes *The House of Mirth.*

Albert Einstein formulates the Special Theory of Relativity.

The Carnegie Foundation for the Advancement of Teaching is founded with a $10 million gift from Andrew Carnegie.

The Royal Typewriter Company is founded.

A U.S. Public Health Service antimosquito campaign ends a yellow fever epidemic that has killed at least 1,000 in New Orleans.

U.S. auto production reaches 25,000, up from 2,500 in 1899.

✢ 1906 ✢

New York architect Stanford White is shot dead at the roof garden restaurant atop Madison Square Garden. The killer is Harry Thaw, who suspected his wife, Evelyn Nesbit, of having an affair with White.

"The men with the muckrakes are often indispensable to the well-being of society," says President Roosevelt, "but only if they know when to stop raking the muck and to look upward…to the crown of worthy endeavor."

U.S. troops occupy Cuba after the government falls and civil war seems imminent.

Evelyn [Nesbit] Thaw. Photographic print, Bain News Service, 1913.

Carnegie Library in Pittsburgh, Pa. Photograph, 1900–1910.

Ruins after San Francisco earthquake. Photograph by Arnold Genthe, 1906.

President Roosevelt takes the first trip outside the United States by a president in office to visit the Canal Zone. U.S. Army Corps of Engineers have begun excavation on the Panama Canal.

The National Collegiate Athletic Association (NCAA) is founded January 12 after a 1905 season that saw 18 American boys killed playing football and 154 seriously injured. The Great San Francisco earthquake is the worst ever to hit an American city. Many buildings in the city are destroyed in a large fire. Congress appropriates $2.5 million for relief aid, and New York bankers loan hundreds of millions to rebuild the city.

J. P. Morgan and steel magnate John W. Gates purchase Tennessee Coal & Iron Co.

Jack London publishes *White Fang.*

Ambrose Bierce publishes *The Cynic's Word Book (The Devil's Dictionary).*

Upton Sinclair publishes *The Jungle.*

The *North American Review* reports that more Americans have been killed by motorcars in five months than died in the Spanish-American War.

✢ 1907 ✢

Oklahoma is admitted to the Union as the forty-sixth state.

A U.S. economic crisis looms as a result of expenditures on the Russo-Japanese War, the rebuilding of San Francisco, and several large railroad expansion programs. The New York Stock Exchange prices suddenly collapse, and in an address, Princeton University president Woodrow Wilson urges an attack on the illegal manipulations of financiers rather than on corporations. "Malefactors of great wealth" are attacked by President Roosevelt in a speech.

Roosevelt permits U.S. Steel to acquire the Tennessee Coal, Iron and Railroad Company, despite questions as to the legality under the Sherman Antitrust Act. The president's action saves the Wall Street brokerage firm

Moore & Schley from collapse, faith is restored, and the stock market recovers.

U.S. senators from Idaho, Montana, Oregon, Washington, and Wyoming force President Roosevelt to sign an appropriations bill that repeals the Forest Preservation Act of 1891. The president signs a proclamation ten days later creating 16 million acres of new forests in the five states, and before the end of the Roosevelt administration it will have set aside 132 million acres in forest reserves.

An immigration act passed by Congress excludes undesirables, raises the head tax on arrivals to $4, and creates a commission to report on immigration issues. Nearly 1.29 million immigrants enter the United States, a new record.

The "Great White Fleet" is sent around the world by President Roosevelt.

Rudyard Kipling receives the Nobel Prize in Literature.

Austria adopts the principle of universal suffrage.

The Ziegfeld Follies opens in New York.

Joel Chandler Harris publishes *Uncle Remus and Br'er Rabbit*.

Booker T. Washington publishes *The Life of Frederick Douglass* and *The Negro in Business*.

New York City horse cars give way to motor buses, but most urban transit is by electric trolley car and subway.

Prince Albert tobacco is introduced by the R. J. Reynolds Company. It will soon be the leading U.S. pipe tobacco.

✦ 1908 ✦

Born this year: Lyndon B. Johnson and Simone de Beauvoir.

President Roosevelt adheres to the tradition against a third term, and the Republicans nominate Roosevelt's secretary of war, William Howard Taft, to succeed him. Taft easily defeats Democrat William Jennings Bryan.

The Supreme Court upholds railroad official William Adair who has fired an employee for belonging to a union. It begins an era in which the Court strikes down regulation of businesses.

The Federal Bureau of Investigation is established as a division of the Department of Justice.

Leopold II hands over the Congo Free State, his private possession since 1885, to Belgium.

Jack Johnson becomes the first black world heavyweight boxing champion.

Muir Woods National Monument and Grand Canyon National Monument are created by President Roosevelt.

Mother's Day is observed for the first time in Philadelphia. Suffragist-temperance worker Anna Marie Jarvis conceived the idea of an annual worldwide tribute to mothers and will agitate for a national U.S. Mother's Day.

E. M. Forster publishes *A Room with a View*.

Kenneth Grahame publishes *The Wind in the Willows*.

The Ashcan school has its beginnings in an exhibition of work by The Eight: artists Robert Henri, William J. Glackens, Everett Shinn, John Sloan, Ernest Lawson, George Luks, Maurice Prendergast, and Arthur B. Davies.

The Model T Ford is introduced by Henry Ford.

Mutt and Jeff, by Harry Conway "Bud" Fisher, which ran in William Randolph Hearst's *San Francisco Examiner*, is the first comic strip to appear daily with the same cartoon figures.

✦ 1909 ✦

Halley's Comet is photographed nearing the sun September 11.

Joan of Arc is beatified.

Died this year: Geronimo and Belgian king Leopold II.

Nearly two decades of Hawaiian plantation disturbances erupt in a strike by exploited Japanese workers. It is the first major strike in Hawaii.

The National Association for the Advancement of Colored People (NAACP) is organized in New York, headed by W. E. B. Du Bois to revive "the abolitionist spirit."

A three-month strike of 20,000 U.S. garment workers begins. The workers belong to the Ladies' Waist and Dressmakers' Union Local 25 of the nine-year-old International Ladies' Garment Workers' Union (ILGWU), and they will win most of their demands.

The United States Copyright Law will protect U.S. authors, publishers, and composers under terms that will remain unchanged for sixty-eight years. The law gives copyright owners exclusive right "to print, reprint, publish, copy, and vend the copyrighted works."

John D. Rockefeller donates $530 million for worldwide medical research. The Standard Oil Company head is the world's first billionaire.

U.S. explorer Robert Peary is the first man to reach the North Pole.

Congress bans the import of opium for anything but medical purposes.

H. G. Wells publishes *Tono-Bungay.*

Booker T. Washington publishes *The Story of the Negro.*

Robert Baden-Powell, founder of the Boy Scout movement, is knighted.

The first military aircraft is built by Wilbur and Orville Wright.

New York's Manhattan Bridge opens.

The first international air races and transcontinental U.S. motorcar races are held.

J. P. Morgan striking a Photographer with a Cane. Photograph, Montauk Photo Concern, 1910.

✣ 1910 ✣

Halley's Comet reaches perihelion April 19, as it did on the eve of Twain's birth, now on the eve of his death.

Died this year: Britain's King Edward VII, Mary Baker Eddy, Julia Ward Howe, and Florence Nightingale.

The Union of South Africa is formed July 1.

China abolishes slavery.

A bomb explodes October 1 at the *Los Angeles Times,* killing twenty men. Authorities arrest James McNamara and his older brother John on charges of having placed the bomb to silence opposition to organized labor.

The "Great White Hope" James J. Jeffries comes out of retirement to challenge heavyweight champion Jack Johnson but loses. Race riots ensue in Boston, Cincinnati, Houston, New York, and Norfolk.

The White-Slave Traffic Act (Mann Act) discourages interstate transportation of women for immoral purposes.

Women in Washington State gain the right to vote in a constitutional amendment.

The U.S. Immigration Commission winds up nearly four years of study with a forty-one-volume report that recommends restricting immigration, especially of unskilled labor.

Glacier National Park in Montana is created by an act of Congress; it encompasses lakes, peaks, glaciers, and Rocky Mountain flora and fauna spanning more than a million acres.

The Boy Scouts of America is founded by Daniel Carter "Uncle Dan" Beard, painter-illustrator of several of Twain's books.

The temperance movement gains more footing as Carrie Nation fights saloons in Kansas and carries her violent crusade across the country.

Father's Day is observed for the first time in Spokane, Washington.

ACKNOWLEDGMENTS

Numerous individuals and institutions supported this project. In the Library of Congress Publishing Office, editor Tom Wiener made this a better book in every way. To quote Twain: "Each of us needed company, also somebody to do half the work." Working with Tom was a joy; our shared vision and passion for the subject drove the narrative and organization. Ralph Eubanks, former Director of Publishing at the Library of Congress and now editor at the *Virginia Quarterly Review,* helped shape the book's form and content from the beginning. At Little, Brown, executive editor Michael Sand was very supportive and helpful with editorial ideas. Editorial assistant Garrett McGrath worked tirelessly to ensure that all editorial and design details were addressed. Pamela Marshall was our trusted production editor, always on top of the flow of materials between New York, Massachusetts, Washington, DC, and California. Denise LaCongo ably handled the production details. I want to give great thanks to Laura Lindgren, our designer, who worked with me on *Baseball Americana* and several other books; she seems to understand just how to meld my words and the images chosen into a seamless whole that is much greater than the sum of its parts. My literary agent, Sandra Dijkstra, and her staff, including Elise Capron and Jennifer Azantian, continued their stellar work on my behalf.

My longtime friend Phyllis Rhodes and her son Chris, self-described Twainiacs (and residents of Redding, Connecticut, where the author lived his last years), first put the idea for this book in my head. They made me question my own understanding of the man and wonder at his evolution from nineteenth-century sensation to twenty-first-century Internet icon.

My extended family on two coasts supported this effort at every turn; I am fortunate in my personal circle. Irvan Ungar offered moral and material support to my work, and I am grateful to Lotty Geremia and Dean Huston, and Maria Esther Geremia, for opening their home and hearts.

Several Library of Congress Publishing Office interns made significant contributions: I want to thank, first and foremost, Julie Thompson and Kristin Ladd; thanks are also due Jaci Moseley, Luke Wilson, Sydney Sznajder, Ashley Smith, Brittany Held, and Derek Moss for their assistance. The staff of the Prints and Photographs Division continue their outstanding work, cataloging and digitizing millions of images annually; my thanks to Chief Helena Zinkham and her staff, especially Sara Duke, Jan Grenci, and Barbara Natanson. In the Rare Book and Special Collections Division, Mark Dimunation, Clarke Evans, and Eric Frazier were helpful in tracking down elusive Twain-related items from the Friedman Collection and other sources. I had help from these Library divisions and personnel as well: in Manuscripts, Alice Birney and Timothy Stutz; in Geography & Map, Mike Buscher; in Newspapers & Periodicals, Megan Halsband and Deborah Thomas; and in the Scan Center, Domenic Sergi. Other former Library colleagues who deserve thanks: Jeremy Adamson, Phil Michel, Susan Reyburn, and Peggy Wagner. At The Mark Twain Project in Berkeley, I received valuable advice and access to the pictorial archives; particular thanks to Victor Fischer and Neda Salem. These institutions and their staffs also supplied illustrations: The Mark Twain House & Museum in Hartford: Mallory Howard; The Mark Twain Boyhood Home & Museum in Hannibal: Henry Sweets; the Mariners' Museum in Norfolk, Virginia: Claudia Jew; the Beinecke Rare Book & Manuscript Library at Yale University: Laurie Klein; the New York Public Library: Andrea Felder; and Elmira College's Center for Mark Twain Studies.

SELECTED BIBLIOGRAPHY

Autobiography of Mark Twain, Volume 1: The Complete and Authoritative Edition. Edited by Harriet Elinor Smith and Other Editors of The Mark Twain Project. Berkeley, CA: University of California Press, 2010.

Autobiography of Mark Twain, Volume 2: The Complete and Authoritative Edition. Edited by Benjamin Griffin and Harriet Elinor Smith and Other Editors of The Mark Twain Project. Berkeley, CA: University of California Press, 2013.

Fishkin, Shelley Fisher. *Lighting Out for the Territory: Reflections on Mark Twain and American Culture.* New York: Oxford University Press, 1997.

Kaplan, Justin. *Mr. Clemens and Mark Twain.* New York: Simon & Schuster, 1966.

Meltzer, Milton. *Mark Twain Himself.* New York: Wings Books, 1960.

Powers, Ron. *Mark Twain: A Life.* New York: The Free Press, 2006.

Scharnhorst, Gary. *Mark Twain: The Complete Interviews.* Tuscaloosa: University of Alabama Press, 2009.

Ward, Geoffrey C., Dayton Duncan, and Ken Burns. *Mark Twain: An Illustrated Biography.* New York: Alfred A. Knopf, 2001.

Other Resources:

Library of Congress Prints and Photographs Online Catalog within the Library of Congress website.

Google Books has the entire text of *The Adventures of Tom Sawyer* available for download in PDF format. The text is also searchable by word or phrase.

Gutenberg.org–online resource for digital editions of Mark Twain's works.

The Mark Twain House & Museum. The mission of The Mark Twain House & Museum is to foster an appreciation of the legacy of Mark Twain as one of our nation's defining cultural figures and to demonstrate the continuing relevance of his work, life, and times.

The Mark Twain Project. A collaboration between The Mark Twain Papers & Project of The Bancroft Library, the California Digital Library, and the University of California Press, this website contains reliable texts, accurate and exhaustive notes, and the most recently discovered letters and documents. Its ultimate purpose is to produce fully annotated, digital editions of everything Mark Twain wrote.

Mark Twain Library, Redding, Connecticut.

Center for Mark Twain Studies, Elmira College, Elmira, New York.

New York Public Library Gallery of Digital Images.

ILLUSTRATION CREDITS

To acquire reproductions of images in this book, note the negative or digital ID numbers that follow page numbers in the chapter lists below. Many images in this book are from the Library's Prints & Photographs Division and can be viewed or downloaded from http://www.loc.gov/pictures/. Items from other divisions are noted using the abbreviations listed below. Contact the appropriate custodial division or Duplication Services of the Library of Congress at http://www.loc.gov/duplicationservices/, (202) 707-5640, to obtain copies of these items. Some of these are also available online.

Collections cited are identified by the following abbreviations:

INFORMATION ABOUT IMAGES

EC	Elmira College, Center for Mark Twain Studies
LCGM	Library of Congress Geography and Map Division
LCMD	Library of Congress Manuscript Division
LCNP	Library of Congress Newspapers and Periodicals
LCPP	Library of Congress Prints and Photographs
LCRB	Library of Congress Rare Books & Special Collections
LCTicknor	Library of Congress Benjamin Holt Ticknor Papers
MM	Mariners' Museum, Newport News, Va.
MTBHM	The Mark Twain Boyhood Home & Museum, Hannibal, Mo.
MTHM	The Mark Twain House & Museum, Hartford, Conn.
MTP	The Mark Twain Project, Bancroft Library, UC Berkeley
MTPapers	Mark Twain Papers, Bancroft Library, UC Berkeley
NYPL	New York Public Library
SCV	Special Collections, Vassar College
YBL	Yale University, Beinecke Rare Book and Manuscript Library

Front endpaper: LCGM. i: LCTicknor. ii–iii: LC-DIG-pga-03106. iii (inset): MTP. vi–vii: LC-USZC4-4615. viii: MTP. 1: LCTicknor. 2: LC-USZ62-28777. 5: LC-USZ62-26239. 6: USZ62-39076. 15: LCRB. Back endpaper: LCGM.

CHAPTER ONE: RIVER OF DREAMS

16: LC-DIG-pga-00192. 18: LC-USZ62-7924. 19: LC-DIG-pga-03815. 20: LC-DIG-pga-01064. 21: LC-DIG-cph-3g12948. 22–23: left LC-DIG-pga-01318, right LC-DIG-pga-03484. 23: bottom right LC-DIG-ppmsca-09855. 24: top left LC-USZ62-24751, top right MTBHM, bottom left LC-USZ62-74794, bottom right LC-USZ62-42568. 25: LCGM. 26: MTP. 27: LCNP. 28: LCNP. 29: LC-DIG-cph-3g03168. 30: LC-DIG-pga-03106. 31: bottom LC-DIG-ppmsca-08888, top SCV. 32: left MM, right MTBHM. 33: LC-USZC4-3102. 34: NYPL. 35: LC-DIG-stereo-1s02500. 37: LC-DIG-pga-03028. 38: LCRB. 39: left LCRB, right LCRB. 40: LCRB. 41: left LCRB, right LCTicknor. 42: LC-DIG-pga-00445. 43: LCGM. 45: top left LCRB, top right LCRB, bottom LCRB. 46–47 top LC-DIG-pan-6a04649. 46 bottom left LC-DIG-cph-3a15269, bottom right LC-DIG-cph-3a14832. 47: MTP.

CHAPTER TWO: WESTERN SWING

48: LC-DIG-ppmsca-23044. 50: top LC-USZC2-2646, bottom LC-USZ62-104557. 51: left LC-DIG-pga-03521, right LC-DIG-pga-03115. 52: LC-USZ6-612. 53: LCRB. 54: LCRB. 55: LC-USZC4-2458. 56: LCRB. 57: LC-DIG-pga-02239. 58: LC-USZ62-11055. 59: LC-DIG-ppmsca-32175. 61: LCRB. 62: LC-USZC4-4615. 63: top LC-DIG-ppmsca-11878, bottom LC-DIG-pga-01999. 64: left LC-USZ62-10437, right LC-USZ62-20159. 65: MTP. 66: top LC-DIG-ppmsca-32101, bottom LC-DIG-stereo-1800427. 68: top LC-DIG-pga-03436, bottom left LC-USZ62-13120, bottom right LC-USZ62-20314. 69: LC-USZ62-13118. 70: LC-USZ62-8197. 71: LC-USZ62-62681. 72: LC-DIG-pga-03906. 73: top left LC-USZ62-27268, top right LC-USZ62-13121, bottom left LC-DIG-highsm-17649, bottom right HABS CAL, 55-JACH1,1-3. 74: LC-USZ6-527. 74–75: LC-DIG-pga-04015. 76: LC-DIG-pga-03140. 77: LCRB. 78: LC-DIG-pga-00315. 79: LCRB.

CHAPTER THREE: TRADE MARK

80: LC-USZC4-4294. 82: LC-USZC4-973. 83: LC-DIG-ds-00694. 84–85: LC-USZC6-79. 86: top LC-DIG-nclc-04495, bottom LC-USZC4-3598. 87: LC-USZ62-114833. 88: LC-USZC4-2388. 89: LC-USZ62-19869A. 90: LC-DIG-ppmsca-28426. 91: top LC-USZ62-43323, bottom LC-DIG-ppmsca-28485. 92: LC-DIG-pga-00025. 93: LC-USZ62-75192. 94: LC-DIG-ppmsca-19510. 96: LC-DIG-highsm-14945. 97: MTP. 98: top LC-USZC4-3437, bottom MTHM. 99: LCRB. 100: LCRB. 102: LCRB. 103: YBL. 104: LC-DIG-ppmsca-28173. 105: LCPP. 106: NYPL. 107: top YBL, bottom MTP. 108: MTHM. 109: top MTP, bottom LC-DIG-highsm-16910.

110: MTP. 111: top LC-D4-34019, bottom HABS CONN 2-HARF, 16-13. 112: left LCRB, right MTP. 113: left LCRB, right LCRB. 114: LCRB. 115: LCRB. 116: LCRB. 117: LC-USZ62-53046. 118: LCPP-POS-TH-KIR, no. 3 (B size). 119: top LC-USZC4-8267, bottom LC-USZ62-3928 PGA. 120: LCRB. 122: left LCRB, right LCRB. 123: top LCRB, bottom LCRB. 124: top LCRB, bottom LCPP–CAI-Beard, no. 9 (B size). 124–125: LC-DIG-ppmsca-06661. 126: LCRB. 127: LCRB. 128: top left LCRB, top right LCRB, bottom LCRB. 129: top LCRB, bottom MTPapers. 130: MTHM. 131: left LCMD, right LCRB.

CHAPTER FOUR: AMERICAN ORACLE

132: LC-DIG-ggbain-05479. 134: LC-DIG-ppmsca-31678. 135: top LC-DIG-ds-00886, bottom LC-DIG-ppmsca-28483. 136: top LC-DIG-nclc-01322, bottom LC-DIG-nclc-04477. 137: LCPP. 138: left LC-USZ62-127064, right LC-USZ62-66364. 139: LC-USZC4-13449. 140–141: LC-DIG-ppmsca-27719. 142: left LC-USZC4-11819, right LC-DIG-ppmsca-28717. 143: LC-DIG-ggbain-00833. 144: LC-DIG-ggbain-01452. 145: top, LC-USZ62-63949, bottom LC-USZC4-13258. 146: MTP. 147: NYPL. 148: top LC-DIG-pga-03330, bottom LC-USZ62-93672. 149: LC-USZ62-114827. 150: LC-USZ62-76205. 151: LC-DIG-ppmsca-05450. 152: MTP. 153: LC-DIG-ppmsca-12516. 155: left LCRB, right LC-USZC4-7693. 156: EC. 157: MTP. 158: NYPL. 161: LC-USZ62-48974.

CHAPTER FIVE: TWAIN'S CIRCLE

162: LCRB. 164: LCRB. 165: LC-USZ62-89286. 166: LC-DIG-cwpbh-00450. 167: LC-DIG-pga-03156. 168: MTP. 169: left MTP, top right LC-DIG-ggbain-03613, bottom right MTP. 170: LCRB. 173: MTP. 174. LC-USZ62-48972. 175: LCRB. 176: top LCRB, bottom LCRB. 177: LCTicknor. 178: left LCRB, right LCRB. 179: LCRB. 180: LCPP. 181: MTHM.

MARK TWAIN'S AMERICA

182: LC-DIG-ds-030915. 183: LC-USZC4-9893. 184: left LC-DIG-pga-00467, right LC-USZC4-894. 185: left LC-DIG-ppmsca-22797, right LC-USZC2-2882. 186: LC-USZ62-47882. 188: LC-USZC4-4557. 189: LC-USZC4-6207. 190: LC-DIG-ppmsca-07635. 191: left LC-USZ62-44563, right LC-USZ62-7816. 192: LC-DIG-pga-04268. 193: left LC-USZC4-4550, right LC-USZC4-2573. 194: LC-USZC4-1362. 195: left LC-USZ62-15887, right LC-DIG-ppmsca-07141. 197: LC-DIG-ppmsca-23764. 198: LC-DIG-ppmsca-19610. 199: LC-DIG-stereo-1s02545. 200: LC-DIG-ppmsca-18444. 201: LC-DIG-stereo-1s02691. 202: LC-USZ62-134452. 203: LC-DIG-stereo-1s02893. 204: top LC-DIG-pga-02496, bottom LC-USZ62-128619. 206: LC-USZ62-42774. 207: LC-DIG-ggbain-13790. 209: LC-USZ62-109591. 210: LC-USZ62-122392. 211: top LC-DIG-cwpb-05341, bottom LC-DIG-pga-04166. 212–213: LC-USZ62-115228. 214: LC-DIG-ppmsca-11484. 215: top LC-DIG-pga-02118, bottom LC-USZ62-42551. 216: LC-DIG-pga-00755. 217: LC-DIG-stereo-1s02813. 218: LC-USZ62-52042. 220: LC-USZ62-52591. 222: LC-USZ62-53334. 225: LC-DIG-ds-01036. 227: left LC-DIG-acd-2a06890, right LC-DIG-ggbain-02174. 228: LC-DIG-stereo-1s03637. 229: top LC-B2-2799-11, bottom LC-DIG-ppmsca-15412. 230: LC-USZ62-26279. 232: LC-USZ62-20579.

INDEX